To "analyze" means to break into components and understand. But new readers find modern mathematical theories of politics so inaccessible that analysis is difficult: Where does one start? *Analytical Politics* is an introduction to analytical theories of politics, explicitly designed for undergraduate classes and for the professional interested in an overview.

Almost all existing work in analytical political theory takes a behavioral perspective, seeking to explain how people act. *Analytical Politics* tries to explain why societies take the political decisions they do and focuses on evaluating these decisions.

We cannot evaluate how well governments perform without some baseline for comparison: What should governments be doing? This book focuses on the role of the "center" in politics, drawing from the classical political theories of Aristotle, Hobbes, Rousseau, and others. The main questions in *Analytical Politics* involve the existence and stability of the center: When does it exist? When should the center guide policy? How do alternative voting rules help in discovering the center? An understanding of the work reviewed here is essential for anyone who hopes to evaluate the performance or predict the actions of democratic governments.

Analytical politics

Analytical politics

MELVIN J. HINICH
University of Texas

MICHAEL C. MUNGER
Duke University

CAMBRIDGE
UNIVERSITY PRESS

PUBLISHED BY THE PRESS SYNDICATE OF THE UNIVERSITY OF CAMBRIDGE
The Pitt Building, Trumpington Street, Cambridge CB2 1RP, United Kingdom

CAMBRIDGE UNIVERSITY PRESS
The Edinburgh Building, Cambridge CB2 2RU, United Kingdom
40 West 20th Street, New York, NY 10011-4211, USA
10 Stamford Road, Oakleigh, Melbourne 3166, Australia

First published 1997

Typeset in Times New Roman

Library of Congress Cataloging-in-Publication Data
Hinich, Melvin J.
Analytical politics / Melvin J. Hinich, Michael C. Munger.
p. cm.
Includes bibliographical references and index.
ISBN 0-521-56287-2 (hardback). – ISBN 0-521-56567-7 (paperback)
1. Political science.   2. Social choice.   3. Voting.   I. Munger,
Michael C.   II. Title.
JA71.5.H56   1997
320 – dc20   96-35419
                                                          CIP

*A catalog record for this book is available from
the British Library.*

ISBN 0 521 56287 2 hardback
ISBN 0 521 56567 7 paperback

Transferred to digital printing 2004

For Rachel and Caitlan Leksana,
and Donna Gingerella

Contents

Preface

> Most of the book presupposes no knowledge of Mathematics beyond
> simple arithmetic, but at the same time it makes use of a mathematical
> mode of reasoning and the student who is acquainted with Mathemat-
> ics will be at a considerable advantage.

These words were written by Duncan Black on the first page of *The
Theory of Committees and Elections* (1958). Nearly forty years later,
they still apply to books that address the analytical theory of politics.
Mathematics is an important language of analysis. Students who know
the rules of grammar and syntax in mathematics will find it easier to
grasp the work immediately. What of students with little math background? Well, by the end of the book you will have learned some mathematics and some political theory. We hope that you will also be per-
suaded that the two go together.

Our hope for this book is that the reader will think of theories of
politics as a form of analysis. The word "political" derives from the
Greek *politicos,* a word that does not translate well into English. In
ancient Greece, politics had to do with the participation of citizens in
the government of their "polis," or city. The Greek word has to do with
both the *process* of decision by government and the *quality* of those
decisions. A nuanced reading of Greek thinkers of the fifth and fourth
centuries B.C. is hard for modern citizens of the West. The reason is
that our conceptions of the scope of government and the individual's

place in it are different. Politics in ancient Greece was clearly "about" *the right thing to do for the good of the polis,* conceived organically.

In our world, because of the tradition of Western liberalism, it is often unreflectively asserted that politics is "about" the will of the majority. One often hears that the majority is (or should be) constrained by the constitutional rights of individuals. Otherwise, though, majority will and morality seem synonymous in the popular mind.

We will argue that this is a misreading of democratic theory. Worse, "majority equals morality" is a misleading basis for educating a society. There is nothing intrinsically moral about the "majority will"; it is just what most people think. Further, the majority may be fickle, changing allegiances or following populist demagogues whose goals have more to do with power than leadership.

In a way, most people already suspect that this is so. The word "politics," to the modern ear, has a definition different from its original Greek meaning. Politics connotes venality, scheming, opportunism, and duplicity. We all look for the "right thing to do," but that is the *end,* or objective, of politics. Majority rule is nothing more than a *means* for discovering that end, and it is not perfect.

In this book, we will reflect on what politics is about. The research we examine consciously compares the coherence, stability, and predictability of the outcomes of different political processes. We also consider "the good" in politics generally on ethical, or normative, grounds. In particular, we will ask how different forms of political choice, or institutional manifestations of particular theories about politics, shape the character and performance of human societies.

Let's start with a warning: The news is not always good. Politics is irreducibly rife with opportunities for scheming and strategizing. It is sometimes said that analytical theories of politics, or "public choice," are cynical and ideologically opposed to government. After reading this book, you can see why: Analyzing politics makes one wonder whether it is possible to have any truths, any real principles at all. Complex menus of political choice make it hard to give a definitive answer to the only question we really care about: What should government do? If we cannot *predict* what government will do, how can we possibly *assess* how well it has done?

The answer is that democracy is frustrating, time-consuming, unpredictable, and even absurd. But there is no defensible alternative, so we had better discover how different forms of democracy work. As John Adams wrote (under the pseudonym Novanglus) in the *Boston Gazette* in 1774: "Metaphysicians and politicians may dispute forever, but they will never find any other moral principle or foundation of rule or obedience, than the consent of governors and governed."

Plan of the book

This book is designed as a classroom text and as a reference for the political science professional who wants to retool. Consequently, most of the material presented is introductory, with exposition oriented more toward examples than formal results or theorems. Nonetheless, to present the basic "spatial" model that we will use to represent political preferences we must use some notation that will appear forbidding to those without much practice in what Black called "simple arithmetic." To make the book useful for several different audiences, we have used an almost purely verbal and graphical presentation of the spatial model, with the more difficult technical material gathered in Chapter 4. Readers interested in learning only the intuition behind the theories we discuss should skip Chapter 4, as there is no new material covered in that chapter. Students who expect to pursue analytical politics in future courses should study Chapter 4 carefully, because the notation introduced there will be necessary for future course work to make any sense.

Chapter 1 presents the main issues in analytical political theory and introduces some examples we will use often in the rest of the text. Chapter 2 outlines the simplest version of spatial theory in politics, if there is only one issue or policy to be decided. Chapter 3 extends this simple model to the more complex (but important) situation where there are multiple issues. Chapter 4 reprises many results from Chapter 3, using matrix notation and a more rigorous statement of the results.

Chapter 5 is an overview of the problems of collective decisions and the paradoxes of social choice, as well as a brief introduction to several voting rules. Chapter 6 extends the basic model to account for policy preferences by elected officials and the uncertainty of voters. Chapter 7 considers the voting decision as a collective action problem. Chapter 8 considers "strategic" voting and the manipulation of outcomes by vote choice, as well as the more technical issues of nonseparability and "probabilistic voting." Chapter 9 departs from the assumptions of most of the rest of the book, because it considers "mass" elections, instead of committee voting. Two models quite different from classical spatial theory, "directional" theory and the theory of "ideology," are presented and discussed.

Acknowledgments

Many people have contributed to the thinking represented by the arguments made here. The truth is that few of the ideas or theories we review are original to this book. Many of the substantive ideas about representing political choices are adapted or reworked versions of work by Hinich with previous coauthors. Two of the foremost of these are Otto Davis and James Enelow. Both gentlemen deserve great credit.

Helpful comments on parts of the work itself were given by Susan Bickford, David Bradley, Holly Brasher, Jay Dow, Todd Ellinwood, James Endersby, Kyle Gray, Kevin Grier, Elizabeth Griffith, Chris Harrison, Steven Hull, Tyson King-Meadows, Susan Kotcher, Robert Nabors, Thomas Oatley, Jon Pierpan, Denise Powers, Thomas Schaller, Richard Schrock, Timothy Vercellotti, Barry Weingast, Carole Wilson, and Frank Zagare. Both comments and research assistance were provided by Judith Russell. Typing assistance was given by Julie Daniel. Alex Holzman at Cambridge University Press suggested the project and helped see it through.

Several people deserve special thanks for commenting on the entire manuscript: John Aldrich, Steven Brams, Jungug Choi, Dennis Coates, William Keech, Scott de Marchi, William Mitchell, George Rabinowitz, and David Scocca. The book is better than it would have been without their suggestions and criticisms. On the other hand, they cannot be held responsible for the inadequacies that remain.

Finally, we wish to thank our families, especially Kevin and Brian Munger. Without you, this book might have been finished sooner, but it certainly would have meant less.

Basics

The basic model of analytical politics addresses both normative and positive questions about human political action. Formal theories help social scientists explore "what if?" questions by deducing the implications of a set of premises. This approach has several advantages over other forms of theorizing, as we shall see. An important advantage of analytical theory is the ability to evaluate different forms of democratic choice.

The middle, or the center of the distribution of enfranchised citizens, is where political power is believed to reside. For at least 2,500 years, philosophers have argued about whether the policies resulting from different forms of democratic choice are just. The contribution of analytical theory is to make precise the consequences of different forms of choice and different sets of desires by citizens.

To make this idea of the "middle" precise, we first consider the idea of the median voter, under the assumption that there is but one policy government must choose. This definition of the middle is then extended to account for the fact that government must make many choices all at once. It turns out that the "middle" may not exist, or that there are many middles, if policy choices inherently involve several issues at once.

Further, this problem of indeterminacy of majority rule is not confined to any one institution or way of choosing. *All* institutions of aggregating arbitrarily chosen preferences exhibit an inability to make a unique choice among three or more alternatives. The only exception is dictatorship, which "solves" the problem of disagreement in democracy by giving only one person a voice in choosing.

The topics covered in this section include:

- The basis of spatial reasoning, including "middle," "left," and "right," as terms to help us understand politics
- The Downsian model and the median voter theorem
- Multiple policies and the median in all directions
- Arrow's impossibility result
- Alternative voting rules

CHAPTER 1

The analysis of politics

Politics is not an exact science.
(Otto von Bismarck, Speech
to the Herrenhaus, 1863)

Politics may be the most complex of all social phenomena and the most difficult to theorize about. There is no lack of theory, of course. Instead, there are many theories, with competing claims, to explain or guide political choices. To make things even harder, theories about politics range from the *normative* (what should be) to the *positive* (what is). Since politics is complex and political theories have both positive and normative elements, newcomers can't tell where to begin or what to believe.

The political theory in this book is "analytical," from the Greek *analysis:* dissolving, or loosening, a complex whole into parts. Analysis helps us understand relations of the parts, as well as the nature of the whole. Without an analytical approach, "politics" is very hard to comprehend, especially if we want to know more than "What will happen tomorrow?" It may be easy to forecast an election from opinion data taken a day before the election, but forecasting issues or elections six months off is difficult. A year before an election, anything could happen.

One might say that theories of politics are not very good if their predictions are so uncertain. One might be right! Still, it is more fair to focus on the distinct nature of the problem: Political phenomena are demandingly, delightfully complex. The *analysis* of politics "loosens" this complexity into more manageable (but still very interesting) components. Analysis helps us understand politics by applying "models" to these components to see how they work. *Models* are internally consistent bodies of theory that describe human behavior or physical phenomena. This process of abstraction helps simulate a reality simpler than (or much different from) the real world of politics.

3

Why use models at all?

Mathematical models are primarily focused on logical consistency, or the internal validity of arguments. Given a set of premises, we can characterize a conclusion in one of three ways:

- *Conclusion is true.*
- *Conclusion is false.*
- *Conclusion is conditionally true,* depending on other variables not accounted for in the model.

The advantage of formal analytic reasoning in clearly distinguishing true, false, and conditionally true arguments may not be obvious. A common reproach is that the simplifying assumptions in formal models are too abstract or unrealistic.

But *simplifying assumptions* makes analysis manageable and helps us focus on the key components of a phenomenon. The reason mathematical models are criticized for their assumptions is simple: *The reader can tell exactly what the assumptions are!* The discipline imposed by this approach means that mathematical models can be falsified, refined, and corrected.

Theories *must be* abstractions, or simplifications from an unmanageably complex reality, whether those theories are stated mathematically, verbally, or in terms of statistical measurements. The basis of any theory is a logical construction, following from premises or assumptions, that can be used to forecast events in the future. These forecasts are based on those data that the theory highlights as important. To put it more simply, theory gives us a way of asking "what if?" in our minds and then deducing implications.

The particular "what if" implications derived from abstract theory may have little to do with the world of directly observable phenomena. The applicability of the argument is irrelevant to the truth or falsity of the propositions *within the logic of the model.* Mathematical statements are either true, false, or conditionally true. A trained person can definitively recognize a set of statements as belonging to one or more of these three categories, without reference to any information outside the model itself. To put it another way, the epistemological basis of mathematical models is pure *deduction.*

Do not be confused: The use of arcane symbols and formidable jargon is different from "science." Using mathematics for discovering simple unifying principles that explain and predict observable phenomena is hard. Good theory is hard even in simple settings such as the behavior of a body moving in a vacuum. Social scientists study human beings, who deal with each other in complicated ways. If symbols make these relations even harder to understand, formal theories would be worse than useless.

We claimed above that a strength of mathematical models is the clarity of the statement of the assumptions. Yet clarity is only a strength if the assumptions themselves are *plausible*. One cannot tell if an argument works outside its own stylized context by looking only at the argument itself. Consequently, the external application, or "testing," of formal theory is by *analogy:* The theory is tested by measuring relationships among observable phenomena, in hopes that the observable phenomena are "like" the relationships the model focuses on.

Without careful empirical tests, models would just be amusing mathematical exercises. Analytical political theory has been subjected to extensive and rigorous empirical testing. Partly because some portions of the theory (such as the classical spatial model of mass voting) *failed* empirical tests, the theory itself has evolved and been improved.

We will review some assumptions and logical forms of several mathematical models in later chapters. In particular, we will consider the "spatial" model at some length. First, though, we ask why politics and governance are important from a *normative* perspective. The brief reason is that these models are more than positive claims about the way the world works. Analytical politics evaluates different ways of choosing and compares ways things *should* be done.

Spatial competition is a simple and intuitively plausible model of political choice. The basic spatial model was originally adapted from economics, but the modern spatial theory of voting is an analytical model of politics. The primary assumption is that policy positions of candidates or parties can be usefully conceived as points in a "space." Policy space can encompass one issue or several. Each issue is associated with a dimension in the space, where "dimension" is an ordered set of alternatives.

We will use spatial models heavily in this text, and it is important for the reader to understand how spatial models represent political phenomena. The spatial model breaks up the analysis of politics into three separate components:

- *Voter choice:* Each voter chooses the candidate or policy "closest" to the voter's ideal conception of what the government should do. In so doing, voters maximize their utility or satisfaction.
- *Party platform selection:* Political parties know how voters choose and make proposals (or choose candidates) that attract the most votes.
- *Quality of outcomes:* In some circumstances, the parties (in a two-party system) or the governing coalitions (in a multiparty or parliamentary system) converge toward the center of the distribution of voters. If the "center" corresponds with ethically defensible notions of democracy and the good society, this outcome is desirable. Alternatively, bias away from the center toward one of the extremes may be observed. In either case, spatial theory presents a detailed set of causal connections for effecting reforms.

Spatial theory has been criticized for the particular conception of voters, platforms, and outcomes it uses. Many of these criticisms are important, as we shall see. For now, let's emphasize why people find spatial models useful: Spatial theory is the only theory that provides an integrated model of voter choice, party platforms, and the quality of outcomes. For a complete model, formal spatial theory is the only game in town.

How should a group choose how to choose?

How should a group of people choose the right action to take? Does the choice of how to choose affect the quality of the choice itself? These are hard questions, but they are important questions in political theory. To make the questions more concrete, consider the Hun–Gats, a tribe of hunter–gatherers living on a long north–south peninsula. The Hun–Gats have to make a collective choice among three mutually exclusive alternatives:

- Stay in their thatched huts beside Muddy River, where they have hunted (and gathered) most of the available food.

- Go north, where there is more food and water, but where the fierce Raouli tribe kills trespassers on sight.
- Go south, where the land is arid and barren, and little is known about the presence of other tribes, game, or water.

If everyone wants to go north or go south, they all go. If all want to stay, they stay. But what if different people want different things? Disagreement tests collective choice mechanisms; conflict strains the ties that gather a group of individuals into a society. What is the best way to tackle this problem of choosing one course of action from several possibilities if people disagree?

At best, the answer to the "What if there is disagreement?" question depends on many factors. These include the nature of the disagreement, how peoples' desires or judgments are aggregated, and the complexity of the set of alternatives over which the group of people is trying to choose. Almost any answer to the "What if there is disagreement?" question is only conditionally true. That means that the assumptions on which an argument rests must be clearly stated. Otherwise, the Hun–Gats can't decide how to decide with any confidence. Worse, their confidence that one form of decision is the "best" way to decide might be misplaced. They may not recognize that (for example) majority rule is "best" only under particular conditions. To illustrate the problem of recognizing conditionally true statements in normative theory, consider the following passage from Rousseau:

As long as several men in assembly regard themselves as a single body, they have only a single will which is concerned with their common preservation and general well-being. . . .

A State so governed needs very few laws; and, as it becomes necessary to issue new ones, the necessity is universally seen. The first man to propose them merely says what all have already felt. . . .

There is but one law which, from its nature, needs unanimous consent. This is the social compact. . . . Apart from this primitive contract, the vote of the majority always binds all the rest. This follows from the contract itself. But it is asked how a man can be both free and forced to conform to wills that are not his own.

I retort the question is wrongly put. . . . When in the popular assembly a law is proposed, what the people is asked is not exactly whether it approves or rejects the proposal, but whether it is in conformity with the general will, which is their will. Each man, in giving his vote, states his opinion on that point; and the general will is found by counting votes. When therefore the opinion that is contrary to my own prevails, this proves neither more nor less than that I was mistaken, and that what I thought to be the general will was not so. (Rousseau, 1973, §§ 315–29)

As Grofman and Feld (1988, p. 568) note, "This passage in Rousseau is often misunderstood." The reason is that in other parts of the *Social Contract,* Rousseau offers a number of qualifications and disclaimers: Even Rousseau thought that the majority will and the general will might sometimes differ. But these qualifications seem like asides and are not identified as what they are: assumptions.

Suppose the Hun–Gats were to read Rousseau. Should they conclude that a majority in favor of either option "binds" all the rest to follow? If they read Rousseau *carefully,* they would end up arguing over what was meant in different (apparently contradictory) text passages. For example, Rousseau notes that "[the argument for the majority] presupposes, indeed, that all the qualities of the general will still reside in the majority: when they cease to do so, whatever side a man may take, liberty is no longer possible" (Rousseau, 1973, IV 2).

Our hunter–gatherers, sitting in cold failing sunlight around a dying fire and reading aloud from tattered old books, are frustrated. They want to know whether they should use a majority vote on whether they should stay or go. But they have no way to find out if Rousseau's claims for the value of majorities in discovering the "general will" are true, false, or conditionally true. They can't tell what his assumptions, or premises for argument, really are. To make matters worse, suppose some Hun–Gat now come across the following text, in another old book: "The tree of liberty must be refreshed from time to time with the blood of patriots and tyrants. It is its natural manure" (Thomas Jefferson, letter to William Stevens Smith, November 13, 1787).

The Hun–Gats face hard questions. Should they accept the will of the majority as just and general, as Rousseau argued? Or should they follow Jefferson in believing that revolution by a minority can be just? Since neither of these extreme positions is *always* true, on what assumptions or premises is the "truth" conditional?

To put it differently, does the "general will" (the just course for a society) always exist, sometimes exist, or never exist? If there is no general will, can we still call majorities "sacred," or are minorities morally justified in rising against the tyranny of the majority to give the tree of liberty the benefits of their blood? No less important, even if the general will does exist in this case, how can the Hun–Gats discover it?

To learn the answers, we must use a form of argument that identifies premises, or assumptions. This approach abstracts from reality, to be sure, but it allows us to focus on the conditional nature of many important truths about politics. The basis of this approach is the spatial model of politics.

The basis of the spatial model of politics

The spatial model is not just an "as if" form of reasoning about politics. People really think this way and routinely use the words "left," "right," and "center" as if those words mean something. This belief that the listener will attach a predictable meaning to a candidate's spatial position is very important. People use the metaphor of spatial position because it helps them understand politics. Communication requires that some part of the meaning of these terms be shared. We will begin with the simplest possible set of assumptions about information and behavior, in Chapters 2 and 3, before moving to more realistic but more complicated models in later chapters.

The first clear use of the left–center–right spatial metaphor was just after the French Revolution of 1789. It is remarkable, given the extensive treatment historians have accorded this period, that so little attention has been paid to the contribution of the Revolution to our everyday language of politics. The extreme differences in the French political system and the novelty of democracy itself evoked important conceptual changes. One of the most durable linguistic innovations was the use of the spatial metaphor as a shorthand for both physical position and political and ideological beliefs.

"Left" and "right" were first used simply to describe the physical positions of political groups in the National Assemblies, and later in the National Convention. Groups that disliked each other sat as far apart as they could. Radical allies of Robespierre sat in the "Mountain," the high benches against the top wall. From the perspective of someone entering the hall, these radical deputies were on the far left. The independent deputies (the "Marsh," or the "Plain") occupied the debating floor in the lower center of the hall. The Girondin deputies held most of the ministries that ran the government, and consequently controlled most of the practical power in the Assembly. They gathered in the far "right" corner of the hall.[1] Over time, it became clear that those on the left (Jacobins) wanted radical change. Those on the right (Girondins) defended the status quo because they ran the government.

These meanings have changed only slightly in being transformed into the modern language of politics: "Left" still generally means those who want change, with the extreme left seeking revolutionary change. The right is conservative, defending either the current policies or the ideas the current policies replaced.

The constancy of meaning of left and right may seem surprising, but it is no accident. The spatial metaphor is not just useful; it is *fundamental* to the way we all decipher democracy. Consider the way disagreements were described before the twin revolutions in the United States and France. Factions in European politics were conceived as struggles among "classes." In France, for example, there were three castes, or "estates." The clergy made up the First Estate; the nobility, the Second. Senior clergy came from noble families, so the first two estates were mutually supporting, protecting institutions and prerogatives that ensured their privileged status. The vast Third Estate, ostensibly representing the rest of France, was in practical terms limited to skilled artisans, lawyers, bankers, and professionals.

The implicit assumption was that the hierarchy in society was natural and just. This hierarchy found its highest realization in the figure of the monarch, who was above all estates (Beik, 1985, pp. 6–31).[2] This conception of politics was descriptively accurate: Social class and political division were identical in prerevolutionary French society. The reason for this is that each person's station in the feudal world was static and categorical. "Position" was defined by birth and political property rights, rather than merit or stands on political issues.

The two dimensions of conflict, social class and politics, were separated by the Revolution. Social class is inherently a set of *vertical* divisions. Politics in a democracy is a *horizontal* division of opinions among putative equals. It is hardly surprising, then, that both Tocqueville and Guizot (1974) use the same word – "leveling" – to describe the major effect of the Revolution. Both men believed that democracies must conceive of citizens abstractly and separate from their stations in life. There are obvious antecedents for such a conception in the religious view of every individual as a soul to be saved. The Revolution, in this conception, did not aim merely at defining the rights of the French citizen, but sought also to determine the rights and duties of men in general towards each other and as members of a body politic. . . . The Revolution set out to replace [political institutions] with a new social and political order, at once simple and more uniform, based on the concept of the equality of all men. (Tocqueville, 1969, pp. 12, 20–1)

With the passing of the old, static caste system, people needed some way of organizing their political world. What was required was a mental construction based on *politics* (horizontal disagreement among equals, over principles), not *class* (immutable vertical distinctions of privilege). The replacing of the old vertical understanding of social hierarchy with the left–right metaphor of political disputes may have been inevitable. Spatial imagery is a consequence of the new way people understood citizenship, and the new alternatives open to them in a democracy.

The "left–center–right" image has led social scientists to develop models that capture spatial political competition. In the next three sections we will consider spatial models that formal theorists use to analyze democracy. These three sections each describe one component of the general model outlined above: voter choices, platform choices, and the quality of outcomes.

Voter choice

The starting point for voter choice in politics is obvious: The candidate or alternative a voter likes best receives that citizen's vote. To say anything useful about the "likes" part of this statement, we need to answer two sets of questions:

(1) What characteristics of a candidate or platform does a voter consider in making comparisons?
(2) If a platform has several characteristics ("dimensions") how does a voter balance these different considerations?

Spatial theory simplifies political choice by beginning with an abstract model of a representative voter's decision on what to support. This mythical voter does not "represent" anyone in the political sense; rather, the voter is a mathematical construct that helps answer the two questions posed above. Specifically: (1) The voter perceives each platform as a bundle of individual issues. The voter then evaluates each platform by comparing it with his or her own ideal set of positions on these issues. (2) The importance of each issue in the voter's mind is represented by a set of weights. A large weight means the voter thinks that issue is more important than issues with smaller weights. If the voter doesn't care at all about some issue, that issue has zero weight.

It is useful to distinguish at the outset two contexts for choices by voters: *committee voting* and *mass elections.*

- *Committee voting* is a decision context where there are few voters, participants can propose new alternatives, the individual implications of the decision may be very large, and participants are well informed about the alternatives. School budget votes by a county commission or voting on a budget bill in a legislative committee are examples of committee voting.
- *Mass elections* are situations where many voters choose among a few candidates. Voters may have only very limited information, and each vote has only a tiny effect on the election. U.S. Presidential elections are one example of mass elections.

Example 1 (Committee voting). Imagine there are three people on a committee charged with choosing an entertainment budget for their club. Suppose we believe that each person would prefer budgets closer to his or her idea of the best budget. Let demure A think the club should spend $50, let regular guy B favor $75, and let party reptile C demand to spend $250. We will call this "idea of the best" the voter's "ideal point." So A, who wants a budget of $50 if it were up to him, likes $54 more than $60, likes $69 more than $81, and so on. Suppose also that we know majority rule is the decision process the committee will use.

Then we can use the spatial model to make a prediction about what the committee *as a group* will decide. As we will see in the next chapter, the prediction is this: If the committee decides by majority rule, the outcome will be a budget of $75, the position taken by the middle person. This example shows one strength of spatial theory: We can make predictions about *aggregate outcomes,* given no more information than (1) *individual goals* and (2) the *decision process.*

Example 2 (Mass elections). Suppose we have survey information on three voters out of a population of millions of people. Figure 1.1 is an

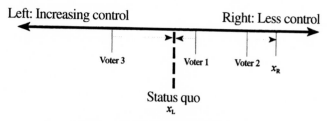

- Voter 1 chooses L, the party now in power
- Voter 2 chooses R, the challengers
- Voter 3 chooses L, but isn't happy!

Figure 1.1. Extent of government control over means of production, with two parties, L and R.

example of how political alternatives and the ideal points of individual voters may be arrayed along a dimension, using left and right as the ideas that organize the space. This is sometimes called the "classical left–right" dimension in spatial theory. Here, *left* means advocacy of increased control of the means of production by government. *Right* implies opposition to intrusions by government against rights to property. Voters have ideal positions along the same dimension. The prediction of the spatial model is that each voter will choose the candidate who is closest to his or her ideal alternative.

If we are to consider an issue (as in a committee vote) or a choice along a classical left–right dimension (an election for president or governor), the spatial model claims that voters will choose the candidate "closest" to their own ideal point on the dimension. In a majority rule election, the party closest to the most voters will win. We will make these statements more precise in Chapter 2 (for one dimension), Chapter 3 (multiple dimensions), and Chapter 4 (alternative voting rules).

In Figure 1.1, it is easy to see that voters, whom we can represent as points along a line segment, will choose between the status quo and support for alternatives. The choice, as was pointed out earlier, is made by comparing which is closer to the way the voter thinks society should be organized. In particular, voter 1 will prefer the status quo; voter 2 will support the party proposing platform "R." Voter 3 will prefer "L" to "R," but finds herself quite far from either of the alternatives. She may not vote at all, but if she does she will choose "L." Consequently, "L" wins the election 2 votes to 1.

Of course, it is important to understand how voters see candidates, or what they think they see. Some clear drawbacks in the model outlined in Chapters 2 through 4 are the restrictive assumptions on voters' information about candidates. In Chapter 5 we extend the model to account for voter uncertainty about candidate positions and for ambiguity in the positions that candidates and parties actually take. Chapter 6 addresses turnout: Under what circumstances will citizens choose not to vote at all? After all, voter 3 in Figure 1.1 may abstain, because the election has little to do with her. This changes everything, because the election is now decided only by those who choose to vote, rather than the entire affected population.

Where do proposals come from?

In the preceding section, we asked how voters choose, *given* the alternatives. Now, we want to know where the alternatives come from. As we saw in Figure 1.1, the distribution of voters determines which platform wins. Consequently, if the party wants to win, it will take the distribution of voter preferences into account. If most voters prefer a platform other than the status quo, then a party proposing such a platform will win the election.

Of course, the "status quo" party can also adjust its position. As long as such movements are possible, the parties will try to outmaneuver each other in a quest for more votes. In a two-party system, according to the classical model, the parties will converge toward the center of the distribution of voters.

What all this means is that platforms are generated *endogenously*, or chosen by the committee members themselves. Committee members make proposals or amend other members' proposals. Then everyone votes on the proposals. How might this work? Consider these extensions of the examples from the preceding section.

Example 1 (Committee voting). In committee voting, with free proposal power, members have an obvious strategy: Propose your own ideal point. That is, A would propose $50, B $75, and C (that wild man) would suggest $250. Suppose the status quo budget is $0 and that proposals and amendments are voted in some fixed sequence. Then a new status quo budget would be established each time a majority voted for the change. How long could this go on? We could impose a time restriction, but then whichever budget happened to win *last* would be adopted. A time restriction seems arbitrary as a basis for choosing the best outcome, but how else can we ensure that a group of people come to a decision?

Interestingly, there is a predictable, stable end to the progression of new status quo budgets (at least, in this example). The final budget is the middle, or median, of the three members' ideal budgets: $75. If this budget is proposed, it beats any alternative, because two people will always prefer $75. A and B vote for $75 versus any *larger* budget. B and C vote for $75 versus any *smaller* budget. We expect to *move toward* $75 as a status quo budget, since B is free to make proposals. Once there, the decision process will exhibit no tendency to change. Consequently, $75 is the "position" adopted by the committee, as a group. We will discuss the process of selection of platforms in detail in Chapters 2–4.

Example 2 (Mass elections). "Proposals" evolve, often chaotically, in response to both ideas and threats. The positions of parties in mass elections may be more vague than the well-defined positions or proposals in committee votes. Nonetheless, parties are associated with positions. Consider again the French National Convention, convened in September 1790.

A majority of the members were "independent," with no formal commitments to any faction. These centrist deputies in the Plain were both numerous and uncommitted, so they determined the results of votes in the Convention. But the deputies in the Plain had no organization and relied on the (relatively) organized left and right parties to provide an agenda or sequence of alternatives to consider.

The Girondins, or party on the right, held to generally laissez-faire economic policies and served as spokesmen for provincial and business interests against the more radical and Paris-oriented Jacobins, the party on the left. The Jacobins became more radically populist in the two years after the Assembly was formed, and their main program was opposing the Girondins. The Girondins ran the government until the spring of 1793, when military defeats and popular unrest led to the purging of most of the Girondin leaders from the Convention.

In the wake of the Revolution of 1789, the first organized support for "issues" led to a focus on reforms of business practices and an opening of markets. The power of the Girondins came from their early organization around the elimination of feudal restraints on trade among cities and within districts of Paris. The Girondins became identified with a "federal" view of France, with much of their support coming from the provinces.

The Jacobins organized against Girondin control of the ministries and offices of government. The populist tendencies of the Jacobins helped them take advantage of general unrest, though they also seized on specific Girondin errors. Most important from our perspective, the Jacobins could *position* themselves so that the Girondins lost support with the independent deputies of the Plain. Consider this description, from Rudé:

[The] economic situation was working to the advantage of the Mountain [Jacobins] and to the detriment of their adversaries. [The government's bond note] had fallen to only half its nominal value in February, and the price of food, after remaining comparatively stable in the preceding summer and autumn, had taken another sharp upward turn in the spring. . . . The riots that followed were, correspondingly, more intense and widespread than those of the year before. . . . But, though none of the Assembly's spokesmen was prepared to condone such activities, it was once more the Girondins, as the governing party and that most thoroughly committed to upholding the freedom of the market, that reaped all the disadvantages, while their opponents correspondingly benefited. (1964, p. 136)

As this excerpt makes clear, parties take positions in complex ways, and the metaphor of spatial position and movement is a simplification. Nonetheless, the metaphor is useful: People associate "left" and "right" with positions on real policies. The differences mattered for the way people expected to live their lives. The Girondins' laissez-faire economics became a terrible disadvantage because as the ruling party they were blamed for the poor performance of the economy. The Jacobins were free to take a position of opposition (in this case, at the center-left). As more voters and independent deputies rejected the Girondins, the Jacobins became ascendant.

Parties may have trouble "moving" in mass elections, once voters associate the name of a party with a set of positions on policies. This is particularly true if the party must govern in times of unrest. We might ask why party "L" and party "R" occupy the positions they do in Figure 1.1. The answer, however, is more likely to focus on history than on strategy.

The quality of outcomes

Models, for the sake of simplifying an unmanageably complex reality, often depict static situations. Consequently, describing change is a great challenge. Nonetheless, models describe situations where *some kind* of change is likely. Therefore, the outcome (not the many intermediate amendments) is the most important notion of "solutions" to problems of political choice.

We wouldn't have much of value, though, unless we can compare outcomes based on their *qualities* as solutions. After all, an outcome is only a solution in the sense that it answers the question "What do we do?" Some things to do are better than others, because the outcomes themselves seem more fair or result in higher welfare for more citizens.

Recall our still undecided Hun–Gats. They care about more than just deciding for the sake of deciding. If they make the wrong choice, they will die parched or be bludgeoned by fierce Raouli. Spatial theory is largely a positive theory, meaning that it considers questions of fact: *Certain patterns of preferences by voters, filtered through certain institutions for aggregating those preferences, result in predictions of particular outcomes.* But the theory must also help us analyze how good the outcomes are if the enterprise of analytical politics is to be of lasting value.

Charles Plott summarized some positive contributions of formal theory this way:

$$\text{Preferences} \times \text{Institutions} \Rightarrow \text{Outcomes}$$

We might think of "preferences" as what individual voters want. "Institutions" are the rules and practices (such as majority rule or a legislative committee system) through which collective decisions are made. Plott's (1991a) equation, sometimes called the *fundamental equation of politics*, illustrates two of the most important principles of formal political theory:

- If *preferences change*, outcomes can change, even if *institutions remain constant*.
- If *institutions change*, outcomes can change, even if *preferences remain constant*.

One might argue, of course, that preferences and institutions are often both changing. Well, yes. But keeping the two types, or sources, of change distinct analytically is fundamental to an understanding of politics. Further, as Plott's equation shows, changes of one type interact with changes of the other type. Relatively small changes in preferences, if multiplied by a change in the way those preferences are counted, may change policy outcomes dramatically.

Almost all political activity falls into one or both categories. A grassroots "get out the vote" campaign tries to change the set of preferences expressed. A constitutional amendment eliminating the Electoral College for electing U.S. presidents represents a change in the institutions of choice. The French Revolution saw the creation of several new governments and new constitutions (i.e., changes in institutions). These were followed by periods of "education" (attempts to change preferences). Groups unhappy with the status quo focus on modifying institutions and preferences as the mechanism for effecting change.

Political theory provides many of the basic criteria for evaluating outcomes in terms of their ethical qualities. Likewise, social choice theorists have pointed out that *democratic means* (widespread participation and shared power) and *democratic ends* (the existence of a coherent "will of the people") may be inconsistent.

Spatial theory has nothing directly to say about either of these questions, but spatial models do provide a forum where students of politics can confront the implications of their ideas. Stripped of rhetorical trappings, it becomes possible to evaluate claims about political theories at their most abstract level, where it is easier to tell if claims are true, false, or conditionally true.

Making judgments and expressing preferences

Before continuing, we should note that the Hun–Gats' problem is different from many problems we will analyze. To put it more generally, there are two forms that fundamental disagreements within societies can take.

(1) *Disagreement over values, or expressions of preference:* If different people have different goals, it is likely they will favor different means. The three people in our social club example earlier in this chapter had different ideas about the "best" budget for parties for

the group. The reason is probably that the three people disagreed about how to weigh parties as a component in all the club's activities. None of the members is confused about how much fun the parties will be, they just differ in the value they attach to the activity. This form of disagreement is not amenable to discussion or persuasion. As we shall see, the collective choice problems that this form of disagreement presents are very difficult.

(2) *Disagreements over judgments, or means:* Disagreement is also possible if all members of a group have the same goal, but are not perfectly informed about the consequences of particular choices. This is the position of the Hun–Gats: They all agree that what they want is a place to live where they can find water, hunt and gather food, and be safe from attack. If they were certain that going south means they will die of thirst, they wouldn't go. If going north means they will be clubbed by Raouli, for sure no one would advocate going north. But they don't know! Consequently, their problem is to discover the *collective wisdom* of the group, not merely add up their *preferences.*[3]

Our discussion of the political theory of Rousseau earlier in this chapter should be viewed from the perspective of making judgments. Rousseau's "general will" is the collective wisdom of the society. He had faith in the ability of voting mechanisms to discover and help carry out this collective wisdom in some circumstances. Throughout most of the rest of this book, we will treat preference aggregations and collective judgments as if they were the same.

The reason is that the politics of choice have a common structure, given either preferences or judgments. In closing this chapter, it is worth repeating that the goal of the analysis of politics is to answer three fundamental questions: (1) How do voters pick candidates to vote for? (2) How are policies or platforms chosen by governments? (3) How good are the results?

Formal theory, or theories that use mathematical models to represent politics, provide a mechanism for *analyzing* real politics by following up the implications of different "what if?" assumptions. Formal theory incorporating the spatial model of political competition provides an integrated framework within which to examine and test claims made by social scientists. Because the three fundamental questions can be integrated, analytical political theory can be used to evaluate the truth of such claims. No less important, we can examine the value of potential reforms or alternative voting systems as policy prescriptions.

The reader may recall that our poor Hun–Gats still don't know what to do. They don't even know how to decide. In later chapters, we will give the best answers that are now available, but most of the basic truths we can offer are conditional, and there may be no single right answer as a matter of definition. Politics is not for the squeamish, and no one said this was going to be easy!

EXERCISES

1.1 The language of everyday politics is full of spatial allusions, including "left," "center," and "right." Look through a few days' worth of newspaper stories or several news magazines. See if you can find three or more examples of explicitly spatial language. Then summarize the differences between left and right that the articles seem to imply, using your own words. Are the terms used consistently in the examples you found?

1.2 "Normative" arguments are disputes over what *ought* to be. "Positive" arguments are claims over what *is*. Yet this distinction often means less than it seems to, because both kinds of arguments are often being made simultaneously. In the following text, identify *at least* two normative and two positive arguments:

Justice is the first virtue of social institutions, as truth is of systems of thought. A theory however elegant and economical must be rejected or revised if it is untrue; likewise, laws and institutions no matter how efficient and well-arranged must be reformed or abolished if they are unjust. Each person possesses an inviolability founded on justice that even the welfare of society as a whole cannot override. For this reason justice denies that the loss of freedom for some is made right by a greater good shared by others. It does not allow that the sacrifices imposed on a few are outweighed by the larger sum of advantages enjoyed by many. Therefore in a just society the liberties of equal citizenship are taken as settled; the rights secured by justice are not subject to political bargaining or to the calculus of social interests. The only thing that permits us to acquiesce in an erroneous theory is the lack of a better one; analogously, an injustice is tolerable only when it is necessary to avoid an even greater injustice. Being first virtues of human activities, truth and justice are uncompromising. (Rawls, 1971, pp. 3–4)

CHAPTER 2

The spatial model of Downs and Black: One policy dimension

You will be safest in the middle.
("Publius Ovidius Naso," or
"Ovid," *Metamorphoses,*
Book II, no. 137)

The idea of spatial competition comes from Hotelling (1929) and Smithies (1941), who used "space" to describe firms' need to be near markets. Spatial theory was adapted for analytical politics by two pioneers: Anthony Downs, in *An Economic Theory of Democracy* (1957), and Duncan Black, in *The Theory of Committees and Elections* (1958). They uncovered two of the most important theoretical contributions of analytical political theory:

- Political power lies at the "middle" of the distribution of citizens *effectively* enfranchised by the society's political institutions.
- The stability of political systems is a variable, or subject of analysis. Stability depends on the distribution and nature of citizens' preferences, as well as the rules used to add up these preferences for social choices.

The contribution of the spatial theorists who have built on the work of Downs and Black has been to state these two principles of political power very precisely. Most importantly, analytical politics works to distinguish situations where the principles are true, false, or conditionally true based on other variables outside the model. The two principles themselves, however, have been recognized by political theorists for more than two thousand years.

The first spatial theorist: Aristotle

Aristotle (384–322 B.C.) was a student of Plato, a tutor to Alexander the Great, and a great thinker. One of his accomplishments has gone

21

unnoted, however, until now: Aristotle was the first spatial theorist. More accurately, he was the first to realize that political conflict has a *spatial* organization. The argument, of which we will give only excerpts, has three distinct elements:

- *Assumption:* The world view of citizens can be described by their position along a single (ordered) dimension. For Aristotle, the dimension is wealth or "class." Further, a citizen's position on this dimension determines the government action he or she likes best.
- *Causal conclusion:* In *any* government, the middle rules. The reason is that power lies at the center of those who can vote.
- *Policy conclusion:* The decision to enfranchise different groups changes the distribution of preferences in the polis. Changing the distribution of preferences alters the political "constitution" of the society.[1]

See if you can pick out these three elements in Aristotle's argument in the following passage:

Now in all states there are three elements: one class is very rich, another very poor, and a third in a mean. It is admitted that moderation and the mean are best ... for in that condition of life men are most ready to follow rational principle. . . . Thus it is manifest that the best political community is formed by citizens of the middle class, and that those states are likely to be well-administered, in which the middle class is large, and stronger if possible than both the other classes, or at any rate than either singly; for the addition of the middle class turns the scale, and prevents either of the extremes from being dominant. . . . These considerations will help us to understand why most governments are either democratical or oligarchical. The reason is that the middle class is seldom numerous in them, and whichever party ... transgresses the mean and predominates, draws the constitution its own way, and thus arises either oligarchy or democracy. (Aristotle, 1979, Book 4, Chapter 11)

For Aristotle "democracy" is a government where the poor are numerous and are allowed to vote. A government where only the wealthy can vote is an "oligarchy." Neither of these societies, Aristotle claims, are really consistent with virtue, because such societies are neither just nor stable. He goes on, in chapter 12 of Book 4:

The legislator should always include the middle class in his government. If he makes his laws oligarchical, to the middle class let him look; if he makes them democratical, he should equally by his laws try to attach this class to the state. There only can the government ever be stable where the middle class exceeds one or both of the others, and in that case there will be no fear that the rich will unite with the poor against the rulers. For neither of them will ever be willing to serve the other, and if they look for some form of government more suitable to both, they will find none better than this.

The nature of institutions, and the good society

The best government is stable and favors neither the poor nor the wealthy too heavily, in Aristotle's view. Such a government is possible only if there is a large group in the center, so that neither extreme can dominate. Consider Figure 2.1, depicting two distributions of citizens by wealth. Panel (a) depicts a society wracked by revolution. If the poor are many and enfranchised, they will favor policies of redistribution and high taxes on the rich. If only the wealthy can vote, they will defend their oligarchy by denying freedoms to the poor, for fear the poor will rise against them.

The society portrayed in panel (b) is more symmetric. Further, the center of the distribution of wealth describes many citizens. It is unlikely that such a society will see wild swings in government form. The middle class gets the government it wants, and the poor and the wealthy have diametrically opposed goals (more democracy versus more oligarchy, respectively).

Aristotle may be right that the first society has an inferior government. We would also have to concede, however, that *it is not the first government's fault.* The flaw lies with the distribution of preferences, which prevent *any* form of government in the first society from being stable. The character of government and the stability of policy can be affected by the distribution of voter preferences. Consequently, the choice of whose votes "count" is tantamount to choosing a specific policy outcome.

In the next section, we begin to analyze the claims about the importance of the center and the stability of outcomes. To do the analysis, we must introduce spatial theory.

The importance of the middle: An example

An appropriations subcommittee meets to decide the budget for construction of river and harbor projects for the coming year. Suppose the government spent $80 million on such projects last year. The subcommittee has already held hearings, so each member knows what he or she wants. Because the debate was public, each member also knows the preferences of other members.

The rules of the committee are as follows:

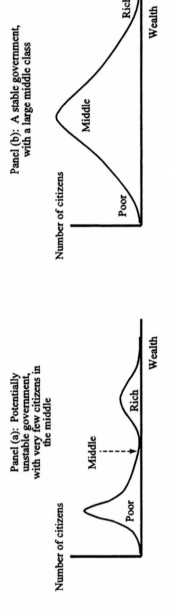

Figure 2.1. Two distributions of citizens, by wealth.

Table 2.1. *Ideal budgets for committee members A–E*

Member	Most preferred budget for rivers and harbors (millions of $)
A	150
B	100
E	*80* ← middle, or ***median,*** voter
C	50
D	10

(→ indicating member E row)

- Each member can make any proposal on the rivers and harbors budget, ranging from zero to an arbitrarily large (but still finite) number.
- New proposals are compared against the *status quo,* using majority rule. *All members must vote,* either for or against, each proposal.
- The initial status quo is last year's budget ($80 million). If a new proposal loses, it is discarded. If it wins, the proposal becomes the new status quo.
- The subcommittee has five members: A, B, C, D, and E. These members all vote based only on their preferences for the proposals then under consideration. This kind of voting is called *sincere.*

Mr. A thinks the subcommittee should recommend almost doubling the budget to $150 million. Ms. B also believes that $80 million was too little, but thinks that $100 million is the right amount. Mr. C believes that the projects built last year are enough and that the committee should recommend just enough money for maintenance, or $50 million.

Conservative Mr. D thinks rivers and harbors legislation is pure "pork barrel" spending, so just $10 million is needed for emergency repairs to existing dams. Moderate Mr. E believes that last year's budget was fine and that $80 million should be allotted again this year. The ideal budgets of all five committee members (in decreasing order) are given in Table 2.1. Two members want budgets larger than Mr. E's ideal. Two other members want to spend less than Mr. E's ideal. Consequently, the "middle" voter is member E, at $80 million.

Now we know who wants what. How can we use spatial theory to predict what will happen when the committee votes? One thing we must know is how unhappy members feel about budgets different from their ideal. Remember, there can be only one budget, and there are five different people, with five different ideals, in our example. Obviously, at least four members are not going to get exactly what they want. Now we will invoke the "ordered dimension" assumption, which allows us to conceive of preferences spatially. The simplest assumption about judgments by members is *distance.* Changes *away from* the ideal make members less happy. Members are more satisfied with changes *toward* their ideal budget.

How members choose: Preferences and representation

The meaning of the words "away from" and "toward" seem self-evident, and the use of distance as a description of preferences seems clear. That is always a bad sign. The fact is that very little is self-evident in analytical politics (or any other kind of political theory), because we have not yet carefully identified our assumptions. It is important to step back and think about what the words mean.

The general problem is to assign a *preference function* to each member. Preference functions describe how people feel about different government policies. In this case, the preference function tells us the level of satisfaction, or acceptance, of each level the budget might take. This is important, because preference functions allow us to rank members' reactions to every possible budget proposal. One way this ranking might take place is based on the difference between the proposal and ideal budget for each member.

There is an "as if" aspect to the assignment of a preference function, of course, since members may not do the calculations implied by a particular function. Preference functions simulate, or *represent,* each member's preferences. To see this, choose two proposals (y and z) arbitrarily, allowing y and z to take any values in the feasible range of budgets. Then we can give two important definitions.

Preference Function. Define a preference function U as follows:

$$\text{Utility of proposal } y = U(y) = \text{(Level of satisfaction)} \quad (2.1)$$

A function U *represents* a member's preferences if it accurately reflects that member's reactions to proposals. To summarize these reactions, we use two key relations: *preference* and *indifference.*

Preference. The member likes one alternative more than the other. Then both of the following must be true:

1. If the member (strictly) prefers y to z, then $U(y) > U(z)$.
2. If $U(y) > U(z)$, then the member prefers y to z.

Indifference. The member likes the two alternatives equally well. Then both of the following must be true:

1. If $U(y) = U(z)$, then the member is indifferent between z and y.
2. If the member is indifferent between z and y, then $U(z) = U(y)$.

If we knew a member's preference function, we could guess how he or she reacts to any proposed budget. But no one, including the member, needs to know the exact preference function to represent preference. In analytical politics, we generally are concerned with a particular kind of function for the representation of preference. These are called "spatial" preference functions, where *satisfaction is higher the closer a proposal is to the member's ideal.* The only properties of spatial preference functions that we will assume for now are the following:

(a) *Unidimensionality:* There is only one issue (here, the budget), and members like their own ideal budgets best. This is the "ordered dimension" assumption mentioned above.
(b) *Preferences are single-peaked:* Each member likes new proposed budgets more the "closer" they are to the member's ideal.
(c) *Voting is sincere:* If $U(y) > U(z)$, the member votes for y, regardless of what other proposals might later be raised if y becomes the new status quo. More intuitively, sincere voting means that the member considers only the two alternatives being voted on and disregards the agenda of future votes.

There is an additional property of spatial preference functions that we will find useful to invoke:

(d) *Symmetry:* A preference function is symmetric if equal departures from the ideal in opposite directions yield equal declines in satisfaction.

Properties (a)–(c) are the assumptions of the spatial model of political preferences, with (d) used only sometimes. These assumptions re-

Intensity of preference

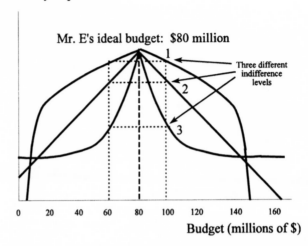

Figure 2.2. Three possible preference functions for committee member E.

strict the set of possible preferences we have to consider. That is not to say that (a)–(d) are always accurate! For example, if members can forecast the sequence of future votes (the *agenda*), they may not vote sincerely, as we will see in Chapter 8.

Likewise, symmetry is a stronger assumption than may be required to say important things about political choice. Let's just consider the preferences of one member, Mr. E. If two alternatives are the same distance from E's ideal point, $80 million (say, $y = 60 million and $z = 100 million) and the preference function is symmetric, then E won't care which proposal is chosen ($U($60m$) = U($100m$)$). We say that E is *indifferent* between the two proposals. If one alternative (say, $40 million) is farther away than another (such as $100 million), E prefers the closer alternative. Remember, there are but two ways E can react to any pair of budget proposals: He can prefer one, or he can be indifferent between them. Both relations are consistent with *many* different spatial preference functions. The graph of a preference function is called the *preference curve*.

Three very different preference curves are depicted in Figure 2.2. The *intensity* of preference (the height of the curve, or the vertical axis in Figure 2.2) is arbitrary. Each curve depicts a preference function that

Intensity of preference

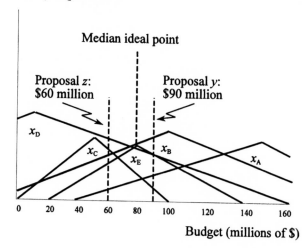

Figure 2.3. Two proposals, z and y, and preference functions for committee members.

satisfies assumptions (a)–(d), so each of the three curves is equally valid as a representation of the preferences of member E in our example. The fact that they are strikingly different reflects the fact that functions that represent preferences are not unique.

Other committee members have preferences, too. One of many possible forms is depicted in Figure 2.3. Note that each of these (linear) preference curves satisfies assumptions (a)–(d), so that they are single-peaked and symmetric. For example, B wants $100 million, prefers $90 million to $80 million, and is indifferent between $85 million and $115 million.

What if we *drop* the restrictive assumption of symmetry? The preference curves wouldn't (necessarily) look like those in Figures 2.2 and 2.3, because increases may look different from decreases, compared with the ideal budget, for each member. We say symmetry is "restrictive" because it rules out plausible forms of political preference, such as that depicted in Figure 2.4. Here, a committee member (G) has an ideal budget of $5,400 per student.

Mr. G feels strongly that spending should be no less than this ideal, because his main concern is that the school budget be *at least* $5,400

Intensity of preference

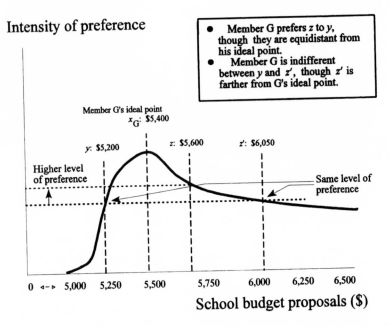

> • Member G prefers *z* to *y*, though they are equidistant from his ideal point.
> • Member G is indifferent between *y* and *z'*, though *z'* is farther from G's ideal point.

Figure 2.4. Example of asymmetric preferences: Member G likes increases in school spending more than cuts.

per student. As the figure shows, increases in spending beyond his ideal don't bother him much. If member G compares proposal *z* with *y*, he likes *z* better ($U(z) > U(y)$), though *y* is closer to his ideal point. We would have to overspend dramatically to find a budget (z') that G values as little as *y*. Mr. G's preferences are asymmetric because he values deviations from his ideal point differently depending on whether the proposed spending level is (from his perspective) too much or too little.

Can we say anything about what the committee is likely to decide, given only assumptions (a)–(c) (leaving out symmetry)? Suppose A proposes to increase spending over last year's level, to *y* million dollars ($y > \$80$ million). How many members will prefer *y* to the last year's budget? Two members (A and B), *at most*, will prefer any $y > \$80$ million. In the example in Figure 2.3, we set $y = \$90$ million. As expected (since $y > \$80$ million, and A and B want increases), A and B prefer *y* to \$80 million.

Imagine C proposes to decrease spending to *z*, where $\$0 < z < \$80$

million. One possibility is the proposal in Figure 2.3, where $z = \$60$ million. Both C and D prefer z to the status quo, but A, B, and E prefer $80 million. What we have shown (informally) is that any budget larger than $80 million will lose by a vote of 3 to 2. We have also shown that any budget less than $80 million will lose by a 3 to 2 vote.

This phenomenon is general, because the same reasoning applies to any status quo in the middle. All that is required is that each member like budgets less the more they differ from that member's ideal budget. Symmetric preference is not required, for any member. The "middle" ideal budget ($80 million) will win a majority against any other alternatives, such as $z < \$80$ million or $y > \$80$ million. Even if groups of members try to form coalitions, the middle member's ideal point will win if each member votes sincerely. What are we to make of this?

Political power rests in the middle of the distribution of voters, that's what. The example we have just seen is a key theoretical result for majority rule decisions on one issue. This result is commonly called the *median voter theorem* (from now on, MVT). Now that we have explained just what is meant by "distance" for representing preference, we can address the technical details that make the MVT result true or conditionally true.

More careful definitions

Let's go back to the beginning. The general problem is that a society of N people must choose *one* position on an issue. This situation is common in public life: There cannot be two different defense budgets in a given year, for example, or two different minimum drinking ages. Assume (perhaps less realistically) that the issue in question can be separated from decisions on other issues. Further, let all members vote sincerely. What will happen? Can we predict what they will decide, as a group, given information only about their individual goals and the decision rule?

The first step is to specify how members rank alternatives. For simplicity, consider a *representative citizen i*, where i can be anyone in the society from 1 to N. Assume i has an *ideal point* x_i, or a unique[2] position strictly preferred to any other alternative. (Notice that for ideal points, and for most other purposes in this book, *subscripts* are used to identify *people*, so x_1 is person 1's ideal point, and x_i is i's ideal point.)

Finally, let $|x|$ denote the absolute value of a number x. For example,

$|-7| = 7$; $|56| = 56$. Consider two alternatives y and z, where both y and z are on the *same side* of x_i (this means symmetry is irrelevant). We can now define two relations, called "preference" and "indifference."

Preference

i *prefers* y to z if and only if $|y - x_i| < |z - x_i|$ (2.2)

Indifference

i is *indifferent* between y and z if and only if $|y - x_i| = |z - x_i|$ (2.3)

The only innovation in these definitions is that now preference intensity varies with distance. Unlike more abstract preference functions, both these definitions clearly require that the issue being considered be continuous and unambiguously ordered along a single dimension (for more detail, see Appendix 2A). For the example we have been considering, the dimension is budget size, but the model is equally applicable to many other spatial settings.

Symmetry is *not* assumed in these formal definitions. Without assuming symmetry, we can define preference and indifference only for the case where y and z are on the same side of the ideal point. If preferences are symmetric, then (2.2) and (2.3) also describe i's evaluation of y and z when y and z are on *different* sides of x_i. This seems a powerful statement, but the power of the claim derives from the restrictiveness of the assumption of symmetry.

Now that indifference and preference have been defined for individual i, we can consider these same relations, and the distribution of ideal points $\{x_1, x_2, \ldots, x_N\}$ for many citizens, and see what happens when they have to vote.

The middle is the "median"

At the beginning of this chapter, we claimed that power resides in the middle of the distribution of voters. But just what does "middle" mean in large groups of voters? Social scientists use at least three different measures of the central tendency of a distribution:

Mean: The sum of the values divided by the number of values. In our subcommittee example, this is:

$$(10 + 50 + 80 + 100 + 150) / 5 = \$78 \text{ million}$$

Mode: The most frequently occurring value. Each of the five ideal points occurs just once in the subcommittee example, so the mode provides little guidance: The "distribution" has five modes.

Median: The middle value. The middle value, as we discussed, is $80 million, because there are two ideal points larger and two smaller than this value.

In *pairwise* majority rule elections (elections comparing exactly two alternatives), a proposal preferred by one half ($N/2$) of the voters is guaranteed to be at least a tie. If an alternative receives more than $N/2$ votes, it wins outright. This property suggests that the median captures an important part of what is meant by the "middle" in politics.[3] Simply put, *the median value beats or ties all other alternatives in pairwise majority rule elections.*

To see this, consider the definition of a median position:

- Choose an arbitrary x_i
- Let N_L be the number of citizens for whom $x_L \leq x_i$
- Let N_R be the number of citizens for whom $x_i \leq x_R$.

Then a median position can be defined as follows.

Median position. A position x_i is a *median position,* or x_{med}, if and only if:

(1) $N_R \geq N/2$

and

(2) $N_L \geq N/2$.

This definition, adapted only slightly from Duncan Black's formulation,[4] is cumbersome. But it is also general, because it encompasses odd and even N and situations where several voters share an ideal point. A more intuitive definition is given by Thomas Schwartz: "x is a median position if 'no majority of individuals have ideal points (peaks) to the left or to the right of x'" (1986, p. 87).

The difference between the two definitions has to do with the treatment of the median position itself. In our definition, N_L and N_R *both* encompass the ideal point(s) at the median position, so $N_L \geq N/2$ and $N_R \geq N/2$. In Schwartz's definition, no majority can have ideal points *strictly* to the left or right of the median position. The advantage of

Black's definition is that it measures directly the vote that the median position will receive in a majority rule election. For any proposal to the left of x_i, the median will receive at least N_R votes. For any proposal to the right of x_i, the median position will receive at least N_L votes.

Odd N, even N, and uniqueness of the median position

In some cases, such as for the congressional subcommittee example (Figure 2.3) the median ideal point was easy to identify. There were *three* members (D, C, and E) who had ideal points less than or equal to x_{med}. There were also *three* (E, B, and A) with ideal points at least as big as x_{med}. E is a median position, since $N/2 = 2.5$, $N_L = 3 > N/2 = 2.5$, and $N_R = 3 > N/2 = 2.5$.

The median is not always so easy to identify. For one thing, the median may not be unique. Suppose that E, whose ideal point is depicted in Figure 2.3, was absent on the day of the vote. Now $N = 4$, and *all positions between 50 and 100* (including $x_C = 50$ and $x_B = 100$) are "medians." Consider, for example, $x = 70$. There are two ideal points above 70 and two below 70. The same is true for 69, or 71, or 98.

If N is odd, and assumptions (a)–(c) are met, there must be a unique median. However, several voters may share this ideal point, so while there is a unique median there may be no unique "median voter." For example, suppose that $x_1 = 10$, $x_2 = 4$, $x_3 = -2$, $x_4 = 0$, and $x_5 = 7$ in a five-person society. Then the unique median position is 4, and x_2 is the median voter.

Now consider a seven-person society, where $x_1 = 10$, $x_2 = 4$, $x_3 = -2$, $x_4 = 0$, $x_5 = 7$, $x_6 = 2$, and $x_7 = 2$. N is odd, so the median position must be unique. A moment's thought shows this is true: There are five citizens with ideals larger than or equal to 2 and four with ideals smaller than or equal to 2. But there is no unique median voter, because the median position is held by two citizens, 6 and 7.

Once we allow citizens to share ideal points, it turns out that a unique median can exist even if N is even. Suppose $x_1 = 9$, $x_2 = 3$, $x_3 = 3$, and $x_4 = -2$. Clearly, $x_{med} = 3$. There is only one median position (though there are two "median voters"), even though the number of voters is even.

It is worth summarizing what we know about the existence and nature of median points, given the distribution of voter ideal points:

- If N is odd, then the *median is always unique.* This is true even if ideal points are shared. (See Exercise 2.6.)
- If N is even and no ideal points are shared, there is a *closed interval*[5] of medians.
- If N is even and some ideal points are shared, then there may be either a unique median or a closed interval of medians.

The median voter theorem

We are now in a position to state and prove the median voter theorem (MVT) and a corollary. The MVT result is based on the two assumptions discussed earlier:

(1) There is a single issue. This means that all the alternatives can be represented as points on one line, and each voter has an ideal point x_i on this line.

(2) Preferences are such that given two alternatives y and z *on the same side* of x_i, individual i votes for y if and only if $|y - x_i| < |z - x_i|$. This type of preference is called "single-peaked."

Median voter theorem. Suppose x_{med} is a median position for the society. Then the number of votes for x_{med} is greater than or equal to the number of votes for any other alternative z.

Proof. Suppose $z < x_{med}$. All ideal points to the right of x_{med} are closer to x_{med} than to z. But since x_{med} and z are both to the left of x_i, all voters with ideal points to the right of x_{med} vote for x_{med} versus z, by assumption (b). Likewise, all voters with ideal points exactly equal to x_{med} vote for x_{med}. Since x_{med} is a median position, there are at least $N/2$ voters such that $x_i \geq x_{med}$. So x_{med} receives at least $N/2$ votes, ensuring victory over any alternative to the left. The same reasoning applies if $z > x_{med}$.

To paraphrase: A median position can *never* lose in a majority rule contest. It can *tie* other alternatives if there is a closed interval of medi-

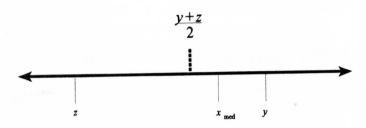

Figure 2.5. Midpoint between z and y is less than the median position.

ans, since any two median points will by definition each receive $N/2$ votes, but it cannot lose. The statement and proof of the MVT is probably best attributed to Duncan Black.[6]

Corollary to the median voter result

The corollary requires two extra assumptions:

(3) The society has exactly one median position x_{med}.
(4) Voter preferences around x_i are symmetric, so that every voter i prefers y to z when $|y - x_i| < |z - x_i|$, even if y and z are on opposite sides of x_i.

Corollary. If y is closer to x_{med} than z, then y beats z in a majority rule election.

Proof. Again, let $z < y$. Since y is closer to x_{med} than z is, it must be true that $(y + z)/2 < x_{med}$, whether y and z are on the same side of x_{med} or not (for an example, see Figure 2.5). The position $(y + z)/2$ is the point that is equidistant from y and z. Thus, all ideal points to the right of $(y + z)/2$ (i.e., the set of x_i such that $x_i > (y + z)/2$) are closer to y than to z, whereas all ideal points to the left of $(y + z)/2$ are closer to z than to y. Since x_{med} is unique, we know that the number of ideal points equal to or to the right of x_{med} is greater than $N/2$. These ideal points are closer to y than to z, because $(y + z)/2 < x_{med}$. Since preferences are symmetric, y receives a majority of the votes.

The MVT says that if the median position itself is one of the alternatives being compared, the median always wins. The corollary implies that for any other pair of proposals, the alternative *closer* to the median wins if preferences are symmetric.

What if preferences aren't single-peaked?

In the passage quoted at the beginning of this chapter, Aristotle noted that one source of instability of governments is wide variations in the distribution of wealth. He assumed that such differences caused disagreement over the basic structure of society: Poor people favor democracy, while the wealthy favor oligarchy. If Aristotle is right, such conflict could cause instability on a grand scale. There is a more common kind of instability in political processes, however, caused by the form of preferences people have over policies. This type of instability is observed when some people's preferences are not single-peaked.

If a significant proportion of voters have preferences that are not single-peaked, there may be no median voter, even if the other assumptions of the MVT are met. Black (1958) showed that single-peaked preference is akin to the assumption of *transitivity,* generally innocuous in economic choice but a crucial and restrictive assumption in the study of politics. Riker (1982) argues persuasively that the possibilities for genuine "popular rule" may be sharply circumscribed by the structure of preferences among voters. It is still not clear whether this incoherence and unpredictability extend to the aggregation of judgments, as opposed to preferences.[7]

It is hard to say who first discovered the difficulties that non-single-peaked preferences cause for the coherence of democratic processes.[8] There is no doubt, however, about the importance of the result: *If preferences are not single-peaked, it may be strictly impossible to arrive at a nonarbitrary outcome, or collective judgment, by majority rule.* This is not some minor mathematical curiosity, because it means that claims about the existence of the middle are only conditionally true.[9]

To see how preferences that are not single-peaked can affect democratic choice, we will consider two very different examples: (1) a simplified characterization of U.S. public attitudes toward United Nations (U.N.) involvement in Bosnia, and (2) the "what do we do now" problem of the Hun–Gats, from Chapter 1.

The U.N. in Bosnia

Imagine it is September 1995. Bosnian government forces are trying to break the siege of the Bosnian capital, Sarajevo. Bosnian Serb rebel forces, with the tacit support of the government of the Serbian Republic (which controlled most of the Yugoslav federal army forces and heavy weapons such as tanks and artillery), are shelling the city of Sarajevo. The rebels are blocking the delivery of truckloads of humanitarian aid by international relief agencies. Suppose (simplifying greatly) that attitudes of U.S. citizens about U.N. involvement in the Bosnian war can be organized into three groups.

Stay Outites. This group thinks that the fighting in the former Yugoslavia is simply a civil war. There is no international threat, unless one or more world powers become involved. They oppose any direct foreign military involvement. This group might allow the use of a limited number of troops to secure routes for humanitarian aid, but would prefer to stay out completely and supply only food and medicine to refugees.

New World Orderists. People with this preference profile consider the conflict to be a threat to the stability of international trade and stability. They are concerned that the war itself will spread beyond the Bosnian borders or that tensions over resolution of the conflict will raise tensions between Russia and the West. Their ideal solution is to insert U.N. peacemakers between combatants, along existing lines of control by both sides. They want to pressure Bosnian Serbs to give back captured territory, but do not advocate actual fighting by U.N. troops. The worst alternative would be to do nothing, because of the potential for unrestricted conflict to spread.

Serb Blamers. This group sees the rebels (and their Serbian sponsors) as the aggressors in the conflict. The Serb Blamers want to punish the Serbs for their attempts at "ethnic cleansing" and force them to relinquish all captured territory, by force if necessary. Second best would be to withdraw all U.N. troops and foreign citizens and end the arms embargo to allow the Bosnians to fight on a more equal basis. The worst solution would be to use U.N. troops to enforce the current (illegiti-

Intensity of preference

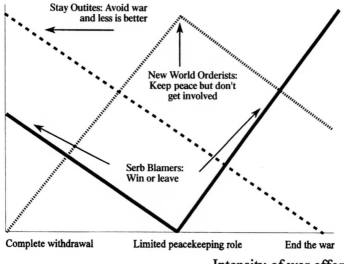

Figure 2.6. Preference profiles for New World Orderists, Stay Outites, and Serb Blamers for intensity of U.N. involvement in the former Yugoslav Republic.

mate) front lines as borders and prevent the Bosnians from lifting the siege of Sarajevo.

Figure 2.6 depicts the preference profiles of the three groups. The reader will note that while the preferences of Stay Outites and New World Orderists are single-peaked, the preferences of Serb Blamers are not. Serb Blamers prefer either of the extremes of the policy dimension to alternatives in the middle. Suppose that the U.N. Security Council is a committee composed of three people, a Serb Blamer, a New World Orderist, and a Stay Outite. The Security Council uses simple majority rule to decide the extent of U.N. troop involvement.[10] Though "intensity of involvement," the horizontal axis in Figure 2.6, is continuous (i.e., it is possible to make small changes in policy in either direction), we will consider only three policy alternatives: complete withdrawal, limited peacekeeping, and assault the Serbian rebel troops. The voters, alternatives, and their rankings are depicted in Table 2.2.

We can choose a starting point (status quo) arbitrarily. Suppose that

Table 2.2. *Rankings of alternatives by three-person committee*

	Member		
Ranking	New World Orderist	Stay Outite	Serb Blamer
Best	Limited action	Complete withdrawal	All-out war
Middle	All-out war	Limited action	Complete withdrawal
Worst	Complete withdrawal	All-out war	Limited action

the U.N. Secretary General has already started a "peacekeeping action," so the committee is meeting to decide if they want to change from peacekeeping to some other policy. The Stay Outite then proposes withdrawal. The Stay Outite and the Serb Blamer prefer withdrawal to the status quo (police action). The New World Orderist prefers the status quo. The withdrawal alternative wins, 2 to 1.

Now suppose the Serb Blamer proposes aggressive threats and air strikes to punish the rebels and take back their ill-gotten gains. Serb Blamer and New World Orderist both vote to stop the war by assaulting the rebels, so aggressive action beats withdrawal, 2 to 1. But the New World Orderist is upset at this escalation of tension and proposes going back to passive peacekeeping. The Stay Outite likes that idea, and of course the New World Orderist does too. Peacekeeping, the original status quo, beats aggressive intervention, 2 to 1, and is reimplemented, while all the world wonders.

What happened here? The sequence of majority rule votes moved us from the original status quo, passive peacekeeping, through each of the other alternatives, right back to where we started! As Figure 2.7 shows, this "cycle" has no end. Majority rule votes on pairs of alternatives will never settle on one outcome in this scenario because preferences aren't single-peaked.

The world was repulsed by its inability to choose a policy in dealing with the war among the former republics of Yugoslavia in the mid-1990s. Ultimately, the international political system was strained almost to the breaking point, and many questioned whether it is possible for an international agency to act effectively. No doubt some of these criticisms were justified. Yet it is hard to avoid noticing that the U.N. ap-

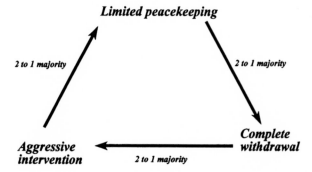

Figure 2.7. The majority rule voting cycle over intensity of U.N. involvement in Bosnia.

peared incompetent because the "middle course" was untenable. A sizable proportion of the world's nations appeared to believe that the U.N. should either go in strong or get out, yet very few of those nations showed much willingness to commit troops to such an intervention.

This is a common problem in majority rule cycles. There is never a majority clearly in favor of any policy for very long. While the political conflict was much more complex than our depiction here, there is some evidence (see, e.g., Russett and Shye, 1993) that *precisely* the sorts of preferences that would lead to a cycle in majority rule voting outcomes can be found in public opinion surveys. In the 1960s, Barry Goldwater and his supporters made very explicit arguments that the United States should either fight an all-out war in Vietnam or withdraw all troops immediately. The "middle" course, a limited action where the United States provided a steadily escalating number of advisors and war materiel to the Army of the Republic of Vietnam, was (for the Goldwater faction) the worst alternative. The preferences implied by this perspective are not single-peaked; the outcome implied by a significant faction with non-single-peaked preferences is a majority rule cycle.

The Hun–Gats

What of our undecided Hun–Gats? The reader will recall we left this tribe of hunter–gatherers sitting around their campfire, trying to decide

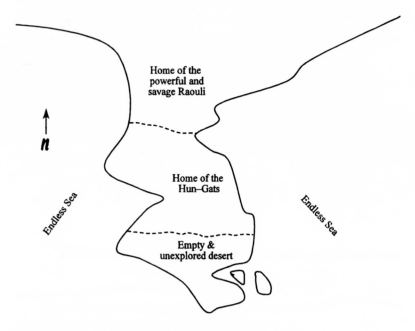

Figure 2.8. The spatial decision problem of the Hun–Gats.

what to do. A map of the Hun–Gats' situation appears in Figure 2.8. Assuming they don't split up, the Hun–Gats must choose among three mutually exclusive courses of action:

- Go north and face the warlike and cannibalistic Raouli, who consider trespassers a chance for a bodacious barbecue. The land of the Raouli is fertile and filled with game and good water.
- Stay at home in the land of the Hun–Gats near Muddy River. There is very little game, fish, or edible plant life left in this "home," but they have water and know the area. Also, nobody else wants it, so they don't have to fight.
- Go south and explore the unknown desert at the end of the peninsula. There may be sources of water far to the south, and there may be game and edible plants around these oases. There also may be nothing to drink or eat.

The Hun–Gats all have identical "preferences," in the sense that they all (1) want to live in a place where they can find food and water and

Table 2.3. *Ranking of alternatives by Hun–Gat factions*

	Faction		
Ranking	Raouli will kill us, stay far away	Anywhere but here	No place like home
Best	Go south	Go north	Stay here
Middle	Stay here	Go south	Go north
Worst	Go north	Stay here	Go south

(2) want to avoid being brained by heavy clubs and then eaten. However, they disagree (i.e., have differing judgments) about the best way to achieve this goal.

There are three distinct factions in the tribe. Each faction has a preference profile induced by a particular judgment about the implications of different courses of action. The three groups and their preferences are described in Table 2.3. The timid "Raouli will kill us!" faction fears the other tribe and believes the farther away they live the better. This group wants to try going south, with staying here second best, and moving north the worst alternative.

The "Anywhere but here!" faction is made up of the younger males of the tribe. They are tired of subsisting near the Muddy River. They are also convinced the Raouli can't be as fierce as the timid old people claim. For this faction, the best action is to move north. Next best is to move south and explore the desert. Worst is staying here and starving by inches.

The "No place like home!" faction thinks the land of the Hun–Gats is not so bad, because they are terrified at the prospect of dying of thirst in the desert. Their best alternative is to remain at home. Second best is to move North, where at least the land is familiar and fertile.

If these groups are of approximately equal size, the result will once again be a cycle. The reason is that the preference profile of the "Anywhere but here!" faction is not single-peaked.[11] They think that the middle alternative is the worst. If the status quo is remaining where they are, then a majority of the tribe (those afraid of the Raouli and those who prefer anything to staying home) will vote to move south. But then a majority (the "Anywhere but here!" and the "No place like home!"

factions) will vote to move north. Finally, a majority will prefer to stay home rather than go north, bringing us back to the original status quo.

There is no general will. There is no way out for the Hun–Gats, no matter how earnestly they try to implement Rousseau's optimistic instructions.[12] For a coherent middle to exist, the preferences of participants must be single-peaked. To put it another way, if a significant proportion of citizens think the "middle course" is wrong, democracy can be unstable and even incoherent.

The discussion in this section represents a slightly different statement of the thesis advanced in William Riker's (1982) *Liberalism against Populism*. In this famous book, Riker argues that too much faith has been placed by political theorists in the power of participatory, or populist, democracy:

> What is different between the liberal and populist views is that, in the populist interpretation of voting, the opinions of the majority *must* be right and *must* be respected because the will of the people is the liberty of the people. In the liberal interpretation, there is no such magical identification. The outcome of voting is just a decision and has no special moral character. (p. 14; emphasis in original)

Riker's interpretation of voting is simple: Elections are a way to control officials and nothing more. Some observers have called this conclusion unduly pessimistic or have objected that the normative conclusions make citizens skeptical about government.

This critique of Riker's conclusions, however, ignores the *positive* character of his argument. The nonexistence of a single best alternative is not of itself good or bad. Rather, cycles are a generic property of majority rule decision processes, under some circumstances. As long as the "middle" either does not exist or exists conditionally and ephemerally, a faith in the ability of majorities *always* to discover objective truth is dangerous and misleading.

The best counterargument for Riker's indictment of populism is probably a focus on arriving at judgments rather than choosing based on judgments already made. Coleman and Ferejohn (1986) point out that voting may be the only way of making good judgments. Their defense of "populism" rests on its ability to identify the right thing to do, just as Rousseau argued. "The desirability of a voting rule will then depend on its reliability – the extent to which the collective judgments it generates converge with what is in fact the correct judgment" (Coleman and Ferejohn, 1986, pp. 16–17). This argument is extended and qualified by Ladha (1996) and Ladha and Miller (1996). A key difficulty with the argument is that it requires choices among exactly two mutually exclusive alternatives. If there are three or more alternatives, then voting on judgments is subject to the problem of cycling majorities, as the Hun–Gats example shows.

Conclusion

In this chapter, we saw both *definitions* and *results*. It is important to keep these two building blocks distinct, as definitions are in effect the premises of arguments, and results are conclusions based on those premises. One key definition was that of *preferences* over a *space of alternatives*. The idea is that voting choices can be predicted by comparing *distances* from an ideal point to an alternative. The two basic results of this chapter can be summarized by restating the MVT and its corollary requiring the additional assumption of symmetric preferences.

> Median voter theorem: *A median position cannot lose to any other alternative in a majority rule election.*

The MVT implies that the middle of the distribution of citizen preferences in a society holds a privileged position in political competition. If the median position is unique (identified with just one voter), we call this very important person the "median voter."

> Corollary: *In a comparison of alternatives that are not median positions, the alternative closer to the median wins.*

The corollary shows that under certain conditions (unique median and symmetric preferences), closeness to the middle is the basis of political power. Consequently, even if the status quo is different from the median, there are pressures for new alternatives to move toward the center until a median position is reached.

Together, these two conditions establish an important benchmark in what we can say about the likely outcomes of political conflict. More important, we have given some formal support for the intuitive claim that the "center" of the society is where political power lies. As we have pointed out repeatedly, this notion of the center as the source of political power is widely held and is taken for granted by the media and political operatives alike.

In the preceding section, we showed that an additional restriction on preferences, called "single-peakedness," is paramount. One of the most famous and influential arguments about the possibility of "populism," or determinate democratic choice in the face of disagreement, was Riker's (1982). Riker's work brought together the results of many other social choice theorists. The primary conclusion of this body of research is that unless preferences are single-peaked, there may not be a viable "center" that leads to stable policy choices. In this view, fear of tyranny by the majority is perfectly legitimate. In the will of the majority there does not, of necessity, inhere the moral force attributed to the "general will" by Rousseau and others.

In the next chapter, we will generalize the MVT to allow for more than one dimension. It will turn out that the simple intuition about distance and voting that led us this far is not reliable. In two or more dimensions, the "center" may not exist at all, even if preferences of individuals are single-peaked.

Appendix 2A: "Space" means ordered dimensions and continuity

We have been using a spatial representation of preferences, but have not properly defined just what it means for issues to be represented as dimensions and for preferences to be points in a "space." The use of a space to represent preferences is usually claimed to have two requirements:

- *Alternatives are ordered:* It must be possible to arrange policy alternatives along a dimension, from "less" to "more." Further, this perception of order must be shared, so that all voters are choosing from the same dimension.
- *Policy space is continuous:* Technically, a space is continuous if between any two feasible alternatives there lies another feasible alternative.

What if dimensions are not ordered?

The assumption that an issue can be thought of as an ordered space may be difficult to sustain for some issues, where there are multiple alternatives distinguished as categories rather than as measured levels of a property. In the Hun–Gats example, the three alternatives (north, stay, south) are *not* ordered. Nothing important would be changed if the choices were north, stay, east, for example. But this means that "preference functions" can handle nonordered alternatives perfectly well. If a Hun–Gat prefers to go north rather than staying home, and wants least of all to go south, all we need is a (transitive) preference function such that:

$$U(\text{north}) > U(\text{stay}) > U(\text{south})$$

Such a preference function is not strictly "spatial," of course, so we cannot use distance between alternatives in defining which alternative is preferred. However, as we have pointed out earlier, there are many ways of representing preference other than using distance. If alternatives are not ordered, it is perfectly possible to define preference functions of a more abstract sort. This more general type of analysis is well developed in the advanced formal theory literature, including Schofield (1985) and Schwartz (1986).

Importantly, the reader should note that defining "single-peakedness" does *not* require ordered dimensions. If one arrays three or more alternatives randomly, all that is required is that a substantial proportion of the voters consider the middle alternative to be worse than at least one of the alternatives on both sides, *no matter what the order of the alternatives.* The question of which preference profile violates single-peakedness then becomes arbitrary, of course. Nonetheless, single-peakedness in the set of preferences is violated, and the result is a cycle in majority rule outcomes.

What if alternatives are not continuous?

The second assumption, *continuity,* is met (at least approximately) for most policy debates on taxes or spending, since between (for example) proposals of $1,000 and $1,500 lies another alternative: $1,250; between $1,000 and $1,250 lies $1,125; and so on. However, for other policies (such as abortion rights and capital punishment), continuity may not be a useful assumption.

Critics of the spatial model have pointed out that continuity may not hold, particularly in elections involving the general public. In some ways this is true, as we shall see when we discuss alternative theories later in this book. However, the criticism may be overblown, because critics have confused two types of assumptions: *necessary* assumptions and *sufficient* assumptions. It is certainly true that spatial theorists often assume a shared, continuous ordering over policy alternatives, because this assumption is sufficient to simplify exposition of the model. But these assumptions (particularly the continuity assumption) are not necessary for the logic of the model to be applied.

EXERCISES

2.1 For a given issue, let $x_1 = 2$, $x_2 = 6$, $x_3 = 9$, $x_4 = 9$, and $x_5 = -2$. What is the median position of the five voters? What is the mean, or average, position?

2.2 Suppose this five-member committee (from Exercise 2.1) is asked to vote (sincerely) on two alternatives, $y = 8$ and $z = 3$. If preferences are symmetric, which alternative will win?

2.3 Suppose $x_6 = 7$ is added to the committee. What is (are) the median position(s) now? If the new, six-member committee is asked to choose between $y = 8$ and $z = 3$, what happens?

2.4 For another issue, let $x_1 = -3$, $x_2 = 21$, $x_3 = 7$, $x_4 = 6$, and $x_5 = -4$. What is the median position and mean ideal point of these five voters? Suppose x_3 is replaced by $x_3' = 25$. Which changes more, the mean or the median position?

2.5 Given Aristotle's discussion of the distribution of citizens that makes for the best society, is "mean" an accurate description of what he meant?

2.6 Three different measures of the central tendency of a distribution were discussed in the chapter: mean, mode, and median. For what sorts of distributions are these three concepts identical?

2.7 The median income for a family of four in the United States is about $28,000. The mean income for a family of four is about $34,000. Which is a better measure of "middle class," as you understand that term? Draw a distribution of income in which the mean is larger than the median. Do you think this type of distribution also describes the patterns of incomes in other countries?

2.8* Prove the following statement: "If N is odd, the median is always

Note: Exercises marked * are advanced material.

a single point, and not an interval." (*Hint: Assume an interval of ideal points exists, and then use the median voter result proved in this chapter to show that an interval of medians implies N is even. It may help to remember that any integer multiplied by two is even.*)

CHAPTER 3

Two dimensions: Elusive equilibrium

> The rights of men are in a sort of middle, incapable of definition, but not impossible to be discerned. . . . Political reason is a computing principle; adding, subtracting, multiplying, and dividing, morally and not metaphysically, or mathematically, true moral denominations.
>
> (Edmund Burke, *Reflections on the Revolution in France,*
> 1790, Part IV)

Is Edmund Burke right? Is the "middle" in complex political choices really "incapable of definition, but not impossible to be discerned"? To answer, we must recognize that real political choices are more complex than the simple choice of one policy. Considering more than one policy also requires a description of voter priorities and candidate strategies.

In this chapter, we will present a verbal and graphical exposition of choice of two policies. All the important concepts and features of two-dimensional political choice will be introduced, but not covered in depth. The specialist reader, interested in the technical details, will want to skim the intuitive overview given in this chapter and then go on to Chapter 4. The reader seeing this material for the first time, however, should master the intuitive presentation before continuing.

The Appropriations Subcommittee

Let's return to the Appropriations Subcommittee from the last chapter. Suppose the members (our friends from the preceding chapter: A, B, C, D, and E) must also budget for a second project, currently slated for $40 million in spending. Suppose Mr. A (that liberal!) wants to increase the amount spent on Project 2 to $120 million, so that it can be finished more quickly. Ms. B also believes more money should be spent, but an increase as large as Mr. A wants is too dangerous a precedent for the many other projects the committee must vote on. Consequently, B favors an increase to only $70 million.

Mr. C is satisfied this is a good project, but thinks the current $40

Table 3.1. *Subcommittee ideal points on two projects*

Member	Project 1 (millions of $)	Project 2 (millions of $)
Mr. A	150	120
Ms. B	100	70
Mr. C	50	40
Mr. D	10	200
Mr. E	80	60
Status quo	80	40

million budget is adequate. Mr. D (that conservative!) loves Project 2. He thinks it contributes to national security (because it creates employment in his district). Consequently, $x_D = \$200$ million. Mr. E also likes the project, but favors an increase to only $60 million. The ideal positions for all five subcommittee members, on both Projects 1 and 2, are listed in Table 3.1.

Though it is not obvious at first, having two (or more) projects changes the voters' problem significantly. Members' priorities on the two projects may differ markedly. Further, preferences about spending levels for Projects 1 and 2 may be related, positively or negatively, and this relation may differ across members. The projects serve different groups of people or different national needs. For example, notice from Table 3.1 that Mr. D wants a *cut* in Project 1 and an *increase* in Project 2. The issues could be linked if the projects affect each other. Members could also want a constant total budget or seek avoidance of duplication. If one project affects another in any of these ways, we will call this a "complementarity"; complementarities can be either positive or negative.

The one-dimensional model of the preceding chapter can't handle this problem, unless the projects are genuinely separable. Separability requires more than just considering the project in different bills: *Preferences* themselves must be "separable." Consequently, we need a model that allows a joint preference rule for the two projects. We will continue to use capital letter subscripts to differentiate committee members. From now on, we will also use number subscripts to distinguish projects (here, Projects 1 and 2). For example, A's ideal point on Project 1 is $x_{A1} = 150$; D's ideal point on Project 2 is $x_{D2} = 200$. It is useful to think of the policy "space" as two-dimensional, with each dimension measuring the budget of one project. Some readers will recognize this two-dimensional space P as a Cartesian product:

$$P = P_1 \times P_2.$$

Practically, what this means is that we can define budget proposals and member ideal points along both dimensions at the same time. Ms. B's ideal, for example, is $\mathbf{x}_B = (x_{B1}, x_{B2}) = (100, 70)$. (Note: The **bold** notation indicates that $\mathbf{x}_B$ is a "vector" with two elements: B's ideal point on Project 1 and her ideal point on Project 2.) Her ideal point is the element of P (the set of all possible budgets for Projects 1 and 2) that Ms. B likes best. Any other point is definitionally less preferred by B.

The key element in the spatial approach is the representation of preference as some weighted function of distance (Davis and Hinich, 1966; Davis, Hinich, and Ordeshook, 1970). Before we can go any further toward the concept of distance in more than one dimension, we must introduce three key concepts: salience, separable preferences, and equilibrium.

- *Salience:* The relative importance of different issues to the member. The more important an issue, the more "salient" for the member's decision about how to vote.
- *Separable preferences:* If preferences are "separable," the expected *level* of one project has no influence on *ideal points* of other projects. If preferences on two issues are not separable, the ideal point on each issue is, in effect, known only conditionally.
- *Equilibrium:* An equilibrium in political decision making is a status quo position in the policy space that cannot be defeated by another feasible position. In principle, such a position could either defeat (or tie) all other proposals. Another possibility is that the status quo is protected by rules or institutions that prevent consideration of proposals that would defeat it.

Voting one issue at a time with separable preferences

To start with, assume that *preferences are separable* for all committee members. Then we can graph the committee's decision problem in Fig-

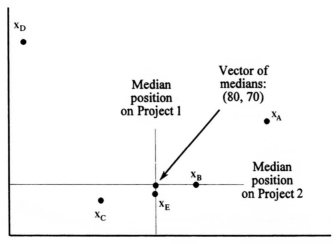

Figure 3.1. Ideal points of committee members and the results of voting one issue at a time.

ure 3.1, which depicts the ideal points of each committee member in a two-dimensional policy space. The fact that there are two dimensions suggests a natural starting point: Let each issue be voted on separately. Committee members may differ on the *relative* importance of budgets on Projects 1 and 2. One member may care mostly about Project 1, and another is concerned more about Project 2. A third member could easily consider the two projects equally salient.

Salience does not matter in the "one-issue-at-a time" vote, however, if on each separate issue all members' preferences are symmetric and single-peaked (Kadane, 1972; Kramer, 1972). Under these assumptions, the corollary to the MVT proved in the preceding chapter applies. Specifically, suppose that preferences are symmetric and single-peaked in each dimension, as well as separable between the dimensions. Applying the corollary to the MVT, we know that simple closeness determines choice on each of the two budgets. Since there is an odd number of members in our example, the median in each dimension is

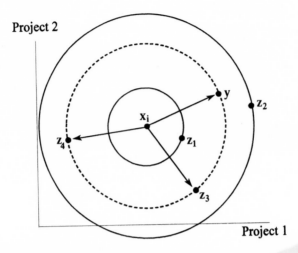

Figure 3.2. If issues are equally salient and preferences are separable, indifference curves are circles.

unique. Assuming free proposal power for all members, the collection of medians in each dimension will be the outcome. The median position on Project 1 is $80 million ($x_{E1}$), and the median on Project 2 is $60 million ($x_{B2}$). Thus, the committee will report out two bills, and the vector of median points ($80 million, $60 million) will be an equilibrium, regardless of the order in which the issues are considered.

In Chapter 2, we defined preference and indifference in spatial preferences. Indifference required (for symmetric preferences) that two budgets be equally far away from the member's ideal budget. In a two-dimensional policy space, where every point represents both a Project 1 budget and a Project 2 budget, indifference is more complicated. Given a budget y, there are *many* budgets the member likes equally well. We will call each set of points that give the member the same level of satisfaction an *indifference curve*. There are three basic cases to consider.

Case 1. *Preferences are separable, and issues have equal salience.*

In this case, indifference curves are *circles*. This case, illustrated in Figure 3.2, is intuitively the closest to the definition of indifference with symmetric preferences in one dimension. A circle has the property that all the points are equally far from the center, or ideal point of the member. Thus, the member is comparing other proposals with budget **y** based on their "distance" from his ideal point x_i. The member likes budget z_1 better, because it is closer than proposed budget **y**. He likes budget z_2 less, since it is farther away. He likes budgets z_3, z_4, and **y** the same, because they are all the same distance from x_i.

Case 2. *Preferences are separable, and issues have different salience.*

In this case, indifference curves have an oblong, or *elliptical,* shape. The indifference curves still join the set of budgets that a member likes equally, but they look different, as Figure 3.3 shows. If preferences are separable, differences in salience simply mean that the indifference curves are "stretched out," because one issue is more important to the member:

- If the horizontal issue is more salient, the indifference curves are "tall."
- If the vertical issue is more salient, the indifference curves are "wide."

The intuition behind these differences is very plausible. The more important an issue is to the member, the more small changes in budget affect satisfaction. In panel (a) of Figure 3.3, it looks as if the circular indifference curves from Case 1 (above) had been squeezed from the sides. In general, if the horizontal issue is more important, then the difference in preference level between any two curves is larger in the horizontal direction. This means that the curves themselves appear closer together, just as lines close together on a topological map indicate a steep slope. In panel (b), the compression is in the vertical direction, reflecting the greater importance of the vertical issue.

Case 3. *Preferences are not separable, issues have the same or different salience.*

This case is very complex. The reader should recognize that nonseparability makes interpretation of preferences much more difficult. Allowing simultaneous consideration of both issues, with nonseparable preferences, it is possible to draw indifference curves, but their shape can take many different forms.

Recall from the definition given earlier that nonseparability means

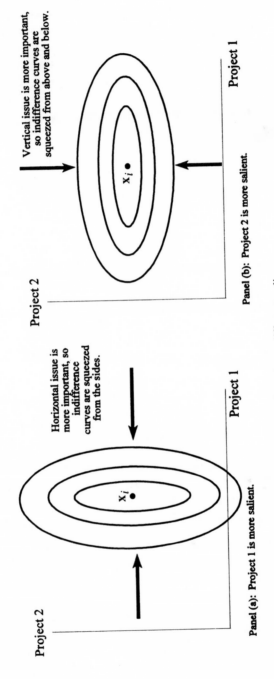

Figure 3.3. If preferences are separable, but projects have different salience, indifference curves are ellipses.

that the *ideal level* on one policy depends on the *expected level* of another policy. Two important kinds of nonseparability can be characterized as positive and negative complementarities. The simplest indifference curves associated with each type of nonseparability are presented in Figure 3.4. Panel (a) depicts "negative complementarity," and panel (b) depicts "positive complementarity." The best way to understand the meaning of negative and positive complementarity is to give an example of each:

Negative complementarity. A city council member may have goals for garbage and parks budgets for next year. But suppose the entire council selects a parks budget that is larger than councilperson *i*'s ideal. How will she react? Suppose she doesn't want to raise taxes, but cares strongly about a balanced budget. The result might very well be that she calls for cuts in garbage collection budgets. In fact, these cuts might be below her "ideal" level. If she could, the councilperson would like to take some money spent on parks and increase money spent on garbage collection. This may not be an option, either for parliamentary reasons or because other members would oppose her. Similarly, if a court order (based on a sanitation complaint from residents) requires more money for garbage collection, *every* council member may favor cuts below his or her package ideal point on parks. In general, if complementarity is negative, having to accept more of one project means the member wants less of the other project (compared with the most preferred budget if he or she could choose on both dimensions simultaneously).

Positive complementarity. A school board member has to decide how many new teachers to hire and how much money will be spent on buying new computers. Suppose the member believes that each teacher who has a classroom also needs a computer to be effective. Imagine that the school board as a group has already decided to hire more teachers than our board member thinks prudent. He disagrees with the decision, but accepts that this choice has been made. He might then vote to support a proposal to buy each of the new teachers a computer. The conditional ideal represents more computers than his package ideal, because (from his perspective) too many teachers have been hired.

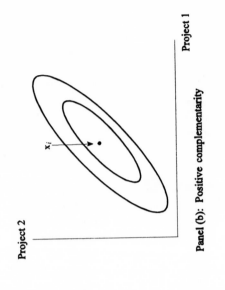

Panel (a): Negative complementarity

Panel (b): Positive complementarity

Figure 3.4. Negative and positive complementarity.

In each of these examples, it appears that preferences are not really "fixed."[1] The reason is that a member's goals for one policy depend on what he or she expects to happen in another budget area. It is important to recognize, however, that the preferences are *fixed.* All that is changing is the context, which modifies the contingent ideal point of the member. It is worth exploring at some length the seeming paradox in preference stability caused by nonseparability.

The paradox of nonseparability

Allowing preferences to be nonseparable makes the process of modeling vote choice much more complex, but also more realistic. One way of stating the "paradox" of nonseparability is:

> *The paradox.* Suppose a voter has an unconditional "package" ideal point x_i, and that preferences are nonseparable. Now, imagine that the position of the committee on issue 1 is fixed at some level $\tilde{x}_1$. The voter prefers movements *away from* x_{i2}.

How could nonseparability make a member vote against his own ideal point?

Nonseparability has a deceptively simple definition: The value the voter places on changes in the budget for Project 1 depends on the level of budget expected for Project 2, and vice versa. To put it another way, nonseparability requires that the member (we will drop the i subscript, for simplicity) consider *all* issue positions before choosing *any.* We can summarize the specific impact of nonseparability in three statements about the voter's conditional preferences.

1. *Positive complementarity:* Let the committee's position on issue 1 be fixed for some reason at $\tilde{x}_1 > x_1$ (i.e., more budget is allocated to issue 1 than the member would like). Then the member's conditional ideal on issue 2 will be *larger* than her ideal budget (assuming separability) x_2. If the position on issue 1 is fixed at $\tilde{x}_1 < x_1$, then the conditional ideal on issue 2 will be *smaller* than x_2.
2. *Negative complementarity:* Again, suppose the budget for issue 1 is fixed at $\tilde{x}_1 > x_1$. Then the conditional ideal on issue 2 will be *smaller* than x_2. If the position on issue 1 is fixed at $\tilde{x}_1 < x_1$, then the conditional ideal on issue 2 will be *larger* than x_2.

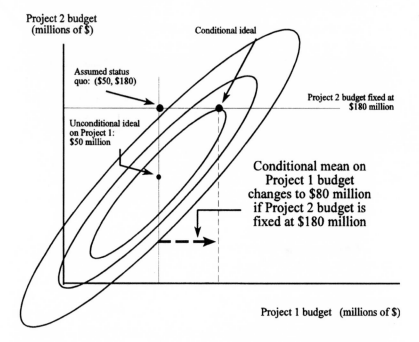

Figure 3.5. The paradox of nonseparable preferences. In this example, negative complementarity is assumed. The case for positive complementarity is analogous.

3. *Separability doesn't matter at the ideal point:* No matter what the form of the complementarity between projects, if $\tilde{x}_1 = x_1$ (the position on issue 1 is fixed at the voter's ideal point), the conditional ideal point is x_2.

If preferences are nonseparable, it must mean that there is some complementarity across budget categories. If the budget on any dimension is fixed at a level different from that most preferred by the voter, all the other "ideal" budgets of the voter change. The direction of the change depends on whether the voter perceives the complementarities in the activities as positive or negative.

The paradox is illustrated in Figure 3.5 for projects exhibiting positive complementarity. As the figure shows, the voter can approve of movements *away from* his one-dimensional ideal if preferences are not separable. In the example in Figure 3.5, the voter's ideal level of spending for Project 1 is the status quo. But the budget for Project 2 is fixed at a level different from his ideal point. He votes for an increase in the Project 1 budget, away from his ideal point.

The resolution of the apparent paradox lies in recognizing that non-separable preferences are conditional on context, though the preference function itself is consistent and unchanging. Though there is a package ideal, there is no unique "best" issue-by-issue ideal point. Consequently, the order in which issues are decided may determine the decision.

In the next section we return to the simplifying assumption of separable preferences and consider decision making on two issues. Accounting for nonseparability is very difficult, though it may be important for understanding the nature of real-world voting and decisions, and even survey responses (Lacy, 1996a). For the rest of this chapter, we will seek simply to illustrate the most basic model of two-dimensional collective choice using majority rule.

Lost in two-space: Voting on packages

Kadane (1972) and Kramer (1972) demonstrated an intuitive but important result: If (1) preferences are separable, and (2) issues are voted one at a time, voting sequence is irrelevant.[2] The outcome of such collective decision processes will always be the collection of median positions. But what happens if this extreme "germaneness" rule is relaxed, so that proposals can reflect changes in both projects simultaneously?

Imagine that there are two projects and three committee members with circular indifference curves (preferences are separable, and projects have equal salience for everyone). Further, let us introduce some concepts for evaluating outcomes.[3]

Pareto set (named after the Italian economist and sociologist, Vilfredo Pareto, 1848–1923). The smallest set of points that contains all ideal points, and the line segments connecting them. These line segments are called "contract curves," because they represent the boundaries of the set of possible unanimous agreements. "Pareto optimality" requires that decision processes select outcomes for which it is impossible to make changes that benefit all participants. For points inside the Pareto set, any change makes at least one member worse off. Status quo points outside the Pareto set are *unanimously* inferior to at least one point in the Pareto set.

   Condorcet winner *(named after the French mathematician and social scientist, Marie Jean Antoine Nicolas Caritat, Marquis de Condorcet, 1743–1794).* A policy position that beats or ties any other alternative in majority rule contests. We have already seen one example of a Condorcet winner: the median position in one dimension when preferences are single-peaked.

   Win set *(Black and Newing, 1951, Section II).* The "win set" of an alternative z (written $W(z)$) is the set of alternatives that will garner more votes than z in a pairwise majority rule election. More formally, let $R_i(z)$ be the set of alternatives that member i likes at least as well as z. Then $W(z)$ is the set of points in the intersection of (at least) a majority of the members' $R_i(z)$ sets. It is quite possible that $W(z)$ is empty (contains no points) for many configurations of x_i, since there is no guarantee that a majority of members prefers any point to z. If $W(z)$ is empty, z is an equilibrium.

One possible configuration of ideal points for the three voters (A, B, and C) is given in Figure 3.6. In addition to the ideal points, Figure 3.6 highlights the set of unidimensional medians ($50 million, $120 million), the Pareto set (the set of alternatives enclosed by the contract curves), and $W(x_{med})$, the win set of the intersection of the unidimensional medians, x_{med}. The win set of any point x is simply the intersection of the sets of alternatives prefered by a majority of members to x. In this case, with three members, we start by drawing each member's indifference curve through the presumed status quo, x_{med}. Then $W(x_{med})$ is the set of all alternatives where two (or more) of the indifference curves intersect or overlap.

   Is x_{med} a Condorcet winner when both issues are voted on simultaneously? No, not in this example and not in most examples. The reason is that $W(x_{med})$ is not empty for most possible configurations of ideal points. Since *any* point in $W(x_{med})$ beats x_{med} by definition, x_{med} is not a Condorcet winner.

   One is led to ask whether there is any Condorcet winner in spaces of more than one dimension, even assuming that preferences are sepa-

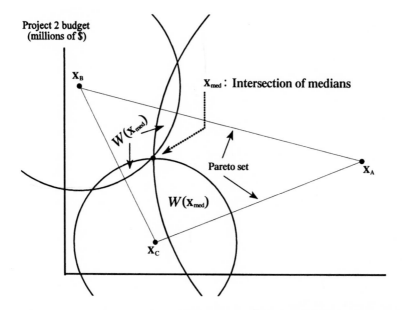

Figure 3.6. The win set of the intersection of unidimensional medians is not empty.

rable and single-peaked. Again, the answer is generally no. As Plott (1967), McKelvey (1986), and Cox (1987), among others, have shown, in the absence of (1) restrictions on the configuration of ideal points or (2) institutions that restrict the sequence of proposals (such as germaneness rules that require members to vote one issue at a time), majority rule processes are chaotic.

This result is substantively important, as we discussed in the previous chapters. From the perspective of the kind of democratic theory Aristotle tried to create, *there is not necessarily a "middle"* we can depend on to lend stability to democracy: Majority rule processes can be arbitrary.[4] On the other hand, we can say something about the circumstances under which majority rule leads to a stable outcome. Further, the "Pareto set" gives us some guidance about the extent of variation in likely outcomes.[5] Edmund Burke's "computing principle" seems to have some merit.

Suppose one point y in $W(x_{med})$ is selected as the new status quo for the committee depicted in Figure 3.6. If we redraw the indifference

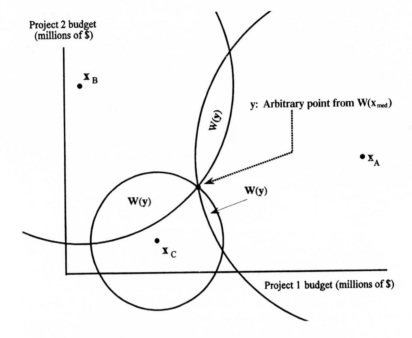

Figure 3.7. The win set of almost any arbitrary point is not empty.

curves and recalculate the win set of the new status quo, we will once again find (as in Figure 3.7) that $W(y)$ is not empty. This process, for most arbitrarily selected sets of ideal points, can continue endlessly.

Furthermore, as is obvious from Figures 3.6 and 3.7, there is no guarantee that the outcomes that are selected as a result of such a chaotic process satisfy even the most basic requirements of value: $W(x_{med})$ and $W(y)$ may contain points that are not elements of the Pareto set! To put it another way, majority rule may lead to an outcome that the entire society, *unanimously,* thinks is worse than other feasible alternatives.

Stability in two-dimensional space: The median in all directions

There are at least two ways out of this predicament. The first is to ask if there are plausible restrictions that can be placed on preferences that make the existence of a Condorcet winner more likely. The second is to ask if institutions of the decision process itself can prevent either endless wandering or manipulation by strategic actors, as has been suggested by Shepsle (1979) and Shepsle and Weingast (1981).[6]

Plott (1967) demonstrated that conditions sufficient to guarantee the existence of equilibrium do exist, but these conditions are highly restrictive. Later work, including that of Davis, DeGroot, and Hinich (1972) and Enelow and Hinich (1983a, 1984b), expanded the set of ideal point configurations for which a Condorcet winner exists, but the conditions are still highly restrictive. The sufficient conditions, sometimes called the "Plott conditions," require an ordinal pairwise symmetry of all voters along any vector passing through the status quo. One configuration of preferences for which there is a Condorcet winner is depicted in Figure 3.8, panel (a). As the reader can see, for each voter whose ideal point x_i is different from the dominant point (Condorcet winner) y, there is another voter j whose ideal point x_j lies on the same line through x_i and y, and lies the same distance as x_i on the opposite side of y.

In panel (b) of Figure 3.8, we see an illustration of a configuration of ideal points that do not satisfy Plott's symmetry conditions, but do imply the existence of a Condorcet winner. Obviously, the "Plott conditions" don't tell the full story. But then just what is the general principle that determines whether a given committee, represented by a set of ideal points in a multidimensional policy space, will come to a unique and determinate outcome by other than arbitrary means?

The answer is best summarized as follows: *An alternative* y *is a Condorcet winner in a society if, and only if, it is a "median in all directions."* We have already seen from Figure 3.6 that the intersection of unidimensional medians is not generally an equilibrium. So the median in all directions must be something different. What is it? The definition, first given definitively by Enelow and Hinich (1983a) is this: An alternative is a median in all directions if *every* line drawn through it, at all angles, divides the ideal points of all members so that at least half are on either side of the line, including those members whose ideal points are on the line in both groups.[7]

As the reader can easily see, Plott's pairwise symmetry condition is *sufficient* to guarantee the existence of a median in all directions. The condition is too strong, however, to qualify as a *necessary* condition.

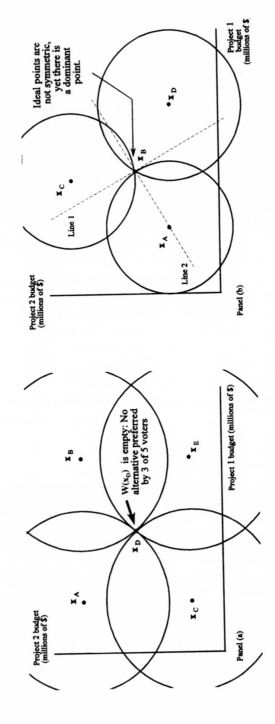

Figure 3.8. Two examples of ideal point configurations that imply Condorcet winners, with and without ideal point symmetry.

As Figure 3.8, panel (b), shows, there exist configurations of ideal points that violate the pairwise symmetry condition, yet yield a Condorcet winner.

The median in all directions, in two dimensions, represents an *exact* analogue to the definition of a median position in one dimension. There, we divided voters into two groups: (1) those whose ideal points were less than or equal to the proposal and (2) those whose ideal points were greater than or equal to the proposal. The difference is that for two or more dimensions, this condition must hold for lines drawn through the median at any angle.

We can't draw all possible lines, but the nature of the median in all directions can be illustrated by looking at lines 1 and 2 in panel (b) of Figure 3.8. There are three ideal points on or to the right of line 1 (x_B, x_C, and x_D), and two ideal points on or to the left (x_A and x_B). Similarly, for line 2: There are three ideal points on or above line 2 (x_A, x_B, and x_C), and three ideal points on or below it (x_A, x_B, and x_D).

Dynamic politics: "New" issues and stability

We have seen that in a single-dimensional world, majority rule leads to a stable policy at a median position if preferences are single-peaked. Even in a multidimensional world, we expect stability if issues are voted one at a time and preferences are separable, as Kramer (1972) showed. Yet if alternatives can be changed in more than one dimension, we have seen that stability and predictability may be rare. We should touch briefly on two sets of issues about the dynamics of politics. We cannot cover the basic research on these questions very deeply, but we can offer some guideposts to the reader. The first set of issues involves the (arguable) ability of institutions to prevent instability. The second is the introduction of "new" issues to change the political space itself.

Institutions and equilibrium

A number of authors have wondered why, in the face of pervasively pessimistic predictions about stability in majority rule decisions, many real-world political processes look stable. In many cases, the answers these authors have given relied on some form of "institution," or what Douglass North (1990) has called the "humanly devised rules of the game," to restrict or prevent instability in majority rule. We will discuss institutions more in Chapter 8, but for now will simply note that the rules that govern the aggregation of preferences may affect policy outcomes, even holding preferences constant. This is exactly the prediction of Plott's "fundamental equation," discussed in Chapter 1 of this book.

One important set of answers was offered by Buchanan and Tullock (1962) and Tullock (1981), who claimed that "logrolling" (vote trading) was the means by which stability could be ensured. Logrolling would allow voters to register the intensity of their preferences by trading votes on issues they care little about for the votes of others on issues about which the vote traders care deeply. Yet "trades" can restrict instability only when such agreements can be enforced.

Another kind of answer was offered by Kadane (1972), Kramer (1972, 1973), and others. Democracy is stable if complex packages of issues are broken apart and considered separately. If (1) preferences are separable and (2) issues are voted on one at a time in a fixed sequence (and no side payments are allowed), the vector of unidimensional medians beats any other alternative.

We are left to wonder, however, how democracies facing complex decisions avoid linkages across issues, either because preferences are nonseparable or because of vote trading. Legislative "germaneness" rules do have something like this effect by preventing "riders" (resolutions dealing with another issue) from being attached to bills. But we are led again to look for institutional arrangements, not to some characteristic of the decision process itself, as the guarantor of stability.

The most explicit statement of the importance of institutions in fostering stability is the "structure-induced equilibrium" theory of Shepsle (1979) and Shepsle and Weingast (1981). "Structure" is taken to mean explicit rules, or binding norms, of political decision-making bodies that preserve stability. Examples include a legislative committee system, with disjoint monopoly jurisdiction over policy dimensions and a system of reciprocity (an enforced, but open ended, logroll) among committees to avoid each other's turf. Other rules (e.g., requiring that the amendment face the status quo last) ensure that many proposals die in committee or in floor debate, rather than being enacted and then modified over and over.[8]

Most recently, Alesina and Rosenthal (1995) have pointed out that votes may reflect a desire to "balance" opposing ideological positions in government. If this explanation is correct, then it need not be true that *parties* move to the center. Instead, voters can achieve a centrist *policy* outcome (in systems with divided government, like the U.S. system with the Congress and a president) by putting one party in control of one branch and the other party in control of other branches. This is a fundamentally institutionalist perspective, with something like stability built in through voter balancing of relatively extreme positions by parties.

New issues and dynamic equilibrium

The notion that the dynamics of party competition can be described by the introduction of new issues or by the realignment of coalitions around issues in particular elections is, of course, a venerable one (Key, 1955; Burnham, 1970; Sundquist, 1973; Sartori, 1976; Kramer, 1977; Aldrich, 1983a, 1983b; Riker, 1986). Of these, only Riker's model and Aldrich's extensions relying on party activists explicitly assume that change comes from professional politicians. The older view is that changes in the preferences of the mass electorate transform the basic "rationale" of political debate (see, e.g., Sundquist, 1973, p. 37).

More recently, several scholars have rethought the relations between political agendas and models of politics. Riker (1990) raised a fundamental challenge:

What are the moving parts in the spatial model of politics? . . . As far as I know, the candidates (or parties) and their platforms or, alternatively, the motions, are all that anyone has proposed as moving parts. But nothing inherent in the model prevents other parts from moving. . . . [Candidates or voters] might change the space itself, distorting it by adding or subtracting dimensions or by expanding dimensions as if they were elastic or elastic in certain distances. . . . *In two dimensions [this] can easily affect the relative location of the center of the distribution.* (p. 46; emphasis added)

Riker (1982, 1986) himself offered the classic example of how the strategic introduction of an issue can change the political world. We can present only a highly simplified version of Riker's account. From the election of 1828 and the accession of Andrew Jackson in 1829 until the realignment of the mid-1850s, the issues that organized political debate were clear: Northeastern states favored high tariffs and tight credit; southern and western states favored low tariffs and relatively easy credit.

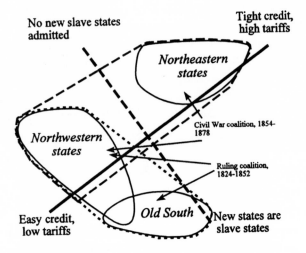

Figure 3.9. A new issue splits the coalition of northwestern and southern states (adapted from Riker, 1982).

As the issue of slavery or (more accurately) the extension of slavery to the western territories became more important, it divided the previously unbeatable coalition of South and West, leading to a political victory by the northeast (and leading to the U.S. Civil War).[9] In Figure 3.9, the prevailing dimension dividing political alternatives is the solid line; the "new" issue, slavery, is the dotted line. The consideration of the strategic addition of new issues makes the implied game dynamic and potentially unstable. What are the implications for political strategy?

Remember, majority rule election processes always have a determinate Condorcet winner at the ideal point of the median voter, provided the relevant strategy set is one-dimensional and voter preferences are single-peaked. While one might quarrel with the assumption of single-peakedness, the obvious problem lies with the assumption of unidimensionality, particularly when we allow for *strategic* introduction of new dimensions. Since there is generally no median position when the number of issues is greater than one, introducing a "new" issue changes everything.

To sum up, the "successful" introduction of a new issue may be a victory for the disgruntled or out-of-power coalition that introduces it, but the victory may be Pyrrhic. Introducing a genuinely "new" issue does not usually mean there will be an orderly transformation or re-alignment. Rather, the effect is to release the genie of chaos from its bottle.[10] The more complex space gives more room for maneuver and strategic action, it is true, but maneuvering is now possible for *all* sides in the conflict. In the higher-dimensional space, and with the collapse of the gatekeeping institutions designed to keep order in one dimension, anything can happen.

Conclusions

A key difficulty with all the structure-induced equilibrium theories is the presumption of separable preferences. As we will see in Chapter 8, equilibrium breaks down if preferences are nonseparable. At a mini-mum, the nature of equilibrium becomes dependent on the order in which alternatives are decided (or even are expected to be decided), which creates crippling opportunities for strategic manipulation.

Even more fundamentally, there is a difficulty with all the institution-ally oriented answers to Tullock's famous "Why so much stability?" question. Even if institutions serve the roles claimed, where do they come from? Why do some institutions disappear, and others survive? These hard questions have been posed in different forms by Riker (1980) and North (1981, 1990). We don't yet have very good answers for them. But the answers, when they come, will tell us much about how some human societies change and grow, while others wither and die. Though in some ways we have come far from Aristotle's ancient specu-lation about the existence of the "middle" and its implications for the good society, these basic questions remain the heart of the matter.

EXERCISES

3.1. Suppose that there are three committee members, A, B, and C, with ideal points in a two-dimensional policy space (issues 1 and 2) as follows: $x_A = (4, 16)$, $x_B = (5, 10)$, and $x_C = (6, 4)$. Suppose the status quo policy is $z = (6, 16)$. Draw a graph depicting the decision problem, including circular indifference curves through the status quo point. Is z a Condorcet winner?

3.2. For the same set of members and ideal points as in Exercise 3.1, imagine that the issues are voted on one at a time, starting with issue 1. What will be the resulting vector of policies?

3.3. Again, for the same set of preferences as in Exercises 3.1 and 3.2, what will be the outcome if two-dimensional alternatives can be proposed? Is there a Condorcet winner? Is there a median in all directions?

CHAPTER 4

Multiple dimensions: Weighted Euclidean distance

> The whole of science is nothing more than a refinement of everyday thinking.
>
> (Albert Einstein, *Physics and Reality,* 1936)

In Chapter 3, we outlined the logic of complex policy spaces in terms of "everyday thinking." In this chapter, we will refine that material, using the language of matrix notation. Instead of two dimensions, however, we will assume that the policy space has n dimensions, where n is an arbitrary number. Technically, the policy space $\mathcal{P}$ is the generalized Cartesian product: $\mathcal{P} = P_1 \times P_2 \times \cdots \times P_n$.

As before, each dimension measures the budget of one project, and members are assumed to have preferences over all the projects. Using matrix notation will allow us to make precise the ideas of *salience* and *nonseparability* that we presented graphically in Chapter 3. Mathematical notation will afford us several refinements that make the additional complexity worthwhile. Matrices and vectors are useful notational devices because they save space and clutter in representing organized arrays of characters. Once you get used to the idea of using matrix notation, you will find it *easier* than using summations cluttered with indexes and brackets.

Matrix notation and definitions

- A *matrix* is an ordered array of numbers or characters. We will use **boldface** type to distinguish a matrix from *scalar* variables. A scalar might be thought of as a 1×1 matrix, but there is no need to be so fussy. Any real matrix has size $r \times c$, or number of rows times num-

Note: This chapter contains technical details of the discussion in Chapter 3 and can be skipped without loss of continuity. However, the reader interested in technical details is advised to study this chapter carefully.

ber of columns. For example, a 4 × 6 matrix **A** will have twenty-four entries, arranged in four rows and six columns.

$$\mathbf{A} = \begin{bmatrix} a_{11} & a_{12} & a_{13} & a_{14} & a_{15} & a_{16} \\ a_{21} & a_{22} & a_{23} & a_{24} & a_{25} & a_{26} \\ a_{31} & a_{32} & a_{33} & a_{34} & \boxed{a_{35}} & a_{36} \\ a_{41} & a_{42} & a_{43} & a_{44} & a_{45} & a_{46} \end{bmatrix} \quad \begin{array}{c} \uparrow \\ 4 \text{ rows} \\ \downarrow \end{array} \tag{4.1}$$

← 6 columns →

Specific entries are denoted by subscripts, with the first subscript representing the row, and the second subscript representing the column. For example, a_{35} is the element of **A** in the *third* row and *fifth* column (see box in figure above).

- There is one special kind of matrix, called a *vector*, that we will find especially useful. A vector may have only one row (a *row* vector) or only one column (a *column* vector). That is, row vectors are $1 \times c$, column vectors are $r \times 1$. Consider these examples of a row vector **R** and a column vector **C**.

$$\mathbf{R} = [a_{11}\, a_{12}\, a_{13} \cdots a_{1c}] \quad \mathbf{C} = \begin{bmatrix} a_{11} \\ a_{21} \\ a_{31} \\ \vdots \\ a_{r1} \end{bmatrix} \tag{4.2}$$

- A *diagonal* matrix is all zeros, except for the elements along the main diagonal (more precisely, $a_{jk} = 0$ for all $j \neq k$). A special case of a diagonal matrix is the *identity* matrix, which consists of 1s along the main diagonal and zeros everywhere else. Here is an example of a diagonal matrix **D** and an identity matrix **I**:

$$\mathbf{D} = \begin{bmatrix} 5 & 0 & 0 \\ 0 & 2 & 0 \\ 0 & 0 & 9 \end{bmatrix} \quad \mathbf{I} = \begin{bmatrix} 1 & 0 & 0 \\ 0 & 1 & 0 \\ 0 & 0 & 1 \end{bmatrix} \tag{4.3}$$

Basic matrix operations

- *Transpose:* The transpose of a matrix is another matrix, with rows becoming columns and vice versa. The matrix being transposed has a superscript T. Transposition is easy in the case of row and column vectors: If the number of rows in **R** is equal to the number of columns in **C**, and they have the same elements, then $\mathbf{R}^\mathsf{T} = \mathbf{C}$, and $\mathbf{C}^\mathsf{T} = \mathbf{R}$. More generally, suppose an arbitrary matrix **M** is size $r \times c$. Then $\mathbf{M}^\mathsf{T}$ will be size $c \times r$.

For example, consider the following matrix **M** and its transpose $\mathbf{M}^\mathsf{T}$:

$$\mathbf{M} = \begin{bmatrix} 6 & 9 \\ -1 & 4 \end{bmatrix} \quad \mathbf{M}^\mathsf{T} = \begin{bmatrix} 6 & -1 \\ 9 & 4 \end{bmatrix} \tag{4.4}$$

Notice that the first *column* [6–1] has become the first *row*, and so on. Importantly, this means that $\mathbf{D}^\mathsf{T} = \mathbf{D}$ if and only if **D** is diagonal.

- *Addition:* Matrices can be added only if they are the same size. We can identify the sum of **A** and **B** as the new matrix **C**, so that **A** + **B** = **C**. The elements of **C** are the sums of the respective elements of **A** and **B**, as the following 2×2 example shows:

$$\begin{bmatrix} a_{11} & a_{12} \\ a_{21} & a_{22} \end{bmatrix} + \begin{bmatrix} b_{11} & b_{12} \\ b_{21} & b_{22} \end{bmatrix} = \begin{bmatrix} (a_{11} + b_{11}) & (a_{12} + b_{12}) \\ (a_{21} + b_{21}) & (a_{22} + b_{22}) \end{bmatrix} \tag{4.5}$$

Subtraction is defined the same way, except that the elements of the resulting matrix are the *difference* of the elements of the matrices being subtracted.

- *Multiplication:* Multiplying a scalar times a matrix is easy and works just the way one would expect. Suppose you have a scalar s and a matrix **A**; then their product would be:

$$s\mathbf{A} = s \times \begin{bmatrix} a_{11} & a_{12} \\ a_{21} & a_{22} \end{bmatrix} = \begin{bmatrix} s \times a_{11} & s \times a_{12} \\ s \times a_{22} & s \times a_{22} \end{bmatrix} \tag{4.6}$$

Multiplying two matrices is a little harder. It is useful to keep three things in mind for matrix multiplication. First, make sure the number of *columns* of the matrix on the left is the same as the number of *rows* of the matrix on the right. If this condition is not met, multiplication is not defined for these two matrices. The reason that this condition is important is that each element in the resulting matrix is the sum of the products of the elements across the columns of the matrix on the left and the elements down the rows of the matrix on the right. Second, the size of the matrix representing the product of any two matrices will be the number of *rows* in the first matrix and the number of *columns* in the second matrix. Obviously, matrix multiplication is very different from scalar multiplication, because the order in which the matrices are multiplied matters. Third, matrix multiplication is associative, just as in scalar multiplication, for a given order of matrices to be multiplied. For example, $(AB)C = A(BC)$, just as in scalar multiplication.

Consider the following three examples:

Multiplication Example 1: Two vectors make a scalar (1×3 times $3 \times 1 = 1 \times 1$, or a scalar).

$$[5 \ 1 \ 3]\begin{bmatrix} 6 \\ -2 \\ 2 \end{bmatrix} = (5 \times 6) + (1 \times -2) + (3 \times 2)$$

$$= 34 \tag{4.7}$$

Multiplication Example 2: The same two vectors make a matrix, if multiplied in the opposite order (3×1 times $1 \times 3 = 3 \times 3$ matrix).

$$\begin{bmatrix} 6 \\ -2 \\ 2 \end{bmatrix}[5 \ 1 \ 3] = \begin{bmatrix} 30 & 6 & 18 \\ -10 & -2 & -6 \\ 10 & 2 & 6 \end{bmatrix} \tag{4.8}$$

Multiplication Example 3: Two matrices make another matrix, with the elements of the product being the sum of the products of the elements across the columns of the first matrix and down the rows of the second matrix. Specifically, for the two matrices multiplied below, the top left element (a_{11}) in the product matrix is $(1 \times 2) + (3 \times 8) + (5 \times 14) = 96$, and so on.

$$\begin{bmatrix} 1 & 3 & 5 \\ 7 & 9 & 11 \\ 13 & 15 & 17 \end{bmatrix} \times \begin{bmatrix} 2 & 4 & 6 \\ 8 & 10 & 12 \\ 14 & 16 & 18 \end{bmatrix} = \begin{bmatrix} 96 & 114 & 132 \\ 240 & 294 & 348 \\ 384 & 474 & 564 \end{bmatrix} \tag{4.9}$$

We are now ready to apply the concepts of matrices and vectors in refining the intuitive exposition of Chapter 3.

SED and WED: Spatial preferences in two-dimensional space

As the reader will recall from Chapter 2, the problem of "representing" preferences for citizens is a very general one. In this book, we have settled on "spatial" representations of preferences, meaning that the distance between a voter's ideal point and a proposal is inversely related to utility. More simply, voters like a proposal less as it differs more from what they want.

But now we must define "distance," or the difference between proposals, in several dimensions rather than just one. Generally, the simplest measure of distance is *simple Euclidean distance* (SED). In a single dimension, the SED between two points y and z is just the absolute value of the difference. Consider *representative citizen i*, who has an *ideal point* x_i. In Chapter 2, we used the absolute value of the difference between budgets to define preference (*i prefers* y to z if and only if $|y - x_i| < |z - x_i|$) and indifference (*i* is *indifferent* between y and z if and only if $|y - x_i| = |z - x_i|$).

The SED between two points in two-dimensional space is more complicated to compute, but has the same meaning. We can define the points in two-dimensional space, using vectors. An element in our two-dimensional policy space will be represented as a column vector with the Project 1 budget on top and the Project 2 budget below it. For example,

$$\mathbf{y} = \begin{bmatrix} y_1 \\ y_2 \end{bmatrix} \qquad \mathbf{z} = \begin{bmatrix} z_1 \\ z_2 \end{bmatrix} \qquad (4.10)$$

are two alternatives ($\mathbf{y}$ and $\mathbf{z}$) in the policy space.

Each member's ideal point is also a vector, with an ideal budget for each project. How are we to represent the distances from ideal points to budgets using vectors? The difference between the vectors is just another vector, giving the difference in the budget *in each project*. But a vector is not, itself, a distance. To compute distance, we apply the Pythagorean theorem. Imagine we are given an arbitrary right triangle with sides measuring α and β and hypotenuse measuring γ. The Pythagorean theorem says that $\gamma^2 = \alpha^2 + \beta^2$. Solving for γ, we get:

$$\gamma = \sqrt{\alpha^2 + \beta^2} \qquad (4.11)$$

As Figure 4.1 shows, the "difference" between proposals $\mathbf{y}$ and $\mathbf{z}$ has two parts: The difference between the two projects has two dimensions. For Project 1, the difference is measured on the horizontal axis (distance α). For Project 2, the difference is measured on the vertical axis (distance β). The *distance* between the two proposals, however, is the hypotenuse γ (dotted line) of the triangle. Consequently, the formula

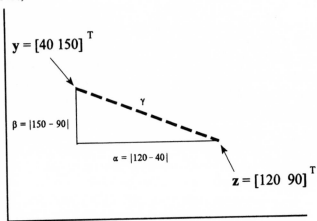

Figure 4.1. Computation of simple Euclidean distance in two-dimensional space.

for SED(**y, z**) in two-dimensional space is derived directly from the Pythagorean theorem.

$$SED(\mathbf{y}, \mathbf{z}) = \sqrt{(y_1 - z_1)^2 + (y_2 - z_2)^2} \qquad (4.12)$$

More generally, for an arbitrary number of dimensions n, the distance between two points **y** and **z** is:

$$SED(\mathbf{y}, \mathbf{z}) = \sqrt{\sum_{j=1}^{n}(y_j - z_j)^2} \qquad (4.13)$$

That is, SED is the square root of the sum of the squared differences in each respective dimension. Using matrix notation, we can rewrite (4.13) as:

$$SED(\mathbf{y}, \mathbf{z}) = \sqrt{[\mathbf{y} - \mathbf{z}]^T[\mathbf{y} - \mathbf{z}]} \qquad (4.14)$$

Here is an illustration of the advantage of matrix notation: Equation (4.13) is different for any number of dimensions, since n (the number of issues) differs. But n does not appear in (4.14); matrix notation is more general and applies to any number of dimensions without modification.

SED is the simplest way to represent preferences in spatial theory, but not the only way. A trivial generalization of SED is the set of order-preserving "affine" transformations of SED. Order-preserving affine transformations are linear rescalings that keep the same direction of increase from small to large. We say y is an affine transformation of x if

$$y = h + (k \times x) \tag{4.15}$$

where h and k are arbitrary scalars ($k > 0$). If $x_1 > x_2$, then a transformation of x is order preserving if $y_1 = h + (k \times x_1)$ and $y_2 = h + (k \times x_2)$ have the same order: $y_1 > y_2$. SED or any affine transformation of SED is equally valid as a representation of preference. To put it more simply, requiring that preferences are spatial does not restrict us to any one preference function.

This "nonuniqueness" seems strange, but it is not an uncommon situation in measurement problems. For example, the concept of temperature can be conceived as a large ordered set, whose elements range from very cold to very hot. The specific units we use to "measure" temperature, as well as the zero point in the scale, are generally arbitrary, however.[1] Zero degrees Fahrenheit is quite arbitrary as a level of temperature. Zero degrees Celsius corresponds to 32° Fahrenheit; 100° Celsius is the same as 212° Fahrenheit. Consequently, both Celsius and Fahrenheit measure the same phenomenon (ambient heat energy), so clearly neither is unique. Measurement theorists say the two scales "are unique only up to an affine transformation." Simple algebra quickly shows the form of the affine transformation – one way of converting between Celsius and Fahrenheit is:

$$C° = 5/9 \, (F° - 32) \approx -17.7778 + 0.556 F° \tag{4.16}$$

Using the general definition of affine transformations in (4.15), we see that in the Fahrenheit–Celsius example $h = -17.78$, and $k = 0.556$.

We want to represent another very complicated concept: political preferences. If we use SED, we have to remember that (as with temperature) the units are arbitrary and need not be "anchored" at any fixed zero point. Differences in satisfaction are only important ordinally. Order-preserving affine transformations don't change preferences in any interesting way: SED or 65 + (4.1698 × SED) are equally valid measures of distance between alternatives as a representation of preferences.

There is another generalization of SED called "weighted Euclidean distance" (WED). To understand why WED is a genuine generalization, rather than just a transformation, notice that SED (and any affine transformation of SED) requires that preferences have two characteristics: (1) *Preferences must be separable* (the expected *level* of one issue doesn't affect the conditional *ideal* for other issues). (2) *All dimensions have equal salience* (distances in all issues "count" the same). Unlike a simple affine transformation of SED, WED relaxes both these requirements. Consequently, WED is substantively more general than SED.

The formula for WED, assuming that the matrix of weights **A** is voter specific (i.e., subscripted by i), is:

$$\text{WED}(\mathbf{y}, \mathbf{z}) = \sqrt{[\mathbf{y} - \mathbf{z}]^{\mathsf{T}} \mathbf{A}_i [\mathbf{y} - \mathbf{z}]} \tag{4.17}$$

Compare Equation (4.17) to Equation (4.14): The difference between SED and WED is the matrix of salience and interaction terms $\mathbf{A}_i$. If there are two projects, $\mathbf{A}_i$ would look like this:

$$\mathbf{A}_i = \begin{bmatrix} a_{11} & a_{12} \\ a_{21} & a_{22} \end{bmatrix} \tag{4.18}$$

We can distinguish two types of terms, salience and interaction terms, in the matrix of preference weights $\mathbf{A}_i$.

- The *main diagonal* elements, a_{11} and a_{22}, are the salience terms. Salience is a measure of the relative value the voter places on Project 1 and Project 2, given the scale of those projects (e.g., dollars or number of people). Salience terms are assumed to be nonnegative by definition, and in practical terms we will consider only positive salience terms. (A salience term equal to zero means the voter doesn't ever consider this project or policy in making decisions.)
- The *off-diagonal* elements are called interaction terms. The interactions measure how much the voter's evaluation of *changes* in one project depend on the expected *level* of another project. For convenience we will generally assume that $a_{12} = a_{21}$, though there is nothing in the theory itself that requires this restriction.[2]

If $\mathbf{A}_i = \mathbf{I}$ (meaning that $a_{11} = a_{22} = 1$, and $a_{12} = a_{21} = 0$), then SED(y, z) = WED(y, z). It is useful to define symmetric preferences for the multidimensional setting:

Symmetric preference. Preferences of voter i are symmetric if and only if the voter likes equally well any two points y and z that (a) lie on a straight line passing through $\mathbf{x}_i$ and (b) are equidistant from $\mathbf{x}_i$ (in terms of SED).

Like SED preferences, WED preferences are symmetric.

We can also define the concept of indifference more generally.

Indifference. A voter i is indifferent between any two alternatives y and y' such that WED$(\mathbf{y} - \mathbf{x}_i)$ = WED$(\mathbf{y}' - \mathbf{x}_i)$. In general, we can identify a set of alternatives y among which the voter is indifferent: $\{\mathbf{y} \mid \text{WED}(\mathbf{y} - \mathbf{x}_i) = K\}$. The variable K is a constant whose value can range from zero (at the ideal point) to an arbitrarily large number. The graph of the elements of this set of points among which the voter is indifferent is called an "indifference curve." Each distinct value of K defines one indifference curve for the voter. Since any particular K defines one indifference curve, it follows that each point in the policy space $\mathcal{P}$ is located on exactly one indifference curve. Consequently, there can be no intersection of indifference curves in preferences measured by WED, just as was true for SED.

Consider the following possibilities for different kinds of indifference curves.

- If $\mathbf{A}_i = k\mathbf{I}$ (k an arbitrary scalar, $\mathbf{I}$ an identity matrix of order n), then indifference curves are *circles* with centers at the voter's ideal point, because issues are weighted equally and preferences are separable.
- For any $\mathbf{A}_i = \mathbf{sI}$ (where s is a $1 \times n$ row vector of salience weights, so that $\mathbf{A}_i$ is diagonal), indifference curves are *ellipses* centered at the ideal point, with major axes parallel to the policy dimensions. The reason is that the voter values issues differently, so equal departures from his ideal have different impacts on his utility, depending on the project.
- For any $\mathbf{A}_i$ that is not diagonal, preferences are not separable. As we

Project 2 budget
(millions of $)

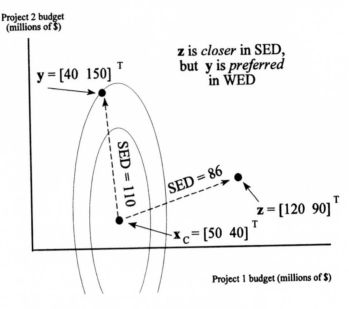

Figure 4.2. Comparison of **y** and **z** using WED for Member C.

saw in Chapter 3, this means that the form of the preference ellipses is complex, with the major axis of the ellipse tilted at an angle rather than parallel to one of the policy dimensions.

An example using (separable) WED in two-dimensional space

Returning to the preferences of the subcommittee members, consider first C's preference rule. We will say he prefers **y** to **z** if and only if **y** is closer to his ideal point, or $WED_A(\mathbf{y}, \mathbf{x}_C) < WED_A(\mathbf{z}, \mathbf{x}_C)$, where as before $\mathbf{y} = [40\ 150]^T$, $\mathbf{z} = [120\ 90]^T$, and $\mathbf{x}_C = [50\ 40]^T$. As Figure 4.2 shows, Mr. C is indifferent among alternatives that lie exactly K units (in WED, not SED) from his ideal point.

Assume that the $\mathbf{A}_C$ matrix looks like this:

$$\mathbf{A}_C = \begin{bmatrix} 15 & 0 \\ 0 & 1 \end{bmatrix} \tag{4.19}$$

Mr. C's preferences for Projects 1 and 2 are separable (you can tell because $a_{12} = a_{21} = 0$). The issue salience values are very different, however: Each dollar difference from his ideal in Project 1 "counts" more because $a_{11} > a_{22}$.

Given the weights in $\mathbf{A}_C$, does C prefer $\mathbf{y}^T = [40, 150]$ or $\mathbf{z}^T = [120, 90]$, remembering $\mathbf{x}_C^T = [50, 40]$? For comparison, first calculate SED($\mathbf{y}$, $\mathbf{x}_C$) and SED($\mathbf{z}$, $\mathbf{x}_C$):

$$\text{SED}(\mathbf{y}, \mathbf{x}_C) = \sqrt{[-10\ 110]\begin{bmatrix} -10 \\ 110 \end{bmatrix}}$$

$$= \sqrt{(-10)^2 + 110^2} = 110.45 \qquad (4.20)$$

$$\text{SED}(\mathbf{z}, \mathbf{x}_C) = \sqrt{[70\ 50]\begin{bmatrix} 70 \\ 50 \end{bmatrix}} = \sqrt{70^2 + 50^2} = 86.02 \qquad (4.21)$$

The definition of WED implies that if $\mathbf{A}_C$ were an identity matrix, WED and SED are identical. Equations (4.20) and (4.21) would then establish that C prefers $\mathbf{z}$ to $\mathbf{y}$. For $\mathbf{A}_C \neq \mathbf{I}$ (as given in Equation (4.17)), however, we must use WED:

$$\text{WED}(\mathbf{y}, \mathbf{x}_C) = \sqrt{[-10\ 110]\begin{bmatrix} 15 & 0 \\ 0 & 1 \end{bmatrix}\begin{bmatrix} -10 \\ 110 \end{bmatrix}}$$

$$= \sqrt{(-10^2) \times 15 + 110^2} = 116.62 \qquad (4.22)$$

$$\text{WED}(\mathbf{z}, \mathbf{x}_C) = \sqrt{[70\ 50]\begin{bmatrix} 15 & 0 \\ 0 & 1 \end{bmatrix}\begin{bmatrix} 70 \\ 50 \end{bmatrix}}$$

$$= \sqrt{(70^2) \times 15 + 50^2} = 275.68 \qquad (4.23)$$

Now, because of the large weight attached to Project 1, C prefers proposal $\mathbf{y}$, though $\mathbf{z}$ appears closer to $\mathbf{x}_C$ in terms of simple distance. The reason can be recalled from Figure 4.2: Member C cares more about small differences in the Project 1 budget. Consequently, horizontal movements cause a larger decline in utility as distance from $\mathbf{x}_C$ increases.

What if preferences are nonseparable?

Allowing preferences to be nonseparable makes the process of modeling vote choice much more complex, but also more realistic. Recall the "paradox" from the preceding chapter:

The paradox of nonseparability. Suppose a voter has an unconditional "package" ideal point x_i, and that preferences are nonseparable. Now, imagine that the position of the committee on issue 1 is fixed at $\tilde{x}_1$. The voter may actually prefer, and vote for, movements *away from* x_i on votes that consider issue 2.

In matrix notation, nonseparability in a two-dimensional policy space has a deceptively simple definition: $a_{i12} \neq 0$. This means that nonseparability has nothing to do with salience. Salience is determined by the *diagonal* terms in A_i; *nonseparabilities* are captured in the off-diagonal terms of A_i. Larger values of the a_{ij} ($i \neq j$) represent larger complementarities, or interactions, in the member's evaluation of issues.

To see this, let's expand the formula for $WED(z, x_i)$:

$$WED(z, x_i) = \sqrt{[y-z]^T A_i [y-z]}$$

$$= \sqrt{[y_1-z_1 \quad y_2-z_2]\begin{bmatrix} a_{11} & a_{12} \\ a_{21} & a_{22} \end{bmatrix}\begin{bmatrix} y_1-z_1 \\ y_2-z_2 \end{bmatrix}} \tag{4.24}$$

$$= \sqrt{[((y_1-z_1)a_{11} + (y_2-z_2)a_{21})((y_1-z_1)a_{12} + (y_2-z_2)a_{22})]\begin{bmatrix} y_1-z_1 \\ y_2-z_2 \end{bmatrix}} \tag{4.25}$$

$$= \sqrt{a_{i11}(z_1-x_{i1})^2 + [2a_{i12}(z_1-x_{i1})(z_2-x_{i2})] + a_{i22}(z_2-x_{i2})^2} \tag{4.26}$$

$$\uparrow$$
Interaction

From (4.26), it is clear why WED simplifies to SED if $A_i = I$ ($a_{12} = a_{21} = 0$ and $a_{11} = a_{22} = 1$). The "interaction" term in (4.26) drops out and the salience terms can be ignored, so the expression simplifies to:

$$WED_A(z, x_i) = \sqrt{(y_1 - z_1)^2 + (y_2 - z_2)^2} \tag{4.27}$$

In general, the only difference between separable and nonseparable preferences is the interaction term in (4.26). The interaction is the product of the differences between z and x_i on each of the two issue dimensions, multiplied by twice the interaction weight a_{12}. Thus, we can summarize the implications of nonseparability by focusing on a_{12}. Since larger values of WED mean less utility for the voter, we have to be careful to interpret the signs on a_{12} carefully. As we saw in Chapter 3, complementarities have to do with increases or decreases in utility when we have to consider two policies together. For example, a positive interaction is an *increase* in WED, implying a *reduction* in utility. Thus, we will adopt the convention (already outlined intuitively in the preceding chapter) that $a_{12} < 0$ is a positive complementarity, and $a_{12} > 0$ is a negative complementarity, where "positive" and "negative" refer to the effect on the voter's utility.

Recall that, intuitively, nonseparability requires that the voter consider *all* issue positions before choosing *any*. We can summarize the specific impact of the interaction term in three statements about the voter's conditional preferences:

1. If $a_{12} < 0$ (*negative* interaction, implying *positive complementarity*) and the position on issue j is fixed for some reason at $\tilde{x}_j > x_{ij}$, then the conditional ideal on issue k will be *larger* than x_{ik}. If the position on issue j is fixed at $\tilde{x}_j < x_{ij}$, then the conditional ideal on issue k will be *smaller* than x_{ik}.
2. If $a_{12} > 0$ (*positive* interaction, implying *negative complementarity*) and the position on issue j is fixed at $\tilde{x}_j > x_{ij}$, then the conditional ideal on issue k will be *smaller* than x_{ik}. If the position on issue j is fixed at $\tilde{x}_j < x_{ij}$, then the conditional ideal on issue k will be *larger* than x_{ik}.
3. No matter what the form of the interaction, if $\tilde{x}_j = x_{ij}$ (position on issue j is *fixed at the voter's ideal point*), the interaction term is zero. Nonseparability has no impact on choices on issue k: The conditional ideal given z_j is still x_{ik}.

We can derive the conditional preference of the voter (dropping the i subscript for now) for Project 2 by fixing Project 1 at an arbitrary budget we will call $\tilde{x}_1$. (Note: The derivation of the ideal for Project 1, given a fixed budget for Project 2, is analogous and will not be presented.) The voter's *conditional* preference for Project 2, or x_2^C can be written in terms of the WED between $\mathbf{x}$ and the policy vector $[\tilde{x}_1 \ x_2^C]^T$. The value of x_2^C that minimizes WED given $\tilde{x}_1$ is unknown, but we can find it in two steps. First, write out the expression for WED:

$$\text{WED}([\tilde{x}_1 \ x_2^C]^T, \mathbf{x})$$

$$= \sqrt{a_{11}(\tilde{x}_1 - x_1)^2 + 2a_{12}(\tilde{x}_1 - x_1)(x_2^C - x_2) + a_{22}(x_2^C - x_2)^2} \tag{4.28}$$

The second step is to find the value of Project 2 budget that conditionally minimizes WED (i.e., maximizes utility). The condition, of course, is that $\tilde{x}_1$ is the (fixed) budget for Project 1. Enelow and Hinich (1984b) performed these two steps and solved for x_2^*, the value of Project 2 that conditionally maximizes the voter's utility:

$$x_2^* \,|\, \tilde{x}_1 = x_2 - \left(\frac{a_{12}}{a_{22}}\right)(\tilde{x}_1 - x_1) \tag{4.29}$$

As (4.29) proves, $x_2^* \neq x_2$ whenever preferences are nonseparable and $\tilde{x}_1 \neq x_1$.

There is nothing perverse about this preference rule. In fact, as Enelow and Hinich demonstrate, the preferences in (4.29) are symmetric and single-peaked around the conditional ideal point on issue 2, x_2^*. But $\mathbf{x}$ is still the *package* of proposals the voter most prefers, and it differs from x_2^* on Project 2.

For the rest of this chapter and most of the rest of this book, we will assume separability of preferences. Still, it is crucial to remember that nonseparability is important in modeling real political choice. We will take up the idea of linkages across issues again in Chapters 8 and 9.

Stability of majority rule: The generalized median voter theorem

In Chapter 3, we outlined the problems of defining a Condorcet winner in more than one dimension. We argued that the general condition for stability is the existence of a median in all directions. As the reader will recall, an alternative is a median in all directions if every line drawn through it divides the ideal points of all members so that at least half are on either side of the line. It is important to note that points on the line are counted as belonging to each of the two groups, or half spaces.

This definition is designed for a two-dimensional policy space and is suitable for graphical examples on a printed page, which is after all a two-dimensional surface. How are we to generalize to situations where there are more than two dimensions? Many people find it hard to visualize three dimensions, and we certainly can't represent three-space very well on a flat printed page. Worse, higher dimensions, with 8, 136, or an arbitrary number of policies, defy graphical interpretations. We certainly cannot use "lines" to split groups of ideal points. Mathematicians use a mental construct called a "separating hyperplane" to understand such a splitting of spaces. We will denote the separating hyperplane $\mathcal{H}$. In general, to split a space $\mathcal{H}$ must have *one fewer dimensions* than the space itself.

As we have already seen, in the one-dimensional example $\mathcal{H}$ was of dimension zero (a point). In two-dimensional spaces, $\mathcal{H}$ must be of dimension one (a line). In more complex spaces, with arbitrary dimension n, $\mathcal{H}$ must always be of dimension $n - 1$. For our purposes, $\mathcal{H}$ must have the same property in a space of any dimension: No matter how $\mathcal{H}$ is tilted or rotated, as long as it passes through the median position, $\mathcal{H}$ must divide all ideal points so that (to use the Schwartz, 1986, definition) no majority of ideal lies *strictly* on either side.

Obviously, this condition becomes harder to satisfy in higher dimensions. But the general principle (McKelvey, 1976a, 1976b) is precisely the same in every case: There must be at least $N/2$ ideal points on each side of the separating hyperplane (including in each case points on $\mathcal{H}$ itself).

This principle implies a generalized statement of the median voter theorem, simultaneously accounting for any number of dimensions from one to infinity. For evolving interpretations of this result, see Davis, DeGroot, and Hinich (1972), Kramer (1973), McKelvey (1976a, 1976b, 1986), Schofield (1978a), Slutsky (1979), Cohen and Matthews (1980), and Enelow and Hinich (1983a, 1984b).

Generalized median voter theorem (GMVT)

Assumptions.

(a) Let there be N voters choosing one set of policies in a space of n policy dimensions.

(b) Let preferences be separable and symmetric around each ideal point $\mathbf{x}_i$, for $i = 1, \ldots, N$.

(c) Define a "separating hyperplane" $\mathcal{H}$ of dimension $n - 1$ as a point (when $n = 1$), line (when $n = 2$), plane (when $n = 3$), or hyperplane (when $n > 3$) that divides the N ideal points into two groups. Each group is made up of the ideal points on one side of $\mathcal{H}$, including those ideal points that lie on the surface of $\mathcal{H}$. Then the number of members in each group is N_1 and N_2, respectively.

Theorem. *An alternative* $\mathbf{y}$ *is a median position for the society if and only if, for every* $\mathcal{H}$ *containing* $\mathbf{y}$, $N_1 \geq N/2$, *and* $N_2 \geq N/2$. *The number of* *votes for* **y** *is greater than or equal to the number of votes for any other alternative* **z**.

Interestingly, we have already seen the "proof" of the GMVT.[3] It is the same as that offered in Chapter 2 for the simple MVT in one dimension. The reason is that although the MVT is a special case of the more general theorem, the principle is the same.

Conclusion

This short chapter has been a more formal presentation of the results summarized in Chapter 3. It may be useful, after mastering the mathematical principles discussed here, to reread Chapter 3 as a way of reinforcing the intuition behind the formal discussion.

There have been four main themes in our presentation of the multidimensional model in Chapters 3 and 4:

- A definition of "preference," using distance in space as a metric.
- A discussion of the importance of different priorities, or "salience," of issues in determining preference over two or more issues.
- A discussion of the importance of separability, or the effect of the expected level of one policy on the preferred level of another policy.
- A consideration of the conditions that cause instability of majority rule decision processes when two or more issues are being decided at the same time.

In the next chapter, we consider the instability, and even indeterminacy, of collective choice processes more generally.

EXERCISES

4.1 Suppose $\mathbf{A} = \ell \times \mathbf{I}$, where $0 < \ell < 1$. What is the specific relationship between the SED and the WED measures of distance?

4.2 Suppose committee member i has an ideal point $(\mathbf{x}_i = [10\ 12]^\mathrm{T})$ on two budget items and that $\mathbf{A}_i = \begin{bmatrix} 2 & -3 \\ -3 & 1 \end{bmatrix}$. Imagine that for some reason the budget for Project 1 is set at $20 and that all members take this as given. Is member i's conditional ideal on Project 2, given $\tilde{x}_1 = 20$, larger or smaller than $12? What is the exact numeric value of $x_{i2}^* \mid \tilde{x}_1$?

4.3 Use the Pythagorean theorem to prove that the SED between two points $\mathbf{z}$ and $\mathbf{y}$ in three-dimensional space (dimensions 1, 2, and 3) is:

$$SED(\mathbf{z}, \mathbf{y}) = \sqrt{(z_1 - y_1)^2 + (z_2 - y_2)^2 + (z_3 - y_3)^2}$$

CHAPTER 5

Social choice and other voting models

She pours, to her spirit's content, a nightingale's woeful lament
That e'en though the voting be equal, his ruin will soon be the sequel.
(Aristophanes, *The Frogs,* Part III, 405 B.C.)

The previous chapters have assumed that society's decisions are made by simple majority rule. In the real world, many decisions really are made that way. Many other decisions, however, are made using other means of adding up or counting people's political preferences. In this chapter we consider public decisions more broadly and look at other ways of choosing. Because we are going to cover many topics quickly, it is well to begin with an intuitive overview.

One of the conventions of social choice theory is to describe each of several important results as a "paradox," a term deriving from *paradoxon,* a Greek word meaning "beyond opinion or belief." Thomas Schwartz described the role of paradox in analytical politics: "Deduce a contradiction from reasonable-looking, widely held assumptions, and you have a paradox; the better entrenched the assumptions, the more paradoxical the paradox" (1986, p. 116).

We have argued that the location of a middle within public opinion, given the voting rules of the society, is the key feature in determining both the nature of policy and its stability in a nation. But we have had trouble *finding* a middle in complicated policy spaces under majority rule. This difficulty suggests that majority rule decisions are susceptible to manipulation, because there is no determinate outcome in many circumstances. At worst, democratic decision processes may be quite incoherent, as William Riker argued.

In Chapter 2 we considered a problem with the stability of majority rule outcomes when preference profiles are not single-peaked. The example itself dates back to the Marquis de Condorcet, who published a lengthy discussion of the mathematical properties of sequences of pairwise majority rule contests in his *Essai sur l'application de l'analyse à la probabilité des décisions rendues à la pluralité des voix* (1785). Condorcet himself considered the result to be merely a feature of majority rule, rather than a paradox. Nonetheless, "Condorcet's paradox" has become part of the language of modern social choice theory. What is the deduced implication that is "beyond belief"?

Before we give the answer, it is useful to define a technical term: "transitivity." Suppose a person is asked to rank three alternatives, A, B, and C. Imagine she responds with a list that has two comparisons:

> C is better than B.
> B is better than A.

Now, it *seems* obvious that anyone who likes C better than B and likes B better than A would also like C better than A. Still, we have no direct evidence because our subject did not tell us about her preferences in a comparison of C versus A.

From a technical perspective, the conclusion "C is better than A" is not obvious, and it is not trivial. In fact, C is *deducibly* preferred to A in our example if and only if the preferences of the person in question are transitive.

> **Transitivity.** Preferences are *transitive* if, for three alternatives, C preferred to B preferred to A necessarily implies that A is not preferred to C (weak transitivity) or that C is preferred to A (strong transitivity).

Note that transitivity is a concept that might be applied to a preference ordering of an individual or a society choosing among alternative policies.

We are now in a position to state Condorcet's paradox.

> **Condorcet's paradox.** Suppose all individual preferences are transitive, but not necessarily single-peaked. Then the social preference ordering under majority rule may be intransitive.

The paradox is that the aggregation of *individually* transitive preferences leads to an *aggregate* intransitivity.[1] The society finds itself in an endless cycle of "best" alternatives, none of which commands a majority against all other alternatives.

Our Hun–Gats, from Chapters 2 and 3, found themselves in such a cycle: A majority preferred staying home to going south. Then a majority preferred going north to staying home. Then a majority preferred going south to going north! To a casual observer, it may look as though this is a group of people who don't know what they want, but that's the paradox: Each person individually knows exactly what he or she wants. It is the society that can't make a decision, because majority rule is intransitive in this case.

In this chapter, we discover that Condorcet's paradox is an example in a general class of paradoxes arising from using *any* social choice mechanism, except dictatorship. The results are called "paradoxes" because the general problem seems so simple, yet turns out to be insoluble.

The meaning of collective choice. Suppose all citizens are perfectly informed about all policies. We then solicit citizens' ordered "lists" of policies, ranking all feasible alternatives from best to worst, assuming that the information on the list is accurate and not strategically misrepresented to manipulate the outcome. Then, given sincere, accurate information in the lists about individual relative valuation of policies, compute the aggregate list for the society. The aggregate list looks like an individual's list, again ranking polices from best to worst. The difference is that "best" now is from the collective perspective.

Social choice theorists have repeatedly demonstrated that there is no sure way of choosing a transitive aggregate list if all citizens' preferences count. This is true even under the best circumstances (perfect information, no manipulation), if no restrictions are placed on the form of individual lists. The objections made by some – that these assumptions are unrealistic – miss the point. If social choice is not tractable under idealized circumstances, then adding imperfect information and manipulation makes the problem harder, not easier. What is beyond belief about paradoxes of social choice is that even the simplest kinds of voting schemes yield surprises.

We will briefly examine the best known of these paradoxical results, Arrow's (1963) impossibility theorem. Arrow laid out a set of properties or conditions that (arguably) are desirable features of a social choice mechanism. The impossibility theorem is a deduction that no social choice mechanism can possess all these features. In particular, all voting procedures must violate at least one of the conditions that Arrow demonstrated to be mutually inconsistent. Since Arrow's paradox applies to *any* nondictatorial aggregation mechanism, it encompasses all of what we might consider "democratic" decisions by societies. We will review briefly a variety of ways of choosing collectively and discuss some of their advantages and disadvantages.

Choosing how to choose

Decisions may be made by one person, by some people, or by everyone. The set of citizens required to make a decision or choice is called the "decisive set."

     Decisive set. A set C of citizens is "decisive" if for two alternatives y and z the fact that all members of C like y better than z is sufficient to ensure that y is selected over z by the society, regardless of the opinions of citizens not members of C. We will call $K(C)$ the "size" of C, or the minimum number of people required to be decisive.

We have seen an example of a decisive set under majority rule: C is any group of $(N/2) + 1$ citizens. Thus, there are many different potential Cs, each of which must have $K(C) \geq (N/2) + 1$ citizens.

    Both the inclusion of a given person's preferences in a decision (enfranchisement) and the decision to use a particular means of summarizing these preferences (aggregation mechanism) can affect the decision. Generally we think of "private" decisions (What will I have for lunch? What shoes will I wear with this outfit?) as being very different from "group" decisions (What is the appropriate budget for education? What is the right speed limit on limited access highways?).

    But distinguishing private and group decisions begs the question. Apparent differences among "kinds" of choices are caused by differences in enfranchisement and aggregation mechanisms, not necessarily by inherent properties of the choices themselves. Lunches and shoes could plausibly be collectively chosen (as in the military or in a school with a dress code). Similarly, levels of spending and speeding might be picked by individuals, at least in principle. Government vouchers could be applied toward the bill at a private school of a family's choice. Drivers might drive as fast as they like on highways, with government road crews occasionally clearing the mangled remains.

Thus, "social choice" has two elements:

- *Public decision:* The choice will have a significant public impact, affecting more than one individual. This might be because the choice affects others; this effect is called an "externality." The effect is called a "positive externality" if the effect is a benefit, or a "negative externality" if the effect is harmful. Alternatively, the choice might involve the level of provision of a "public good." Public goods (e.g., national defense) are characterized by zero marginal cost of production and high cost of exclusion from consumption.

- *Collective decision:* It is mandated, by rule or practice, that the choice will be made by more than one person. Technically, all this means is that $C > 1$. If collective decisions are made by majority rule, $K(C) \geq (N/2) + 1$. If the rule is unanimity, the decisive set may be all enfranchised citizens: $K(C) = N$.

The two aspects of choice may appear to go together, but they are distinct. Choices might be public but not collective: Suppose I build a factory that produces sooty smoke and my downwind neighbors suffer. There may be no institution that *enfranchises* them in the decision to build the factory.[2] Their preferences receive zero weight in the public (but not collective) decision, because $C = 1$. In the extreme, *all* decisions might be made by one person (a dictator), with no collective enfranchisement whatsoever, though all the dictator's choices might be "public."

Conversely, choices may be collective but not public: A society may decide to outlaw some consensual sexual practice involving two mentally competent adults. Another society might require that cyclists wear helmets. In both cases peoples' choices are being regulated, even though these activities affect no one else.[3] In this case, other people are enfranchised to decide individual behavior: The sexual partners and the bareheaded biker get a voice in the collective decision, but their preference counts only as a few among many. It is no longer true that $C = 2$ (for the consensual sexual activity) or that $C = 1$ (for the cyclist).

Our primary concern in this chapter will be with the implications of different *aggregation mechanisms,* not alternative *enfranchisement rules.*[4] The following section lays out the limits of the abilities of aggregation mechanisms to solve collective choice problems. The rest of the chapter considers several specific collective choice rules and their implications.

Arrow's paradox and the limits of social choice

Condorcet showed that majority rule may be intransitive, even if each individual has transitive preferences over the alternatives. Intransitivity is a kind of breakdown, assuming that some choice is required. That choice may be to preserve the status quo, and do nothing, but the choice itself must be clear and determinate. Intransitivity means the society is incapable of choosing among several mutually exclusive outcomes, without resort to random or imposed "choice." One might ask whether this potential for incoherence extends to other aggregation mechanisms. The definitive answer is less than fifty years old and dates to Arrow (1952; revised 1963).

That answer is disturbing for defenders of democracy or for advocates of any particular form of collective choice. We will present a simple overview of Arrow's technical result, but it is worth beginning by summarizing the intuition of the result first:[5]

Arrow's paradox. The only collective choice mechanism that is always transitive, allowing for any possible fixed set of pairwise preferences over alternatives, is dictatorship.

The "paradox" is that the only transitive collective decision rule that obeys the technical criteria Arrow sets out is dictatorship, or rule by one. Such a decision rule is not "collective" at all! Dictatorship resolves disagreements by restricting the decisive set to contain only one person. How did Arrow arrive at this conclusion?

The "impossibility" result

We will consider only a simplified paraphrasing of Arrow's theorem and will not consider the technical aspects of the proof of the theorem at all. The reader interested in pursuing this subject more deeply can find an introduction to the literature in Mueller (1989, especially chapters 19–20) and a treatment in depth by Schwartz (1986) and Kelly (1988). Our exposition of the logic of Arrow's result can be summarized this way:

(1) Specify a set of desirable characteristics for an aggregation mechanism, or way of "counting" preferences registered by enfranchised citizens.
(2) Determine the set of collective choice mechanisms that have these desirable characteristics.
(3) Ask how many of these choice rules are *not* dictatorial. The answer is: Not one! Any social choice mechanism exhibiting all the characteristics Arrow listed as desirable *must* be dictatorial.

Some scholars have questioned the merit of Arrow's list. Others have suggested substitute axioms that are weaker or quite different, but Arrow's original set of desirable characteristics is not implausible. The version of these characteristics we will use is adapted from Mueller (1989), itself adapted from Vickrey (1960). To describe the list of desirable characteristics for social choice mechanisms, we will need to define some terms and concepts.

Consider three different states of the world, S_1, S_2, S_3, representing discrepant policy vectors 1, 2, and 3, respectively. We can then describe the set of desirable characteristics as follows:

1. *Unanimity (also, the Pareto criterion):* If all enfranchised citizens agree (for example) that S_1 is better than S_2, then S_1 is selected by the collective choice rule over S_2.
2. *Transitivity:* The collective choice mechanism is transitive, so that if S_1 is selected over S_2, and S_2 to S_3, then S_1 is selected over S_3.
3. *Unrestricted domain:* For any individual and for any pair of alternatives S_1 and S_2, any of the following six preference orderings (from best to worst) is possible:

	1	2	3	4	5	6
Best	S_1	S_1	S_3	S_2	S_2	S_3
Middle	S_2	S_3	S_1	S_1	S_3	S_2
Worst	S_3	S_2	S_2	S_3	S_1	S_1

4. *Independence of irrelevant alternatives (IIA):* The social choice between any two alternatives must depend only on the individual rankings of the alternatives in question in the preference profile of the group. Thus, if S_1 is socially preferred to S_2, then it will still be socially preferred if we rearrange the orderings of the other alternatives

while leaving the paired rankings of S_1 and S_2 the same. For example, the following two sets of preference profiles of three citizens must yield the same social ordering for S_1 and S_2, if the social choice rule is IIA:

Preference profile set I (for persons 1, 2, and 3)

	1	2	3
Best	S_1	S_2	S_1
Middle	S_2	S_1	S_3
Worst	S_3	S_3	S_2

Preference profile set II

	1	2	3
Best	S_1	S_3	S_1
Middle	S_3	S_2	S_2
Worst	S_2	S_1	S_3

Notice that the relative rankings of S_1 and S_2 are the same in profile sets I and II. All that is different is the position of S_3 in the rankings. For example, in set I, person 1 ranks the alternatives S_1, S_2, S_3. In set II, person 1 ranks them S_1, S_3, S_2. In both cases, 1 likes S_1 better than S_2. Independence of irrelevant alternatives requires that this pairwise comparison of rankings does not depend on the position of other, "irrelevant" alternatives (such as S_3 in our example).

The final "good" characteristic of mechanisms for the democratic aggregation of preferences is probably the most obvious: No one person possesses all power to decide.

5. *Nondictatorship:* There is no dictator. If person 2 (for example) is a dictator, then if person 2 ranks S_1 above than S_2, then "S_1 better than S_2" is the social ranking, regardless of how anyone else, or even everyone else, ranks S_1 compared with S_2.

With these conditions established, we can state a version of the "impossibility" theorem more precisely.

Impossibility theorem. *Consider the set of all collective choice rules that satisfy requirements 1–4 (unanimity, transitivity, unrestricted domain,*

*and IIA). Every element of the set of collective choice mechanisms satis-
fying these requirements violates requirement 5, implying the existence of
a dictator.*

What does the impossibility result leave us? A menu of choice: Any
mechanism for aggregating individual preferences must lack at least
one of the desirable properties 1–4. We have listed nondictatorship separately because tyranny is incommensurable with democracy. To put it
another way, nondictatorship is a starting point if the goal is to compare ideal forms of government.

Clearly, this outright exclusion of dictatorship is a normative choice
and could be quarreled with. Plato might well have disagreed, arguing
that it is democracy that causes tyranny:

> Democracy is precisely the constitution out of which tyranny comes; from ex-
> treme liberty, it seems, comes a slavery most complete and most cruel. . . .
> When a democratic city gets worthless butlers presiding over its wine, and has
> drunk too deep of liberty's heady draught, then, I think, if the rulers are not
> very obliging and won't provide plenty of liberty, it calls them blackguards and
> oligarchs and chastises them . . . and any who obey the rulers they trample
> in the dust as willing slaves and not worth a jot. (Plato, *The Republic,* Book
> VI, 560A–564B)

The only way to have justice is, in Plato's view, to have a just dictator:

> It is no wonder that the multitude do not believe what we are saying. For they
> have never seen in existence the project now being discussed . . . a man, bal-
> anced and equated with virtue as nearly as possible to perfection in word and
> deed, and, moreover, holding sovereignty in a city perfectly equated with
> him. . . . Let there be one man who has a city obedient to will, and he might
> bring into existence the ideal polity about which the world is so incredulous.
> (Plato, *The Republic,* Book VI, 498D–502B).

Still, Arrow disallows dictatorship. A similar argument (for restricting the menu of choice for ideal forms of government) applies to
the Pareto criterion, though on more practical grounds: It is hard to
imagine adopting a rule that would prevent change if literally *everyone*
favored the change. If nothing else, society could unanimously change
the rules![6]

If we insist on nondictatorship and the Pareto criterion in our social
choice rules, we are left with three options: decision rules that allow
intransitivity, rules that allow *independent alternatives* to affect pairwise
choices of other alternatives, and rules that restrict the set of *preferences*

that will be allowed (i.e., violate universal domain). A complete discussion of the implications of relaxing the postulates of the impossibility theorem are beyond the scope of this book; the interested reader should consult Schwartz (1986) or Kelly (1988).

What we will do instead is look at some alternatives to simple majority rule. People have come up with many different ways to choose. Each of these methods of aggregating preferences has some advantages and some drawbacks. The search for an "optimal" system is very difficult, however. All systems have potential problems with fairness, and all systems can be manipulated.

Alternative decision rules

There is a difficulty with majority rule as a normative prescription for all members of society. That difficulty is that the majority's will must serve all, though it is only selected by most. Such a process must rely for its legitimacy on the majority's forbearance: "To be governed by appetite alone is slavery, while obedience to a law one prescribes to oneself is freedom" (Rousseau, 1973, Book I, chapter 8). If the majority does not act on "appetites," but rather enacts only good laws, *the same policy would be chosen* by one person, by a group, or by the whole society, provided the choosers are wise, well informed, and well intentioned. Such an approach begs the question of collective choice by assuming the problem away: The collective is organic, not fractious.

This moral force of unanimity can be achieved for majorities by artifice, as in Rawls's (1971) "veil of ignorance." Rawls posits a thought experiment: Suppose you didn't know what your position would be in the society. Then what laws, rules, and policies would you select? The answer, Rawls claims is that "each is forced to choose for everyone" (p. 140). Since you don't know what your self-interest is, you must choose for society, rather than for your own "appetites." If each chooses for everyone, the distinction between private and collective choice vanishes.

But what if the majority decides to act on its appetites? Suppose, for example, most of the society wants simply to enslave the rest. Even on a smaller scale, it is perfectly possible that the majority may want to enrich itself at the cost of the minority, and ultimately at the cost of virtue and order for the society. The reader may recall that such a pessimistic prediction was Aristotle's view of unfettered majoritarianism, or what Riker (1982) called "populism." Abraham Lincoln, harking back to Jefferson's belief that revolution, even in a democracy, could be just, said: "If by the mere force of numbers a majority should deprive a minority of any clearly written constitutional right, it might, in a moral point of view, justify revolution – certainly would if such a right were a vital one" (Inaugural Address, March 4, 1861).

How can we choose rules that determine how we choose policies and have any faith in the justice of the choice? The choice of aggregation mechanism will determine, in part, the nature of the society by advantaging certain alternatives. We will consider three major sets of alternatives to simple majority rule: (1) optimal majority rule, (2) the Borda count and approval voting, and (3) proportional representation.

Optimal majority rule

The first variation on majority rule is some form of majority rule itself, allowing the size of the required "majority" (i.e., decisive set) for an affirmative decision to be different from the simple majority $C = (N/2) + 1$. After all, what is so special about 50% (plus one voter) as the minimum group in favor? In theory, as we have discussed above, the size of the group making a decision can vary from one person to the whole society.

In practice, lots of normal collective business is done by majority rule. But even within the context of real-world collective decisions, the size of the proportion of enfranchised voters required to make a decision varies widely. In many legislative assemblies, unanimous consent is required to amend or waive temporarily the rules of procedure. To change the U.S. Constitution, two different supermajorities (two-thirds of a national assembly to propose, three-quarters of state assemblies to ratify) are required. There are examples of decisive sets smaller than even simple majority, including the U.S. Supreme Court's practice of affirming a writ of *certiorari* based on a vote of less than one-half of the seats on the court (four out of nine). What is the "best" decisive set as a proportion of the polity? The answer to almost all important questions, of course, is that "it depends." But what does the answer depend on?

The classic analytical treatment of optimal majority is Buchanan and Tullock's *The Calculus of Consent*. Taking an economic approach,

Expected costs

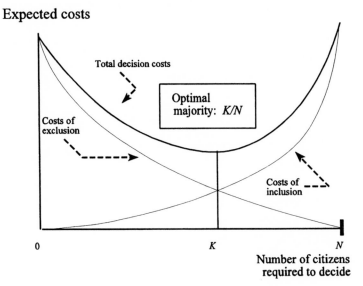

Figure 5.1. Buchanan and Tullock's "optimal majority" analysis.

Buchanan and Tullock note that there are *costs* of widely shared decision power as well as *benefits*. The costs of *including* more people in the required majority entail defining and amending the proposal, explaining it to the voters, providing payoffs to solve strategic maneuvering of swing voters, and so on. These are called "decision costs," because the costs fall on those whose preferences count in the decision. The costs of *excluding* members of society from the required majority can be thought of as the costs of being forced to obey a policy that one opposes. We will call these costs "external costs."

We can depict the problem of optimal majority graphically, as in Figure 5.1. Decision costs rise dramatically as we near a rule of unanimity, because each voter becomes a potential swing voter. Anyone can threaten to withhold approval unless certain concessions or payoffs are made. Similarly, external costs fall as we near unanimity, because by definition there is less chance a policy can be enacted without approval of everyone affected.

The optimal majority is *K/N*, because it minimizes the sum of the costs of inclusion and the costs of exclusion. These costs, though hard to quantify, clearly figure in how we choose how to choose, as public decisions fall into three categories:

(a) *Access decisions: $0 < K < (N/2) + 1$.* One member of the U.S. House or Senate is required to introduce a bill. If no one introduces the bill, it is completely blocked. At least four members of the U.S. Supreme Court are required to grant a writ of certiorari, or petition for a case to be heard. Neither of these decisions by any means ensures success; all that is granted is access.

(b) *Routine decisions: $K = (N/2) + 1$.* The smallest strict majority is a very common value for the decisive set in democracies, from tiny private clubs to the U.S. Congress and Supreme Court. This value for K is the smallest value that ensures no simultaneous passage of two directly contradictory measures. Thus, both inclusion and exclusion costs are moderate. For simple majority rule to have such wide real-world application, it must minimize the (perceived) costs of making routine collective decisions.

(c) *Changing the Rules: $(N/2) + 1 < K \leq N$.* The rules of choice govern the kinds of outcomes that the choices represent. A decision to change the rules has more far-reaching and unpredictable effects than a decision made under a fixed set of rules. Consequently, the costs of excluding enfranchised members is higher for rule change decisions, and the optimal majority for rule changes is more than 50% + 1.

In most cases, there is no single decision rule used for all choices; it depends. For example, in the U.S. Congress the introduction of a bill requires just one member. The passage of a bill requires 50% + 1 of the members present and voting. A resolution to propose an amendment to the Constitution requires a two-thirds majority. A motion to suspend the normal rules requires unanimous consent. Business in the Senate can be held up almost indefinitely by dilatory tactics or "filibuster," unless three-fifths of the membership vote for a resolution of "cloture," closing off further debate.

If there is a general rule, it does appear that we require larger majorities for larger questions, just as Buchanan and Tullock suggested. This conclusion is also quite consistent with some of Rousseau's thought, though his justifications are very different from those given by Buchanan and Tullock:

A difference of one vote destroys equality; a single opponent destroys unanimity; but between equality and unanimity, there are several grades of unequal division, at each of which this proportion may be fixed in accordance with the condition and needs of the body politic.

There are two general rules that may serve to regulate this relation. First, the more grave and important the questions discussed, the nearer should the opinion that is to prevail approach unanimity. Secondly, the more the matter in hand calls for speed, the smaller the prescribed difference in the numbers of votes may be allowed to become: where an instant decision has to be reached, a majority of one vote should be enough. (Rousseau, 1973, Book II, chapter 2, p. 278)

Equilibrium for larger majorities

It appears that different decisive sets are appropriate for different choice situations. But now we must ask what effects these differences may have on the existence and nature of equilibrium. We will still face the generic failing of majority rule systems, of course: The society may cycle among alternatives within a subset of the overall space of feasible political choices. But given this caveat, is there a generalization of the MVT that applies to optimal majorities K/N, where $K > N/2$?

The answer is yes.[7] As in Chapter 3, define N_1 as the number of points on one side of a hyperplane $\mathcal{H}$ (including points on $\mathcal{H}$), and N_2 as the number of points on the other side (again, including points on $\mathcal{H}$). The generalized K-majority voter theorem' (KMVT) is then just an obvious generalization of the GMVT.[8] The KMVT can be stated as follows:

KMVT. *An alternative* **y** *is a K-majority equilibrium for the society if and only if $N_1 \geq N - K + 1$ and $N_2 \geq N - K + 1$ for every $\mathcal{H}$ containing* **y**.

Interestingly, the KMVT reduces to the MVT for majority rule, since for majority rule $N - K + 1 = N/2$, where $K = N/2 + 1$. Thus, a more general statement of the GMVT in the preceding chapter might have been to require the numbers of voters on each side of the separating hyperplane to be at least $N - (N/2 + 1) + 1$.

The practical difficulty with supermajority rules is the dramatic increase in the number of equilibria for the society. There is no way of choosing one over another at the outset. Further, there is no way of

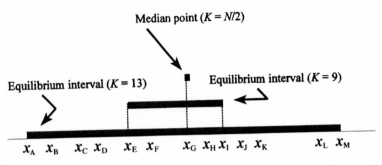

Ideal points for 13 committee members

Figure 5.2. An example of supermajority rule: many equilibria, little change.

changing the choice once any equilibrium position is established as the status quo. Another way to think of the KMVT, as Figure 5.2 shows, is to realize that supermajority rules profoundly advantage the status quo position. The larger the required majority, the more difficult is any kind of change, *once a status quo is established.*

As the figure shows, larger majorities imply broader equilibrium intervals, illustrating why the KMVT is a generalization of the GMVT. If $K = N$, the set of equilibria is the Pareto set. For $N > K > N/2$, the set of equilibria is an interval. As K shrinks to $N/2$, the set of equilibria is the median ideal point (as in our example), or a median interval containing two ideal points (if the median is not unique, under the conditions outlined in Chapter 2).

If any point in the set of possible equilibria is established as the status quo by accident, practice, or strategic action, it is protected from change under supermajority rules. Consequently, supermajority rules ensure stability, but at the expense of flexibility. The status quo is preserved like an insect in amber, even if most citizens support some other alternative.

Runoffs and pluralities. One other consideration remains in our discussion of majorities. We have required that votes be conducted in a series of pairwise comparisons. That is, though the set of alternatives may be quite large, our consideration of majority rule has required that each new proposal be voted against the status quo, with the winner becoming the new status quo. Majority rule can also be applied to more than two alternatives, but analysis becomes much more complex. Further, the existence of equilibria (particularly "centrist" equilibria) becomes problematic. One solution is to have a modified form of majority rule over three or more alternatives: If any alternative receives more than half the vote, that alternative wins and becomes the status quo. Otherwise, the top two alternatives (in terms of votes received) are selected for a *runoff* election.

An apparently similar (but very different) procedure is *plurality rule.* In plurality rule systems, whichever party or candidate receives the most votes wins, regardless of whether a majority of the vote is received. To see the difference, consider the following vote shares, for a four-candidate election: candidate 1, 27%; candidate 2, 26%; candidate 3, 24%; candidate 4, 23%.

In a majority rule with runoff election, candidates 1 and 2 would have to stand for election again. The outcome is very much in doubt, since we have no idea how the 47% who cast ballots for candidates 3 or 4 compare candidates 1 and 2. Importantly, the candidate who wins will be the one who appeals to more of the 47% of the voters who did not vote for candidates 1 or 2 in the first round. Under plurality rule, the leftover 47% are irrelevant: Candidate 1 wins the election outright, and the other three candidates get nothing.

While majority rule with runoff and plurality rule are fairly widely used in the real world of politics, it is interesting to note that neither has quite the direct centralizing tendency so apparent in the two-alternative, majority rule world of the median voter result. Plurality rule, in particular, may lead to the nonexistence of equilibrium if candidate entry or movement is free and unrestricted. Plurality rule may also lead to equilibria that are "decidedly noncentrist" (Cox, 1987). Cox shows that some candidates (if there are several) will take positions outside the two central quartiles of the distribution of voter ideal points even in equilibrium. This point is elaborated, for a variety of voting systems, in Cox (1990).

Borda count and approval voting

Majority rule and its variations are based on the premise that each person gets one, and only one, vote. It is simple, easy to understand,

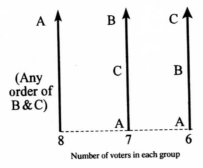

Number of voters in each group

Figure 5.3. Borda's example of how majority rule picks the "wrong" alternative: A wins, but either B or C is better. (From Borda, 1781; reprinted in Black, 1958, p. 157, Fig. 156)

and technically defensible when the polity is seeking a choice of a single "best" outcome from the set of alternatives. The blunt and decisive quality of majority rule is a disadvantage, however, if the goal is to select a set of alternatives, or if the polity is trying to rank alternatives in a way that reflects voters' preferences from best to worst, rather than just choosing a single outcome or candidate.

In this section, we will consider some aspects of two types of voting over "lists" of alternatives (or candidates), with the presumption that the number of alternatives may be much larger than the two we have generally assumed so far. These two voting rules are the *Borda count,* and *approval voting.*

Borda count. Jean-Charles de Borda (1733–99) anticipated some of the observations of Condorcet, whose achievements we outlined earlier. His objection to majority rule was different from Condorcet's, however (see Black, 1958, for discussion and background). Condorcet's criterion for value in elections was that if a majority preferred an alternative, that alternative should be selected. Borda was concerned that majorities might pick the *wrong* alternative, even if Condorcet's criterion was satisfied.

Suppose there are twenty-one voters, who must choose over three alternatives A, B, and C. Suppose further that the preference rankings of voters fall into three categories, as in Figure 5.3. If we use a majority (actually, plurality) choice rule, only first-place votes count. We don't know the second- and third-place preferences of voters in the first group. All we know for sure is that they like alternative A best, and they are the most numerous (eight first-place votes for A). Since B receives seven votes and C gets only six, A is the chosen policy.

Borda's point was that thirteen voters, a clear majority, may actually like alternative A *least*. The problem with plurality rule, he felt, was that it counted only first-place votes. Borda suggested several possible alternative decision rules, but the one most often associated with him is the "Borda count": Let each voter assign to each alternative a number corresponding to his or her ranking of that alternative.

Thus, each voter in the middle group in Figure 5.3 gives alternative B a rank of 1, C a rank of 2, and A a rank of 3. (If there were more alternatives, say, q of them, then the ranks would go down to the worst, or qth, alternative on each voter's ballot.) The authority conducting the election then adds up the scores, or "marks," for each alternative, and that alternative with the *smallest* number (for Borda, the most "merit") wins.

Borda left the exact distribution of preferences for C and B in the first group unspecified (again, see Black, 1958). For the sake of example, let us suppose that four of the eight voters like B better than C, and the others prefer C over B. What would be the result of using the Borda method? Alternative A has eight first-place votes, zero second-place marks, and thirteen third-place marks, for a Borda count of forty-seven. Alternative B has seven first-place votes, ten second-place, and four third-place, for a count of thirty-nine. Alternative C has six first-place marks, eleven second-place, and four third-place, for a count of forty. Using the Borda count, then, B wins over C in a close race, with A well back in the voting.

We might change the preferences of the first group for B over C in the example, but the basic result would be the same: No matter what preference for B over C is used, A always comes in *last*, rather than first as under majority rule. When the preferences of voters beyond their first-place rankings are considered, A is eliminated from serious consideration in this example.

Approval voting. The Borda count has been criticized as requiring of citizens too much character and information. Borda requires that voters rank all alternatives. If some do not, the outcome will depend on the way abstention is counted. Further, though Borda noted that "my scheme is intended only for honest men,"[9] the Borda count provides opportunities for voting strategically, misrepresenting one's preference ordering to change the outcome.[10]

An alternative that preserves some of the qualities of the Borda count is *approval voting:* Each voter votes for as many of the candidates as he or she likes, and the candidate with the most votes wins.[11] Another way to think of approval voting is to imagine that each voter makes a list of candidates, ranked from best to worst. The voter then draws a line between the worst acceptable candidate and the best unacceptable candidate. Every candidate the voter approves gets a vote, but those below the line get nothing.

Returning to the example in Figure 5.3, suppose that voters in the first group think that only A is acceptable. Imagine that voters in the middle and last groups consider both B and C acceptable. What will be the result under approval voting? A will receive eight votes, just as under plurality rule. Candidates B and C will each receive thirteen votes, so that the specific outcome will depend on how we assume ties are broken. The point is that A will not have a chance as long as A is judged not acceptable by a majority of voters, which is the spirit of Borda's example.[12]

Both the Borda count and approval voting must violate one of Arrow's axioms, but which one? The answer is independence of irrelevant alternatives (IIA). The social choice under the Borda rule or approval voting may depend on the relative positions of two alternatives compared with other (irrelevant) alternatives. Violation of IIA is the basis of the manipulability of the Borda count. This may be more of a disadvantage in small-group settings than for mass elections, of course. In any case, IIA is almost always violated for any choice rule that requires scoring an entire list of alternatives rather than making a single best choice.

A simple example (adapted from Arrow, 1963, p. 27) illustrates another property of the Borda count: It is not *independent of path.*[13] This is actually a different problem from independence of irrelevant alternatives, since it involves the presence or absence of particular alternatives, not their relative locations in the preference rankings of voters. The interesting thing about Arrow's example is that it reveals an access point for strategy: For the Borda count and related social choice rules, outcomes can be sensitive to the set of alternatives that appear on the ballot, even in a single-stage decision.

Imagine there are three voters (A, B, and C) and four alternatives (x, y, z, and w). Further, suppose that all voters use the Borda count and vote sincerely. Consider two different ballots, one with four alternatives and another with only three.

Vote 1: A comparison of x, z, and w, with y also considered

	Voter			
Rank of alternative	A	B	C	Borda count
x	1	2	2	5
z	4	1	1	6
w	2	4	4	10
y	3	3	3	9

Clearly, x wins, because it has the smallest Borda count. Now, however, suppose that one alternative, y, is eliminated from the contest.

Vote 2: A comparison of x, z, and w, without y

	Voter			
Rank of alternative	A	B	C	Borda count
x	1	2	2	5
z	3	1	1	5
w	2	3	3	8

The outcome is now different: x and z tie, though nothing about their *relative* value has changed. All that is different is the decision context: For vote 1, y was on the ballot, and for vote 2, y did not appear. Furthermore, if there is now a run-off between x and z, z actually wins. Consequently, dropping y from consideration changes the outcome. This sensitivity to the inclusion or absence of other alternatives is different from the relative rankings of irrelevant alternatives, having more to do with how alternatives are retained or dropped in the early stages of elections or amendment procedures. That is the reason the "path" is important in this example.

Table 5.1. *Plurality rule and proportional representation compared*

Party	% Vote received	Pluralities won	Seats (plurality)	Seats (PR)
Green	45	55	55	45
Red	35	45	45	35
Blue	20	0	0	20
Totals	100	100 Elections	100 Seats	100 Seats

Proportional representation

A wide variety of collective decisions, particularly choices of political representatives in national assemblies for geographic districts, are made using "proportional representation" (PR) rules. There are many PR rules, but they share the characteristic that *each party's share of seats in the assembly is approximately that party's share of votes in the last election.* The ideal for a pure PR system, then, would be:

$$\frac{Party's\ seats}{Total\ seats} \approx \frac{Party's\ votes}{Total\ votes}$$

In practice, this ideal is violated in many ways and for very practical reasons. One of the most common modifications made to pure PR systems is the *threshold,* or minimum vote required for a party to seat members in the assembly. For example, Greece requires that a party receive at least 15% of the votes. Israel has an "exclusion threshold" of only 1.5% (Sartori, 1994). Such rules have two effects: (1) There is a departure from the ideal of pure proportionality, since a party can receive up to the vote threshold, minus one vote, and receive no seats in the legislature. (2) Consequently, people may vote strategically, eschewing sincere votes for small parties that have no chance and concentrating on one of the larger parties.

To contrast a PR system with a plurality rule system, consider Table 5.1.[14] In the table, we see a contrast between 1-seat allocations under plurality rule and a pure PR rule for three parties. The implications of plurality and PR rules, even given identical vote totals in either case, for the distribution of power in a 100-seat assembly are strikingly different.

Notice that the table does not give individual election results, but only nationwide totals. The number of pluralities won was chosen arbitrarily, but represents a possible outcome: The Green party comes in first in fifty-five races, the Reds come in first forty-five times, and Blues don't win any races outright. Under a plurality rule, these are exactly the proportions of seats the two parties hold: Greens 55%, Reds 45%. (The Blue party is presumably demonstrating in favor of electoral reform.)

Under a pure PR system, the Blue party would get fully 20% of the seats, corresponding to its 20% of votes in the election. There is no clear majority party, since the largest number of seats is held by the Greens, who have only 45% of the assembly under their control. The Greens will be obliged to form a coalition if they want to govern, or face the possibility that a Blue–Red coalition government (the Purple) will form and control 55% of the votes, a working majority.

The process of coalition government formation is complex and quite beyond the scope of this book; the interested reader should consult Laver and Schofield (1990). Our point is simply that once a PR election has been held, it is by no means clear that a government has been selected; in fact, the process may have barely begun. Any two of the three parties in our example are capable of joining and forming a government. On the other hand, no one party can govern. Consequently, the nature of the government is very much in doubt. Cycling over coalition partners simply moves the incoherence of the democratic process from voter choice to bargaining among elites.

A summary of the difference between plurality and PR rules is given by Dennis Mueller:

> If the purpose of the election is to select a government, a chief executive, a single party to rule the country, then the plurality rule for electing representatives, or for electing the chief executive, should be employed. This rule will tend to produce two parties or candidates. . . . If the purpose of the election is to select a body of representatives that mirrors as closely as possible the preferences of the citizenry, then PR is the appropriate electoral rule. . . . PR is a system for choosing *representatives,* not for picking between final packages of outcomes. (1989, pp. 222, 226; emphasis in original)

In some ways, the consideration of whether plurality/majority rule (sometimes called "first past the post" elections) or PR is better mimics our earlier discussion on the optimal size of majorities. If a single decision among several mutually exclusive alternatives is required, then plurality rule, or majority rule with runoff, has clear advantages. The polity may simply need to decide something *right now,* so the costs of delay from deliberation and negotiation in a PR system may not be worth paying.

On the other hand, questions of far-reaching consequence for all citizens may require a representation of many points of view. In such decisions, representation may even be an end in itself, since not just the decision but the legitimacy of the decision is crucial to the survival of the society. For such decisions, voters may want to be sure they have a representative of their own choosing. PR systems are appealing in such circumstances because the deliberative process of the legislative assembly mimics, in proportions of perspectives, the population as a whole.

Summary and conclusions

In this chapter, we have outlined some intuition behind alternative voting institutions. The use of the word "alternative" means "ways of choosing other than simple majority rule," for majority rule holds a privileged status as a benchmark in social choice. Gary Cox (1987), in discussing alternative voting institutions, notes:

Another way to organize the findings herein is along a "degree of centrism" axis. Holding down one end of this axis would be the Condorcet procedures, under which candidates have a dominant strategy to adopt the position of the median voter. Other procedures (such as Borda's method and approval voting) under which the unique convergent Nash equilibrium is the situation in which all candidates adopt the median position would come next, followed by systems (such as negative voting) under which there are multiple convergent equilibria. Finally, holding down the other end of the centrism axis would be procedures such as plurality rule, under which candidates will not converge at any point, instead spreading themselves out more or less evenly along the policy dimension. (p. 99)

Dictatorship, for most of us, is unacceptable as a way of organizing government. In the weighing of order versus liberty on the scales of choosing a "good" society, dictatorship provides only order. But liberty without order may lead to chaos. The signal contribution of Arrow and the social choice theorists that have followed him has been to demonstrate that there is no perfect alternative to dictatorship. Ultimately, dictatorship may always be with us, because order without liberty may be better than liberty without order. The design of government institutions that can preserve order and still protect liberty is perhaps the most difficult, yet most rewarding of all human enterprises.

EXERCISES

5.1. Suppose that there are seventeen members of a committee, with ideal points on a policy line that correspond to their identities (Mr. 1 most prefers a policy of 1, Mr. 11 likes a policy of 11, and so on). Suppose that the current policy is 7. According to the KMVT, what is the *smallest K* that preserves the status quo (7) as an equilibrium?

5.2. Suppose five voters (Messrs 1–5) have the following preference rankings for three candidates (A, B, and C).

	Voter				
	1	2	3	4	5
Best	A	B	C	B	A
Middle	C	C	A	C	C
Worst	B	A	B	A	B

Which candidate will win under the following decision rule:

a. *Majority rule,* each voter gets one vote for first preference, *with runoff* in the event of no majority on first ballot.

b. *Borda count,* each voter ranks candidates from 1 (best) to 3 (worst). Smallest total "score" wins.

5.3.* Give a formal proof of the KMVT.

Note: Exercises marked * are advanced material.

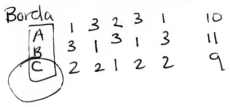

Borda

A	1	3	2	3	1	10
B	3	1	3	1	3	11
C	2	2	1	2	2	9

Extensions

The basic analytical theory of politics uses assumptions to simplify an impossibly complex world. But assumptions limit the external applicability of the model. The assumptions we have used so far include: Candidates know the distribution of voter preferences; voters know where candidates will locate in the policy space; candidates have no goals other than winning the election; finally, all enfranchised citizens vote.

In this section, some important extensions of the basic model are introduced. The extensions represent applications of more realistic assumptions to the problems we have discussed in earlier chapters:

- Candidates with policy preferences
- Candidate uncertainty about voter location
- Voter uncertainty about candidate location
- Abstention out of indifference or alienation
- Voting is a collective action problem

These extensions make the model more complex, but dramatically improve the model's ability to explain real-world politics. Interestingly, the main prediction of the basic classical model, that there is a fundamental centralizing tendency in political competition, is robust with respect to alternative assumptions.

CHAPTER 6

Uncertainty and policy preference

Better it is to die, better to starve,
Than crave the hire which first we do deserve.
In this wolvish toge should I stand here,
To beg of Hob and Dick, that does appear,
Their needless vouches? Custom calls me to't;
What custom wills, in all things should we do't,
The dust on antique time would lie unswept,
And mountainous error be too highly heapt
For truth to o'er peer. Rather than fool it so,
Let the high office and the honour go
To one that would do thus. I am half through;
The one part suffer'd, the other will I do.
                    (William Shakespeare, *Coriolanus,*
                              1608, Act II, sc. III)

Downs (1957) created the foundations of the classical model. But Downs clearly saw the need for a more comprehensive model. He tried hard to build better assumptions into his discussion of politics. As John Ferejohn points out:

The spatial metaphor has by now become such a common and powerful way of portraying electoral competition that students and journalists unselfconsciously depict electoral phenomena in its terms, without recognizing either its limitations or its foundational assumptions. But in his original introduction of the spatial model Downs is actually quite cautious with regard to the applicability of the spatial theory to actual elections. He spends a good deal of effort and space in his book examining the conditions under which electoral competition could be understood in terms of the spatial model. Specifically, he tries to develop a theory in which parties compete for office by making promises and voters base their votes on a comparison of these promises. (1993, p. 107)

The classical spatial model simplifies candidates' "promises" and their reasons for making those promises. First, all participants know the distribution of voter ideal points. Second, platforms and candidates are indistinguishable. In the classical model, platforms and candidates are both nothing more than vectors of policy positions. These simplifications are crucial to the exposition of the model, but now that the reader has mastered the basics, it is time to incorporate some of Downs's own caution about applying the spatial theory to actual elections. What actually happens when a candidate must don his or her "wolvish toge" and seek out Hob and Dick in pursuit of those "needless vouches"?

In this chapter, we allow uncertainty about voter positions, as well as a distinction between platforms and candidates, by introducing three extensions of the classical model. As we explained in Chapter 1, a key advantage to abstract analytical theorizing is the ability to ask "what if?" questions. In this chapter we will look at three "what if?" questions, comparing the answers to the answers implied by the classical model:

- *What if* candidates are not sure how voter ideal points are distributed?
- *What if* voters are not sure what candidates will do once in office?
- *What if* candidates have some preferences of their own about outcomes?

The classical model requires that (1) the distribution of voters is known, (2) any participant can propose any platform, and (3) participants care only about winning and have no policy preferences. We have shown that the proposal power assumption is not crucial: Even if proposals can only be made by two parties, the outcome will be the same as with free proposal power, provided the parties care only about winning.

Further, the candidates take identical positions, because *equilibrium requires convergence to the median position.* Because the model advanced so far allows no place for comparisons of uncertainty about what the candidates will do, they might as well be clones. This Tweedledum and Tweedledee quality of the classical model has been criticized from several quarters, both for the lack of realism of its assumptions and for the (arguable) inaccuracy of the basic prediction of convergence. By considering *candidate uncertainty, voter uncertainty,* and *candidate policy preferences,* we can investigate the robustness of the predictions of the classical model under more plausible assumptions about political competition.

Where the voters are

In political campaigns, lots of time and money are spent asking voters questions, conducting focus groups, or looking at demographic characteristics of different parts of the electorate. Why would politicians and their staffs do this? Candidates need to know what voters want, what their preferences are. In the parlance of spatial theory, campaigns try to learn the distribution of voter preferences so candidates can locate at the middle of that distribution.

Suppose we don't know what voters want. How can we predict what politicians will *do*? The outcome might be random: If voter preferences cannot be directly observed, then politicians just pick a platform based on a guess about the distribution of voter preferences. The candidate closer to the center of the (unobservable) distribution of voter ideal points will win the election. But then, what of the prediction of convergence to the center?

Suppose candidates pick the platform representing their best guess at the ideal point of the median voter (or the interval of median positions). If the two candidates have access to the same information (polling data, consultants, etc.), then their "best guesses" about the location of the median voter will also be the same. If the (expected) position of the median voter is the same for both candidates, the prediction of convergence will be preserved. Further, if pollsters' estimates are (on average) correct, the point of convergence will center on the *actual* location of the median voter.

To see how this works, consider the distributions of expected median positions in Figure 6.1. The middle distribution (solid line) represents one distribution of the probabilities candidates attach to the event that these are the actual median positions for voters in the upcoming election. Most positions have no probability of being a median position, of course. Positions near the center of the distribution are fairly likely, however, because there is a good chance that the median voter will have one of those ideal points. The solid curve is labeled "convergent expectations," meaning that the two candidates (Y and Z) have similar data about the voter preference distribution.

Clearly, if candidates care only about winning and have the same information about the location of the median voter, they will choose

Probability x is a median position

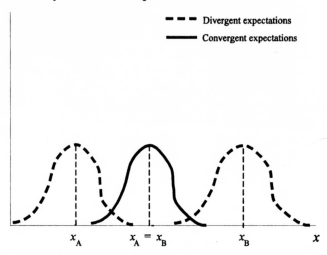

Figure 6.1. If expectations converge, candidate platforms converge; if expectations diverge, platforms diverge.

the same platform x. The optimal platform (assuming the distribution of expected median positions is single-peaked and continuous) is the "mean median," or center of the distribution of medians.[1] Thus, in Figure 6.1, $x_Z = x_Y$ if expectations are convergent.

On the other hand, if expectations about the location of the median voter's ideal point are not identical, neither are candidate locations. If candidate Z chooses a platform based on one set of interviews or advice, and candidate Y uses different information, the two candidates may have different expectations about the location of the median. Consequently, as in Figure 6.1 (dotted curves depicting distributions), the candidates may *initially* choose different platforms ($x_Z \neq x_Y$).

This "result" means little, for two reasons. First, broadly divergent expectations don't occur in large electorates, unless one of the polling firms is incompetent.[2] Political professionals, faced with similar information, draw similar conclusions. Second, and more important, *whatever the initial positions of the candidates,* divergence is not an equilibrium, given the logic of political competition. If one candidate takes a position different from the opponent's position, each would immediately notice he could increase his vote share by moving toward the opponent.

It is useful to summarize the discussion above in three theorems, which will be stated without proofs (for early work on the importance of the mean preference under uncertainty, see Davis and Hinich, 1968; for a more detailed discussion and proofs of these results, see Calvert, 1985, Theorems 3–7; and Wittman, 1990). The assumptions of the theorems are more restrictive than required, to simplify the intuition.

Theorem 6.1. *Suppose exactly one median position is known to exist, but that its location is unknown. If the distribution of possible median positions is unimodal, symmetric, and shared, then candidates will adopt identical positions at the location of the mean of the distribution of medians.*

Theorem 6.2. *If the distribution of possible median positions is unimodal and symmetric but candidates have different perceptions of this distribution, then candidates will initially adopt divergent positions at the location of the means of the perceived distributions of medians. These divergent positions are not an equilibrium, however. If candidates can move they will adopt identical positions somewhere between the two divergent perceived means of the distributions of medians.*

Theorem 6.3. *If candidates are uncertain about the location of voters and candidates seek some mix of policy and reelection, then candidate positions will diverge in equilibrium. In fact, no convergent equilibrium exists under these circumstances. However, the extent of the divergence depends on the extent of uncertainty and the mix of policy–reelection motivations by the candidates. Only if uncertainty is extreme and reelection motivations are trivial will the degree of divergence be substantively significant.*

Uncertainty about the location of the median is not, by itself, sufficient to reject the convergence prediction. The center still rules, even if the location of the center is now hard to identify before an election, as long as perceptions of the distribution of voters is shared. If perceptions differ, positions may diverge, but as a product of difference in expectations, not uncertainty per se. Further, even if expectations diverge, candidates will adjust to a convergent equilibrium if they can.[3]

Voter uncertainty about what candidates will do

The classical model has voters choose based on what candidates say. Real voters may care about what a candidate says, because that may be the only way to tell what the candidate will do. However, as Jeffrey Banks points out:

[The] strong assumption implicit in the [classical] model is that the positions the candidates announce prior to an election will be the positions they subsequently enact once in office. Since voters typically have preferences defined over policy outcomes and not over electoral announcement per se, but their only information at the time of voting consists of these announcements, the equivalence of announced position and policy outcome appears to be one of analytical tractability at the expense of realism. (1990, p. 311)

In this section we are concerned about the distribution of voter expectations about what candidates will do once in office, *given what the candidates claim they will do.* The classical model depicts candidates as *points* in policy space. Allowing voter uncertainty over candidate positions implies a *distribution* defined over an *interval.* Within this interval (assuming the set of possible policies is continuous), many different policies have some chance of being implemented after the election. Consequently, we are allowing that there may be some difference in voters' minds between what politicians say they will do and what actually will happen.[4]

Figure 6.2 depicts three very different levels of voter uncertainty about the policy consequences of a candidate's election. Panel (a) depicts a candidate about whom there is no uncertainty: The distribution of expected policy consequences is a point. Panel (b) depicts a candidate whom voters perceive as moderately committed to a particular policy. Voters recognize that this candidate may choose some other policy or for some other reason fail to do as promised. Panel (c) shows a candidate with no credibility at all. As in the first two panels, this candidate's "expected" (i.e., mean) policy action is the same as his or her professed platform; but the distribution of actual policies is uniformly distributed over all feasible policies.[5]

The question of how these distributions might be induced in voters' minds is very complex, and is outside the scope of the present book (see Bernhardt and Ingberman, 1985; Ferejohn, 1986; Banks, 1990; Austen-Smith, 1990; Enelow and Munger, 1993; or Hinich and

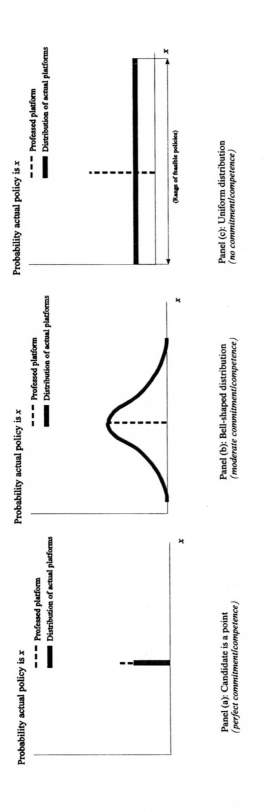

Probability actual policy is *x*

- - - Professed platform
■ Distribution of actual platforms

Panel (a): Candidate is a point
(perfect commitment/competence)

Probability actual policy is *x*

- - - Professed platform
■ Distribution of actual platforms

Panel (b): Bell-shaped distribution
(moderate commitment/competence)

Probability actual policy is *x*

- - - Professed platform
■ Distribution of actual platforms

(Range of feasible policies)

Panel (c): Uniform distribution
(no commitment/competence)

Munger, 1994; for possible origins of voter expectations, given a candidate's espoused platform).[6] If voters have such expectations, we can incorporate the difference between panel (a) in Figure 6.2 (certainty) and the other panels (moderate or complete uncertainty) into our model of voter choice.

Suppose candidate Nagaer is a committed conservative and has taken consistent positions for the past twenty years in many different political environments. Imagine Nagaer's opponent, Sikakud, has taken a variety of positions on issues, but has been a liberal. In the campaign, suppose Nagaer continues to argue for rightist positions, though his expected policy is clearly to the right of the most preferred policies of the median voter. Sikakud, seeing this, gleefully proclaims himself to be the candidate of the center and awaits the landslide victory that must be his. (Sikakud read as far as Chapter 2 of this book and knows that the MVT is on his side!)

Of course, the voters (A, B, and C) have read the whole book or act as if they had. Such voters' choices are more complex and sophisticated than Sikakud realizes. Consider Figure 6.3, which depicts the comparison of voters' perceptions of the distribution of expected policies from the two candidates. Sikakud's distribution (solid line) is *centered* at the median position (x_B), just as he had hoped. Because he has taken a variety of positions in the past, however, the *dispersion* of his expected actions once in office is high. By contrast, Nagaer's distribution (dotted line) is centered some distance away from the median. But because of Nagaer's consistent conservatism, there is very little perceived variance around this central tendency.

The intuitive keys to the choice of the median voter, B, are the crosshatched areas in the left and right tails of the Sikakud distribution. These areas represent the probability that the *actual* policy carried out by Sikakud, if he is elected, is worse (further from B's ideal point) than the *mean* value of Nagaer's expected policy distribution. Suppose voter utility functions are quadratic, meaning that the utility from candidate Y being elected is $- (x_Y - x_i)^2$. Such voters may accept an expected policy *slightly* away from their ideal point if the risk of being *very* far off is reduced. In that case, the probability that policies far from x_B may be implemented hurts Sikakud's chances.

The following section gives an overview of the more fully fleshed-out model for the reader familiar with basic statistics. Before continuing

Probability x_i is implemented after election

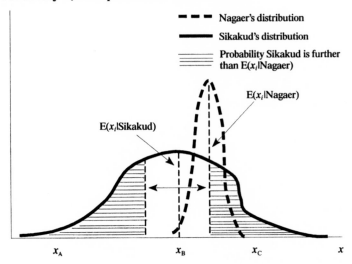

Figure 6.3. Voters trade off expected policy against uncertainty: Median voter prefers Nagaer, because of high probability Sikakud will be even worse.

to the next section, however, a disclaimer: The candidates in the above example are fictional characters. The fact that Nagaer spelled backwards is "Reagan" and Sikakud is "Dukakis" is just coincidence.

Details for the statistically minded

Suppose there is a single policy dimension x, preferences are quadratic, and that the voter's ideal point is x_i. Suppose there are two candidates, R and D, with policy positions x_R and x_D. These random variables are distributed with means $\bar{x}_R$ and $\bar{x}_D$, and are assumed to have known variances. If i chooses the candidate who provides him the highest expected utility, this implies the following decision rule (note: $E[\cdot]$ is the expectations operator):

$$E[(x_i - x_R)^2] < E[(x_i - x_D)^2] \qquad \text{Vote for R} \qquad (6.1)$$

$$E[(x_i - x_R)^2] > E[(x_i - x_D)^2] \qquad \text{Vote for D} \qquad (6.2)$$

$$E[(x_i - x_R)^2] = E[(x_i - x_D)^2] \qquad \text{Choose randomly} \qquad (6.3)$$

We can represent the random variables as (symmetrically) distributed about their means:

$$x_R = \bar{x}_R + \epsilon_R \tag{6.4}$$

$$x_D = \bar{x}_D + \epsilon_D \tag{6.5}$$

where ϵ_R and ϵ_D are zero-mean random error terms. But this means we can rewrite the decision rule by substituting in the definitions of the random variables. For example, i will vote for R if:

$$E[(x_i - (\bar{x}_R + \epsilon_R))^2] < E[(x_i - (\bar{x}_D + \epsilon_D))^2] \tag{6.6}$$

and so on. If we actually complete the square on both sides, take expectations, and gather terms, we find i will vote for R if

$$(x_i - \bar{x}_R)^2 + E(\epsilon_R^2) < (x_i - \bar{x}_D)^2 + E(\epsilon_D^2) \tag{6.7}$$

Since $E(\epsilon_R) = E(\epsilon_D) = 0$, the expected value terms on both sides of (6.7) are simply the variances of the expected positions of R and D, respectively. The following results are then obvious:

- If $\bar{x}_R = \bar{x}_D$, the candidate with the lower variance will always win.
- If $\bar{x}_R \neq \bar{x}_D$, it is possible for the candidate located at x_i (in expected value) to lose if that candidate has a large variance of expected policy. (See Exercise 6.3.)

Convergence or divergence if voters are uncertain

We began this section by asking if voter uncertainty about candidates causes divergence in equilibrium in the spatial model. A quick reading of this section might lead one to believe the answer is yes. Well, no. We have shown that, if positions diverge, the candidate further from the median *may* win, provided her variance is less than that of the centrist candidate. But this is true only if the candidates are for some reason fixed in position: Divergence is not, in a technical sense, an equilibrium result. A low-variance candidate is better off at the center than anywhere else, just as before.

There is one possibility for generating divergence in equilibrium, however, which is just beginning to be understood by social scientists. This possibility is that the "technology of commitment," by which we mean the cognitive process by which voters form expectations about what candidates will likely do in office, advantages extremists.[7] To put it another way, it is possible that one cannot commit to being a centrist with the same low variance as it is possible to commit to more extreme positions on either the right or the left. The center, after all, is the region of compromise and protection for the status quo.

Political extremists may be more doctrinally pure and consistent, and therefore have lower perceived variance, than candidates in the middle. If this is so (as we shall discuss further in Chapter 9), then the technology of commitment itself may imply divergence in equilibrium. Without this assumption, however, there is nothing about voter uncertainty that *necessarily* upsets the prediction of convergence to the center by both candidates.

Candidates with their own policy preferences

Candidates (or the parties that nominated them) may have specific policy goals. Politicians might plausibly be motivated, in other words, not just to work in government, but to change government. Such candidates would care *both* about winning and about what policies are actually enacted.

There are several reasons candidates might have policy preferences. One is the need to satisfy partisans who have policy preferences. People who volunteer labor or contribute money are necessary to make campaigns work. If supporters and contributors have policy preferences, then candidates may have to act as if they do, too. Further, doesn't it make sense to expect that politicians genuinely care about what policies are enacted? Having and arguing for a specific set of policy goals may be the reason that the member was selected as a candidate in the first place.[8]

The extension of the spatial model to allow candidates to have policy motivations has been suggested by several authors, including Bental and Ben-Zion (1975), Wittman (1977, 1983, 1990), Cox (1984a), Calvert (1985), and Enelow (1992). Rather than reproduce their analysis, we can simply give a flavor of the logic of candidate location when candidates care about policy. Consider Calvert's apt summary:

It does not matter, in the electoral model, whether we treat the candidates themselves as having a vote or not, since we could think of the voting candidate as two separate people for the purposes of the model: one just a voter, the other a candidate whose ideal point happens to be identical with that voter's. *The voting, policy-oriented candidate for election faces exactly the same problem as a committee member with that power.* His task is to choose a proposal which, when matched against an opposing one, will give an outcome closer to his ideal. . . . It is plausible, of course, to expect that candidates have preferences about policy and prefer to win elections. Indeed, *the payoff to winning, itself, is really the only feature that might formally distinguish between the usual models of committee decision making and electoral competition with policy oriented candidates.* . . . The outcome of a two-party committee is exactly the same as the outcome when every member has proposal power, because the parties are forced to compete away their advantages in order to win. (1985, p. 79, emphasis added)

In these passages, Calvert captures the key difference between committee decisions and elections from the point of view of those making proposals. In the classical committee decision, people care *only* about policy and have free proposal power. The model predicts that the ideal point of the median voter will be the outcome. In an election between two candidates, if candidates care only about winning, the ideal point of the median voter will again be the outcome, though for different reasons: Since other positions lose, candidates go to the median to win.

To make this point clear, it is necessary to introduce a technique social scientists call "game theory." The following brief section introduces some elementary concepts of noncooperative game theory. Though the results generated from this approach are very similar to those of the classical model, the differences in how the idea of equilibrium is defined are important enough to merit their own section.

Game theory and political competition

The classical spatial model uses "decision-theoretic" reasoning. This means that the researcher assumes "rational" (informed and optimizing) behavior by each participant, but treats each participant as if his or her actions do not affect the expected payoffs of other participants. Thus, it is possible to evaluate the actions of each participant in isolation.

Game theory provides a way of incorporating the actions of others by accounting for strategic context. This may be important: What is best for A to do may depend on what A expects B to do. The trick is that B is also thinking about what A might do before choosing. The existence of a "best" choice is no longer obvious, because the best choice for each player may depend on what other people are expected to do.

This appears to lead to an infinite regress: "A thinks that B thinks that A thinks. . . ." But that is not necessarily true. In fact, there are some elegant solutions to the problem, though most are beyond the scope of this book. We will consider only the most elementary solution concept in game theory, "Nash equilibrium."[9]

The behavioral assumptions underpinning Nash games are these:

- Players move simultaneously, but blindly, or take turns moving.
- All players know (and know they all know) the context – the rules of the game, the set of feasible strategies, and associated payoffs and utility functions for all players.[10]
- In each turn, each player assumes that *the most recent play of the other players is fixed* and chooses the best response to this vector of positions.

The myopic behavioral assumption in Nash games seems silly. In fact, the presumption that actions are fixed is often dismissed as absurd by people who encounter it for the first time. In fact, the approach is both theoretically powerful and practically useful. The reason is that *in equilibrium* it must be true that nothing changes. This set of mutually consistent actions ("my play is the best response to your play, which is the best response to my play") provides the very definition of Nash equilibrium.

Nash equilibrium. For two players, let (for example) $U_1(S_1, S_2)$ be the utility of player 1, given his own strategy choice S_1 and the strategy of his opponent, S_2. For n players, let $U_1(S_1, S_{-1})$ be the utility of player 1 given his own strategy choice and the vector of all other players' strategies ("~1" means "all players other than 1"). Then for two players a strategy pair (S_1^*, S_2^*) is a Nash equilibrium if and only if the following two expressions are both true:

$$U_1(S_1^*, S_2^*) \geq U_1(S_1, S_2^*) \tag{6.8}$$

$$U_2(S_2^*, S_1^*) \geq U_2(S_2, S_1^*) \tag{6.9}$$

where S_1 and S_2 are any strategies different from S_1^* and S_2^*, respectively. The general, or n-player, Nash equilibrium is a strategy vector $\mathbf{S}^*$ such that for each player i's strategy, given all the other players' strategies,

$$U_i(S_i^*, \mathbf{S}_{-i}^*) \geq U_i(S_i, \mathbf{S}_{-i}^*) \tag{6.10}$$

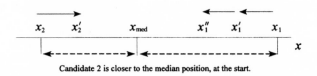

Candidate 2 is closer to the median position, at the start.

Figure 6.4. If candidates care about winning at all, platforms converge to the median position.

To put it another way, the only time the Nash behavioral assumptions make sense is in equilibrium. But then, that is the only time the assumptions need to make sense!

Nash behavior gives a way out of the infinite regress. Players' expectations are fulfilled in equilibrium, and there is no regret or possibility of having done better, taking the other players' positions as given. In the specific context of the two-player electoral game between candidates Y and Z, we can see that no position but the median is an equilibrium, as long as both candidate-players care about winning and policy.

There is no hint of the dynamic process by which equilibria are achieved in the Nash equilibrium concept. The point is that once an equilibrium is reached, it is sustained by the fact that none of the candidates has any incentive to move. One way that the candidates *might* reach equilibrium, a point where no one has any incentive to change position, is reminiscent of a description used by Cournot (1897) to describe duopoly competition.[11]

Suppose that there are many voters (with symmetric preferences), but that there is a unique median x_{med} at the ideal point of the median voter. Suppose that candidates Y and Z have taken divergent positions at the location of *their* respective policy ideal points, x_Y and x_Z. For the sake of example, suppose that x_Z is closer to x_{med} than x_Y is. This situation is depicted in Figure 6.4.

What will happen if the election were held today? Candidate Z would win (remember, preferences are symmetric!), so Y gets neither office nor his desired policy. Clearly, Y should move. His new platform, x'_Y, is closer to x_{med}, maybe just close enough to win by a whisker: $x'_Y = x_{med} + (|x_{med} - x_Z| - \epsilon)$, where ϵ denotes an arbitrarily small number. In words, Y's platform is just barely closer to the median, but now Y wins the election and, as a bonus, gets a policy much closer to his ideal (though it is less than his ideal). What is Z's best response to the new position by Y? To move even closer to the center, of course: $x'_Z = x_{med} - (|x_{med} - x'_Y| - \epsilon)$. But then, Y would respond, taking x'_Z as fixed: $x''_Y = x_{med} + (|x_{med} - x'_Z| - \epsilon)$.

This process of moving to the center will continue until both candidates converge to x_{med}. Surprisingly, this is true *even if the candidates care mostly about policy.* At the median point, the best response of Y to Z's position at the median is to remain at the median. Similarly, Z's best response is to stay at the median. There is no way to improve either candidate's level of satisfaction by moving to any other position. Any movement loses the election (whoever stays at the median wins), and *there is no change in policy anyway,* because the mover lost.

The strategy pair $[x_Y = x_{med}, x_Z = x_{med}]$ is the only equilibrium of the two-player Nash game. The important thing to remember is that both candidates care about policy and about winning. The fact that they care about winning *at all* is enough to guarantee convergence to the median. This is the result from Calvert (1985), though he used a more sophisticated game and a more general set of assumptions.

To summarize, the fact that winning and policy are both valued doesn't change the prediction of convergence. If the candidate cares about winning at all, then the fact that the median will be the winning policy proves irresistible. "It might as well be me up there signing those bills and getting my name in the paper," rationalizes the aspiring Solon. "The outcome will be the same no matter what; it might as well be me." If just one candidate chooses the median, the other must also. If one candidate moves closer to the median, the opponent will respond by edging inward. This is the logic of the classical spatial model, and that logic is confirmed by equilibrium models relying on game theory.

What if candidates are policy motivated **and** uncertain about voters?

The tenacious reader will recall a loose end in the discussion. In Theorem 6.3 in the section on voter uncertainty, we noted that equilibria are divergent if (a) candidates are uncertain about what voters want and (b) candidates have at least some policy motivation.

The particulars of this argument are beyond the scope of this book, partly because the relevant theorem requires a thorough knowledge of "probabilistic voting" (see Hinich, Ledyard, and Ordeshook, 1972;

Hinich, 1977; and Coughlin, 1992), which we will touch on in Chapter 8. More important, the question of the practical extent of divergence predicted by the model is still being decided (Green and Shapiro, 1994). We will simply point out the possibility that a relatively simple variant of the standard spatial model is capable of generating predictions of nonconvergent equilibrium.

Several interesting conjectures are suggested by the nonconvergence result:

- Policy-motivated candidates will lose more often because they will choose positions further from the median. But policy motivations, or noncentrist positions, may be an advantage in primaries. Which "type" is really more prevalent, policy seekers or pure office seekers? Why? For what offices?
- If the emoluments of office (salary, benefits, prestige, etc.) are increased, then at the margin holding office becomes relatively more attractive for its own sake. There is some evidence that careerism and platforms may be correlated (Parker, 1992; Fiorina, 1994), but many questions remain unanswered: Do existing politicians change their positions, giving up policy satisfaction to protect office satisfaction if salaries or benefits increase? Or do changes in salary induce a new wave of politicians whose main goal is a political career for its own sake? Finally, is paying high salaries and benefits "good" for society, in the sense of ensuring both accountability and leadership in government?
- Does the institution of recurrent elections select candidates whose policy preferences match the middle of the distribution of voter preferences, as Ferejohn (1986), Lott (1987), Lott and Reed (1989), and Dougan and Munger (1989) argue? If it does, the fact that politicians take central positions may reflect not convergence, but selection.[12]
- Do politicians trade off electoral "slack" and policy? That is, if a politician wins by wide margins, does he drift over time toward his ideal point? Conversely, if electoral pressures grow more binding, do politicians try to "vote their constituencies" more closely? Again, there is some evidence this is true (Kau and Rubin, 1981; Kalt and Zupan, 1984, 1990; Nelson and Silberberg, 1987; Bianco, 1994;

Coates and Munger, 1995), but no systematic investigations have been conducted on these questions.[13]

Though these questions have not yet been answered, it is clear that the various extensions to the classical model we have considered in this chapter represent exciting areas for future research.

Conclusions

In this chapter, we have presented an overview of the logic of spatial competition when the model is extended to account for uncertainty and policy preferences. The main prediction of the classical model outlined in earlier chapters is that the center rules, if it exists. The theme of the extensions we have considered is largely the same: Even if candidates are uncertain about where voters are, voters are uncertain about where candidates are, or if candidates have independent personal policy preferences, the center is the focus of political power.

There are four important qualifications for this claim:

- If two candidates are uncertain about the distribution of voters, have different perceptions of the location of the median, and *cannot move* after taking initial positions, they will take divergent positions corresponding to the mean of the respective distributions of median positions. But this result derives from the *divergence of expectations,* not from uncertainty itself. Nonetheless, different information or beliefs is a source of potential divergence.

- If voters are uncertain about the true position of candidates, then they will evaluate candidates both on what they expect the candidate will do and on the confidence they have in this prediction. Under these circumstances, it is possible for a candidate with a mean different from the median, with consistent commitment, to beat an unpredictable centrist candidate. If the technology of commitment is uniform across the spectrum of positions, however, the *equilibrium* is still at the center. The only difference is that now, instead of flipping a coin, the median voter chooses the centrist candidate who is more reliably centrist.

- If it is possible to commit credibly only to the extremes of the policy dimension (i.e., centrists have more variance), then divergence may be observed in equilibrium. But this result derives from an *additional assumption* (the technology of commitment hurts centrists), not from the logic of spatial competition with uncertainty alone.

- The most important qualifications to the convergence result, arising when both candidates are policy motivated and uncertain about what voters will do, is still being worked out theoretically, and tested empirically. The practical extent of the implied divergence is still unknown.

Finally, it is important to note that the debate over convergence versus divergence has evolved far from our original motives for considering the middle. The basis of the claims for the value of the center in political theory is exclusively *normative:* The center is the best policy, and institutions that lead to the center create the good society. The attractions of the center we have discovered in the spatial model are all *strategic:* If candidates want to avoid losing, they move to the center.

If the institutions of society create the means for democratic processes to attract politicians to the center, it is *possible* that the result is normatively good. But it is not necessary to assume that politicians are altruistic, or that any moral force inheres in the will of the majority, to appreciate the positive results of the classical model. The center, if it exists, is where political power resides. We get the government we think we want. Whether it turns out that we want the government we get is another question entirely.

EXERCISES

6.1 Suppose that voter i must choose between candidate R, with mean expected policy position $\bar{x}_R$, and D, with mean expected policy position $\bar{x}_D$, using the following information:

$$x_i = \bar{x}_D = 12$$
$$\bar{x}_R = 14$$
$$E(\epsilon_D) = E(\epsilon_R) = 0$$
$$E(\epsilon_D^2) = 16$$

    a. Suppose i's choice is described by the utility function in Equation 6.6 and that $E(\epsilon_R^2) = 2$. Who will i vote for?

    b. What is the largest variance candidate R can have and still win the election?

6.2 Suppose two candidates, Y and Z, care *equally* about policy and winning. Let the unidimensional policy space be the unit interval [0,1], and let $x_Y = 0$ and $x_Z = 1$. (Note: These are *candidate* ideal points!) Assume the candidates have the following utility functions:

$$U_Y = -.5[(x - x_Y)^2] + .5[W_Y]$$
$$U_Z = -.5[(x - x_Z)^2] + .5[W_Z]$$

where x is the winning platform (assume platform and actual policy implemented are the same), and W_Y and W_Z each take one of three discrete values: 1 if the candidate wins, 0 if the candidate loses, and .5 if there is a tie.

Finally, assume voter preferences are symmetric, so proximity to x_{med} determines the winner. What platforms maximize each candidate's utility if x_{med} takes the following values?

a. $x_{med} = .95$
b. $x_{med} = .10$
c. $x_{med} = .50$

[handwritten: answers — go to median, losing is weak than maintaining policy]

6.3 Consider a two-dimensional policy space, where voters have preferences over both policies. Suppose there are three voters, 1, 2, and 3, with preferences described by the ideal points $\mathbf{x}_1 = [6\ 0]^T$, $\mathbf{x}_2 = [0\ 6]^T$, and $\mathbf{x}_3 = [2\ 4]^T$, and matrices of salience/interaction terms:

$$\mathbf{A}_1 = \begin{bmatrix} 2 & 0 \\ 0 & 3 \end{bmatrix} \quad \mathbf{A}_2 = \begin{bmatrix} 2 & -1 \\ -1 & 1 \end{bmatrix} \quad \mathbf{A}_3 = \begin{bmatrix} 5 & 0 \\ 0 & 2 \end{bmatrix}$$

The two candidates, Y and Z, care only about winning. But they don't know voter preferences, so they aren't sure where to locate. Each candidate hires his own polling firm. Each of the two firms takes a poll, from a slightly different sample and using slightly different survey questions. The candidates are told to take the following positions:

$$\mathbf{x}_Y = \begin{bmatrix} 3 \\ 4 \end{bmatrix} \quad \mathbf{x}_Z = \begin{bmatrix} 2 \\ 3 \end{bmatrix}$$

Which candidate wins the election, and which should hire a better polling firm next time he runs for office?

CHAPTER 7

The voting decision and collective action

When bad men combine, the good must associate; else they will fall one by one, an unpitied sacrifice in a contemptible struggle.

(Edmund Burke, *Thoughts on the Cause of the Present Discontents,* April 23, 1770)

Not everyone votes. In some elections, almost nobody votes. County and city officials in the United States are elected by less than 20% of the eligible electorate. Bond referenda are voted on by 10% or less of those legally entitled to vote. In October 1973, Pinellas County, Florida, had an election, but nobody came! Here is an excerpt from a newspaper account the following day:[1]

Not even the three candidates on the ballot Tuesday bothered to vote in the countywide election for the Pinellas County Soil Conservation District board of supervisors. In fact, no one seemed to know anything about the election except the man who put it on, said Art Day, district conservationist. . . . Under the law, the board conducts its own elections. The only problem is it doesn't have any money for voting machines, clerks, and publicity. . . . "My total budget is $28, and I need more stationery!" Day said. . . . Day placed legal advertisements about the election in [local newspapers], but even the board's chairman, Wendell Salls, didn't know the election was being held. "I missed the last meeting," he said. Day said he will have to write the state office to find out what to do next. In the last election two years ago three people turned out. (Helen Huntley, *St. Petersburg Times,* November 18, 1973).

Perhaps people don't vote because their vote doesn't matter. At least, one vote doesn't affect the outcome of most elections. Of course, in the "election" in Pinellas County, *any vote would have mattered* because it would have decided the entire election. On the other hand, lots of people do vote. Some of them even seem to enjoy it or think it is important. In any case, voting is how we decide things, like how much to spend on new schools and who will represent us in public offices. What is the right way to think about voting at the mass level?

In this chapter, we will consider the implications of formal models for participation in the political process. There are several problems with making useful predictions about voter turnout and citizen participation, so it is worthwhile to reprise the set of questions we are investigating. There are three main sets of questions that concern analytical political theorists:

Question 1: Why are citizens presented with the alternatives they see on a ballot or referendum and not some others?

Question 2: Given the choices presented, (a) why do citizens vote or participate in politics at all, and (b) why do they make the choices they make?

Question 3: Are the results good, in an ethical or normative sense, for the society?

So far in this book, we have worked a little bit on Questions 1 and 3, but we have made only the simplest assumptions about Question 2. Most important, we have assumed that all "voters" vote, and have constructed our models under the conjecture that spatial "distance" determines each voter's choice. What does the spatial model have to say about turnout, or the decision of citizens to become voters?

As was noted in Chapter 2, the decision of the society to enfranchise only part of the potential electorate is a fundamental one. Enfranchisement might be restricted based on age, sex, ethnicity, moral worth, or other more complicated characteristics such as ownership of property. Enfranchisement in the United States has been steadily expanded from the creation of the Republic, as Table 7.1 shows.

Thus, with some fits and starts (it took from 1871 to 1965 to enfranchise African-Americans, though reading the XVth Amendment would make it seem the events of 1871 should have been enough), the size of the American electorate was dramatically expanded. Beginning with white males over twenty-one, the electorate has grown to include nearly all citizens over eighteen who are not in jail or mentally incompetent.[2]

However, as Table 7.2 shows, turnout in the United States is still low compared with other democracies. Part of the reason may be that the franchise in the United States is universal and the population is large, so people feel their vote doesn't "count." That can't be the whole story, however. After all, the comparison in Table 7.2 is based on national elections, where turnout is highest. Turnout is even *lower* for local elections and bond referenda, as we discussed above, and that is where individual votes have the greatest impact on the outcome.

Table 7.1. *Enfranchisement in the United States*

Year	Event	Enfranchisement of citizens
(Early)	Design of Republic	Considered restricting to white male property owners.
1781	U.S. Constitution	Requirements left to states; mostly white males over twenty-one years old, not convicted of any crimes.
1870	XVth Amendment	Right to vote cannot be restricted by states based on race, color, or previous condition of servitude. (*Followed XIVth Amendment, making all residents citizens, regardless of state law*). African-Americans effectively enfranchised in the North, and in the South during the period of Reconstruction (1867–77). However, after the end of Reconstruction, "Jim Crow" laws significantly encroached on the effective enfranchisement of black citizens, in some states making it impossible for them to vote.
1913	XVIIth Amendment	U.S. senators popularly elected for first time.
1920	XIXth Amendment	Right to vote extended to women, subject to same other state restrictions as men. (*Note: several states had already enfranchised women, through their own constitutions.*)
1962	XXIIIth Amendment	Right to vote in U.S. presidential elections extended to citizens of the District of Columbia.
1964	XXIVth Amendment	State "poll" taxes charged as a condition on voting in federal elections are outlawed. Harassing tactics had been used primarily by southern states to exclude African-Americans from voting.
1965	Voting Rights Act	Law passed by U.S. Congress to enforce the XXIVth Amendment. States were prohibited from using poll taxes, literacy tests, or other impediments that deny minorities voting rights. Also, federal examiners determined where discrimination had been practiced, and federal marshals enforced the law of no restrictions.
1971	XXVIth Amendment	Minimum voting age lowered to eighteen years, regardless of state law.

What does the classical spatial model say about the voting decision? To analyze voting, we have to recognize that the voting decision itself is only the last in a series of decisions, or reactions to costs and constraints, by the citizen. To see this, consider the results of Fort (1995), who elaborates and tests a "sequential barriers" model of turnout sug-

Table 7.2. *Voter turnout in fifteen democracies*

High-turnout countries (Average more than 80% of eligible age groups)	Australia Belgium Germany Italy Netherlands Sweden
Moderate-turnout countries (Average between 65% and 75% of eligible age groups)	Canada France Ireland Japan United Kingdom
Low-turnout countries (Average less than 60% of eligible age groups)	India Turkey Switzerland United States

Note: Figures on which the table is based are for national legislative elections, unless there is a president (as opposed to parliamentary) system of government. If there is a strong president, figures are for that office. The original data generally are taken from elections occurring in the period 1960–75. The authors updated the long-term averages using country-specific sources. *Source:* Adapted from G. Bingham Powell, Jr., "Voting Turnout in Thirty Democracies: Partisan, Legal, and Socio-Economic Influences," Table 3-1, p. 35. In R. Niemi and H. Weisberg, *Controversies in Voting Behavior,* 2nd ed., pp. 34–53. Washington, DC: CQ Press, 1984.

gested by Cox and Munger (1989, 1991). The point is that the "participation rate" of voters in any given election j is *definitionally* the product of four ratios:

$$\underset{(1)}{\frac{\text{Vote}_j}{\text{Population}}} \equiv \underset{(1)}{\frac{\text{Enfranchised}}{\text{Population}}} \times \underset{(2)}{\frac{\text{Registered}}{\text{Enfranchised}}}$$

$$\times \underset{(3)}{\frac{\text{Enter booth}}{\text{Registered}}} \times \underset{(4)}{\frac{\text{Vote}_j}{\text{Enter booth}}} \qquad (7.1)$$

In words, for a citizen to vote in election j, (1) the citizen is part of the population enfranchised by the laws and practices of the society, (2) the enfranchised citizen has chosen to register, (3) the registered citizen has chosen to enter the voting booth, and (4) the citizen in the voting booth has chosen to cast a vote in election j. The $\equiv$ sign means "equals by definition." We use it here because each of the intervening steps (enfranchisement, registration, entering booth) occurs in both the numerator and denominator, so they cancel in the product.

Though they cancel out in the *definition,* each of the intervening steps affects the observed turnout rate, of course. Attempts to analyze turnout empirically in any one election must account for all of the choices the citizen makes or has made for her by the rules of her nation, state, or city. For example, if the political jurisdiction that makes voting rules restricts enfranchisement by race, gender, age, or income, then ratio (1) in Equation (7.1) may be small. If registration is expensive, time-consuming, or complicated and intimidating, ratio (2) may be small. Finally, there is an important interaction between ratios (3) and (4): The number of registered people who vote may depend on how groups of elections are packaged. If elections are held separately, it may be that few people vote (ratio (3) will be small), but that everyone who enters the booth casts a vote in election j (ratio (4) would be near 1.00).

We started this chapter with an example, where "they had an election, but nobody came." That election, for the Pinellas County Soil Conservation District board of supervisors, was the only race on the ballot. For that race, ratio (3) was 0.0, and ratio (4) was undefined (0/0). Suppose this election had been held on the same day as a United States presidential election, with the same candidates for Soil District board appearing at the bottom of the ballot. Ratio (3) may have been as large as 0.5 or 0.6, as people turned out to vote in the presidential election. Ratio (4), however, might have been as large as 1.0 or as small as 0.0. Even if they are in the booth, voters may have gotten bored or simply felt ignorant: "Just what the heck is a Soil District, anyway?" This phenomenon of abstaining from obscure races, often listed at the bottom of the ballot, is called "roll-off" (Burnham, 1965). Roll-off may occur because voters are tired, apathetic, or uncertain.

Having "analyzed" voter participation (breaking it up into components), we see that several different explanations are required to understand the process. The task of explaining variation in ratio (1) (legal enfranchisement) across countries is interesting, but quite beyond our scope. Explaining variation in ratio (2) (registration) across nations or U.S. states is an interesting policy question, but the decision whether to register is clearly a different decision from deciding whether to vote (though, as Erikson, 1981, points out, registration may be the more important decision overall).[3]

If we are to analyze the voting decision, we must restrict our attention to ratios (3) and (4). The simplest case, which we will pursue, is to assume that the race in question is the only one on the ballot. The reason is not that most elections actually look like this (they don't; ballots are often quite long). We already *know* that multiple elections have complicated effects (Cox and Munger, 1989; Fort, 1995; Hamilton and Ladd, 1996). By considering a single race and a single decision on whether to go to the polls and vote, we isolate the logic of the citizen's choice. In the next section, we discuss the two major reasons the classical model gives for abstention: indifference and alienation.

The classical model: Indifference and alienation

We have assumed, in earlier chapters, that all citizens vote. This is a very limiting assumption if the goal is to understand or predict real-world events. There are at least two circumstances where enfranchised citizens might not choose to vote in an election. One of these is *indifference,* or the perception that there are no important differences (in terms of citizens' welfare) among the alternatives presented on the ballot. The other is *alienation,* or a voter's sense that the issue positions of the candidates are far removed from what she cares about. One candidate may be closer, but all candidates are outside the range of policy alternatives where the voter has any interest in participating.

The classical spatial model can handle either indifference or alienation.[4] To understand the meaning of, and distinction between, the concepts, it is useful to portray indifference and alienation graphically.

In Figure 7.1, panel (a) depicts a single voter's ideal point x_i and two sets of positions for candidates A and B. Notice that the voter is indifferent between x'_A and x'_B. She is also indifferent between the much closer x''_A and x''_B. Of course, if the candidate positions were x'_A and x''_B, the voter would choose candidate B. But paired as the platforms are, she finds herself indifferent in each case, though at two very different levels of utility.

Panel (b) gives the analogous diagram for alienation. If the race is between x''_A and x''_B, the voter will cast her vote for candidate A. But if

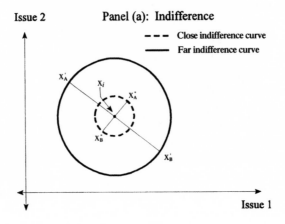

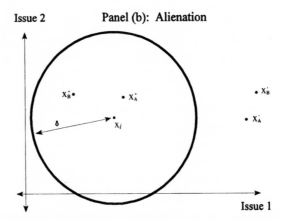

Figure 7.1. Indifference and alienation as explanations for abstention.

the race is between $\mathbf{x}'_A$ and $\mathbf{x}'_B$, both alternatives are so far away that the voter sees no point in participating. It doesn't matter which is relatively closer; both are too far, in an absolute sense, for the voter to care about the election. More precisely, abstention from alienation requires that beyond some threshold distance (defined here as δ) the voter loses interest in the election. She may perceive herself as lacking efficacy because she is so distant from the campaign she hears about in the media. More

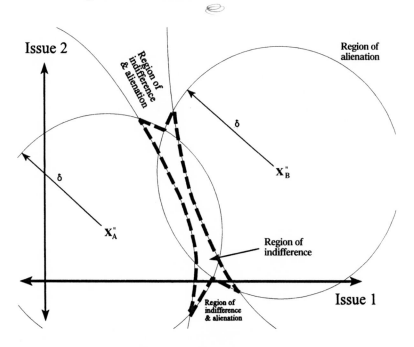

Figure 7.2. Integrated indifference–alienation example.

formally, the voter is alienated if *no candidate p* has a platform x_p such that $WED(x_p, x_i) \le \delta$.

Enelow and Hinich (1984b) present an integrated two-dimensional example, corrected slightly by Hinich and Munger (1994). This figure is adapted in Figure 7.2. The best way to understand the information in Figure 7.2 is to focus on two arbitrary candidate positions, x_A and x_B. We will not specify where voters are, but will identify the ideal point locations where, given x_A and x_B, a citizen will abstain out of alienation, indifference, or both.

A citizen whose ideal point is more than δ (the radius of the circles in Figure 7.2) away from both candidates abstains out of *alienation*.[5] If (not as we have drawn Figure 7.2) the two circles with radius δ do not overlap, citizens between the two circles abstain out of alienation. This observation gives rise to an interesting prediction about alienation of the center in extemely polarized systems: If the parties are too extreme, then voters in the middle may abstain because they feel no connection with either party.

If, but only if, the candidates are close enough so that the two circles overlap, there may also be a group of citizens who abstain out of *indifference*. This group need not be depicted as a narrow line, but (as we present it here) can be a region with nontrivial area, provided an "almost" indifferent citizen does not vote. A wide indifference region might arise because a small (though nonzero) difference between the candidates is not enough to offset her costs of voting.[6] For example, suppose that a voter prefers candidate A to candidate B, but only by a small amount. If the costs of voting are negligible, the voter may go cast a ballot for A. If the costs of voting are significant, however, the almost indifferent voter does not vote.

This effect is observed in actual elections in at least two ways. First, polities have widely varying rules governing the number of polling places and how long the polls stay open. If the polls open late and close early, many "almost indifferent" voters won't make it to the precinct.[7] Second, the weather on the day of the election may determine turnout. If it rains, the almost indifferent voter stays home.[8] If it snows, she laughs at the very idea of going to the polls. However, if she prefers A to B by a wide margin, she will brave storm or snow to cast her ballot. Consequently, the impact of bad weather is not random, because it drives down turnout from voters in the middle.

The classical spatial model's depiction of the decision to abstain is useful, because it identifies circumstances when citizens are less likely to vote from the perspective of a particular election. Since turnout varies across elections, it is important that we can identify variables (such as voter perceptions of candidate locations) that differentiate elections. The problem with the classical model, however, is that it is deterministic and does not allow for the possibility that voters consider what other voters will do before deciding whether to abstain.[9] In the next section, we consider this problem, which has been called the "paradox of not voting."

Voting is a collective action problem

We said earlier that no one's vote matters, and in a sense that is true: Mass elections are almost never decided by a single vote. But suppose a group of voters all agree on who would be the best candidate. If that group can induce its supporters to go to the polls, then all members of the group benefit because their candidate wins. On the other hand, any one voter might prefer to stay home and let everyone else ensure that the "right" candidate wins.

This conflict between what is good for the individual and what is good for the group is common in analytical politics. The problem is called the "free rider" problem and is most widely associated with the work of Mancur Olson, particularly in the *Logic of Collective Action* (1965). Olson claims that the key to success in providing collective goods is to induce people to contribute to the creation of collective benefits. "Free riders" are people who enjoy collective benefits provided by the efforts of someone else, without contributing any effort or resources themselves. Olson makes the free-rider argument explicitly for voters:

> Though most people feel they would be better off if their party were in power, they recognize that if their party is going to win, *it will as likely win without them, and they will get the benefits in any case.* . . . The point is that the average person will not be willing to make a significant sacrifice for the party he favors, since a victory for his party provides a collective good. (1965, pp. 163–4; emphasis added)

To analyze turnout as a collective action problem, we need to consider the "Downsian" model of voting, from Downs (1957). This model was elaborated by Riker and Ordeshook (1968).[10] According to this model, an individual will vote if and only if:

$$P \times NCD + D \geq C \qquad\qquad (7.2)$$

where, for each voter:

P = The probability that this individual's vote will affect the outcome of the majority rule election.

NCD = Perceived net benefits of one candidate over another in the eyes of the individual ("net candidate differential" in Downs's parlance). If there are two candidates A and B, then the NCD is $|x_i - x_A| - |x_i - x_B|$. If $NCD > 0$, B is closer to x_i. If $NCD < 0$, A is closer.

D = The individual's sense of civic duty. This is the utility derived from voting, regardless of the outcome.

C = The costs associated (at the margin) with the act of voting, including the opportunity cost of time spent, chance of inclement weather, and so on.

The logic of this model is cost–benefit analysis: If the (expected) returns exceed the costs, the citizen becomes a voter and casts a vote for the candidate he most prefers. Otherwise, he abstains. But notice how complex the model truly is. The decision of *whether* to vote is made simultaneously with the choice of *for whom*. Imagine that the duty term is negligible ($D \approx 0$). Then the citizen votes if and only if $P \times NCD > C$. We know that $C > 0$, because voting entails some identifiable costs, including time spent traveling to the polls and waiting in line, and filling out registration forms. This leads us to predict that $P \times NCD >>> 0$ is a *necessary condition* for voting.

To put it another way, if either P or NCD is zero, the simple Downsian model predicts abstention. The P term is the individual's belief (in probability terms) that her vote will transform a loss into a tie, or a tie into a victory, for her preferred candidate. If an individual knows how all the others will vote, she knows the outcome: P is either 1 (her vote changes the outcome) or 0 (it won't). Such a perfect information outcome is highly unrealistic, even in small electorates, because no one knows how everyone else will vote.

Now, suppose we allow that $D > 0$. Though this seems like a simple matter, the intuition behind the D term is actually very intricate. As John Aldrich points out:

Adding a D term is the same as subtracting a C term. Thus, C can be thought of as "net costs," that is, as costs of voting, less any positive values, such as doing one's duty. A positive C says that duty only partially outweighs costs of voting. . . . Thus, the D term does not change the fundamental analysis, unless $D > C$, in which case it is better to vote for [the more preferred candidate] than to abstain in all circumstances. (1993, pp. 251–2).

This is a very important point: If $D > C$, the voter *always* votes, regardless of the locations of the candidates. Whether the motivation is the avoidance of guilt or the enjoyment of the act of voting itself, the point is the same. But then voting is simply a *consumption* activity, more like attending a baseball game than an act of rational investment.[11] Some scholars (Barry, 1970; Green and Shapiro, 1994) have argued that this means rational choice models are not useful for explaining levels of turnout, since turnout is simply a matter of taste within the model.

This criticism is not without merit, but neither is it completely correct. We will return to taste and turnout at the end of this chapter.

There is yet another problem, as a simple example from Hinich and Munger (1994) shows. The number of cases where $P = 1$, assuming perfect information, is practically zero. Suppose that each voter thinks of the electorate (i.e., those who vote, rather than those who are eligible) as a random sample from the eligible electorate. Suppose, further, that the polls show that the election is a dead heat between candidates A and B. The probability of a tie then depends on the sample size. Let N be the individual's guess as to the number of people who will vote, not counting himself. Then the number of potential tie outcomes T is:

$$T = \left[\frac{N!}{N/2! \times (N - N/2)!} \right] \tag{7.3}$$

(Note: ! means factorial.) For example, using this formula, if $N = 6$, then $T = 20$.

To get P, we divide T by the total number of outcomes 2^N. The reason there are 2^N outcomes is that each of the N voters has two choices: Vote for candidate A or vote for candidate B. Again using our $N = 6$ example, there would be $2^6 = 64$ outcomes. Putting this all together, we get $P = 20/64 = .31$. That is, in an electorate of six, there is approximately one chance in three that a rational voter will believe her vote will influence the outcome, assuming that (1) the polls predict a dead heat ex ante, and (2) each voter is equally likely to vote for either candidate. As N grows, P falls dramatically, as Table 7.3 shows. For an N of 100, $P = .08$; if $N = 150$, $P = .06$. If $N = 100,000$, P is zero to more than five decimal places. For all practical purposes, this number is indistinguishable from zero. Yet 100,000 is still a fairly small electorate, far smaller than the number of registered voters in a medium-sized city.

The probability gets smaller even faster, if the election is not perceived as "too close to call" ex ante. The candidate who has the lead is almost certain to get a majority if (1) most people have decided how to vote by the time of the poll, and (2) the poll itself is competently conducted and statistically accurate. If either candidate is far ahead in the polls on the day before the election, that candidate's victory seems assured.

So why would anyone vote? To put it another way, in terms of

Table 7.3. *Number of voters and the probability of affecting outcomes*

N	P
2	.5
6	.31
8	.27
10	.24
20	.18
100	.08
150	.06
100,000	.00

Downs's model, who would vote if the P term is zero? The answer is obvious: no one. Of course, this answer is also obviously wrong. One is reminded of Yogi Berra's famous line about a restaurant in New York: "No one goes there anymore. It's too crowded!" In our case, if no one votes because it won't matter, it *will* matter. If no one votes, then one vote determines the election. But then P isn't really zero. In fact, $P = 1$, because *anyone* who did vote would have decided the outcome, with certainty!

As before, we are in the infinite regress of "He thinks that I think that he thinks. . . ." Ferejohn and Fiorina (1974) call this the "paradox of not voting": If everyone knows the chances of affecting the outcome are trivial, no one votes. But then any one voter's chances of affecting the outcome if he or she *had* voted are very large. Game theory provides a way out, by allowing us to see if any level of "rational" turnout can be sustained in the face of Ferejohn and Fiorina's paradox. Ledyard (1981, 1984), building on the probabilistic voting model of Hinich, Ledyard, and Ordeshook (1972), demonstrated that such a game among voters has a "mixed strategy" equilibrium.

Mixed strategies require the voter to randomize over pure strategies (in this case voting and not voting). Ledyard showed that each voter might plausibly choose to vote in any given election with only a small probability. But then it will turn out that some voters will actually vote in any given election, and turnout exceeds zero in equilibrium.

This was an important achievement, because the act of turning out was rationalized: Positive levels of political participation were shown to be consistent with purposive, self-interested behavior. Palfrey and Rosenthal (1983, 1985) showed, however, that as the size of the electorate rises, equilibrium turnout shrinks, even in Ledyard's game. In the limit, as the potential electorate goes to infinity, the "rational" level of turnout goes toward zero. Palfrey and Rosenthal show that the maximum level of turnout predicted in equilibrium (for plausibly sized electorates) is about 3 to 5%. But actual rates of turnout in the United States exceed 30%, and may be much higher in U.S. presidential races or elections in other countries.

This conflict between theory (no more than 5%) and data (more than 30%) suggests something else is going on. That "something else" is the attempt by parties and other political elites to persuade voters to vote. The quotation at the beginning of this section has a clear, rational choice implication: Securing the "right" policy from government is a collective good. Somehow, groups of citizens are overcoming the free-rider problem. More people are participating than would be predicted by a purely self-interested investment strategy. Incorporating groups into an individual decision calculus is difficult, but some progress has been made (Uhlaner, 1989a, 1989b; see Aldrich, 1993, for a broader review). Still, the attempts to use private returns, or Olson's (1965) "selective incentives," have not solved the problem of explaining levels of turnout. After all, if people vote because they like to vote, then what more can be said?

Quite a bit. We have used the model of narrowly self-interested behavior to generate hypotheses about turnout rates. Those hypotheses, that turnout will not exceed 5% in any reasonably large electorate, have been proved false. This has led analytical political theorists to look to mechanisms by which pure self-interest motives are overcome and collective action problems are solved. Further, though the *levels* of turnout are hard to explain, voters respond to costs of voting, opportunity costs of time, and other factors as the "rational" model predicts, by being less likely to vote.[12] As we noted earlier, rain or bad weather drives turnout down (Morton, 1991; Knack, 1994) because traveling to the polls is harder. Difficult or time-consuming registration makes people less likely to vote (Kelley, Ayres, and Bowen, 1967; Wolfinger and Rosenstone, 1980; Nagler, 1991). People with few resources find it hard to take time to vote (Tollison and Willett, 1973; Wolfinger and Rosenstone, 1980).

There are two other important insights from the early game-theoretic literature on strategic influences on turnout (Ledyard, 1981, 1984; Palfrey and Rosenthal, 1983, 1985). These results hark back to our earlier concern with elections as a means of eliciting truth, the "best" policy, or the "general will." As has been our practice, we will present the results in the form of theorems, without proofs, and refer the interested reader to the original article for the details.

Theorem 7.1 (Ledyard, 1984, p. 26). *Under certain circumstances, one equilibrium of the game among voters, choosing whether to vote or abstain, is for no voters to turn out. However, under the assumptions of the classical spatial model (if a median in all directions exists), the optimal location for parties to have chosen in such an "election" is optimal from the point of view of the median citizen. More simply, candidates act as if all voters were going to vote, but if candidates act that way voters may, in equilibrium, not vote.*

Theorem 7.2 (Palfrey and Rosenthal, 1983, pp. 42–3, 47). *The proportions that split the vote among two alternatives is a biased measure of the actual distribution of preferences in the population of enfranchised voters. Majorities have greater incentives to free ride, so large majorities will be harder to sustain if victory seems certain. Elections can be fairly close, even when one alternative is supported by a large majority of the electorate.*

The verbal paraphrasing of the two sets of results appears obvious at first glance, but both are substantively important. Further, each demonstrates the importance of formal analytical reasoning applied to politics. Theorem 7.1 addresses a common concern among observers of democracies, who say, "Turnout is too low!" Presumably, the object of elections is to ensure a coincidence between the desires of the people and the actions of government. Ledyard showed that low turnout could be a sign that parties and candidates are occupying the positions in policy space that would win the most votes even if everyone voted. Ledyard did warn that the outcomes of such a process were not necessarily Pareto optimal, but this problem would exist even if turnout were universal.

Theorem 7.2 calls into question the use of polls and other forms of election prediction, based on proportions in populations. Proportions in populations may be very different from election percentages, because turnout is itself a strategic choice. The reverse is also true, of course: Using percentages of the vote as signs of a "mandate," or the lack of one, represents an unsupportable conclusion about the opinions held by proportions of the population. Election results may be all that politicians or the media have to go on, but the rational turnout model suggests extreme care should be taken in assuming the election results are meaningful for anything other than the simple selection of one alternative over another.[13]

Conclusions

The formal theory of turnout is worth studying. The model has several important things to teach us:

- The two main causes of abstention in the classical spatial model are *indifference* and *alienation*.

   Indifference. If voters perceive little (no) difference between alternatives, they are less likely to vote. This prediction has both *cross-sectional* and *time series* implications: Voters who perceive little distance between alternatives are less likely to vote than other voters who perceive large net candidate differentials. Similarly, any given voter is more likely to vote in an election where the perceived difference is large, compared with other elections where the same voter perceives the difference as small.

   Alienation. If both (all) alternatives in the election are far from the voter's ideal point, that voter is less likely to vote. Again, the prediction is made both across voters and over time: The greater the difference between the voter's ideal point and the nearest alternative, the less likely is that voter to turn out, compared either with other voters or other elections where perceptions of the difference are smaller.

- Voting appears to be primarily an act of consumption, broadly conceived, rather than investment, because the prediction of the investment model of very low turnout is not borne out empirically.[14] Rational choice has a well-developed theory of consumption, making it possible to specify "determinants" of voting, in terms of costs and benefits at the margin, that affect the satisfaction the voter receives from voting. As Aldrich (1993, p. 261) pointed out, "Turnout is a decision almost always made 'at the margin.'" What this means, in simple terms, is that an analytical model may not be able to predict the general level of turnout very well, but that the factors that cause turnout to vary around that level are amenable to treatment by the models described in this chapter.

- Benefits to the voter may be both individual and collective. One of the key *collective* benefits to voting is selection of the "best" candidate. Yet, like any collective action, these benefits are obtained only if groups of like-minded voters are able to overcome the free-rider problem. We are led to look to institutions such as grassroots party organizations, as well as personal group identification, as the means by which political contests are won.

- Consequently, the conditions for overcoming free riding must be added to the conditions specified in earlier chapters for predicting outcomes in democratic politics. Specifically, it is the median *voter,* not the median *citizen,* who represents the center. It is still true that the center rules, but the location of the center is very much in doubt until the actual election determines which preferences are registered. If turnout is uncertain, because of either incomplete information or strategic decisions by voters, the median citizen may still represent the center, as Ledyard showed.

There have been numerous attacks on the idea that "rational" choice theories can explain political participation. In fact, there have been some significant falsifications of analytical theories of turnout. But the fact that portions of the theory can be falsified is an important advantage over other approaches that simply *measure* "determinants" using statistical correlations. Further, the theoretical framework of a consumption or "contribution" decision, coupled with the implication that solving collective action problems is necessary for people to "associate" and vote, has proved fruitful.

EXERCISES

7.1 Suppose you are hired as a consultant by a state governor, who is concerned that too few people in her state voted in local elections.

You ask for more information and find the following facts in a state elections guide:

Some 740,000 people voted in local elections last November. Our state has a population of 5,600,000. There were 1,200,000 people in our state registered to vote last year. State election laws restrict eligibility to register to those who are not in jail or mental hospitals, and have not been convicted of a felony, about 96% of the adult population. The last statewide election, held at the same time as the local elections and on the same ballot, saw 810,000 votes tallied.

The governor wants to know whether the state elections board should try (1) "motor voter" registration to make it easier to register or (2) "get out the vote" drives to get more registered voters to the polls. Use Equation 7.1 as a way of analyzing the problem. What would be your advice to the governor? *Lot of people not registered*

7.2* Suppose a particular citizen 1 has ideal point $x_1 = [8 \ -3]^T$, with $A_1 = I$, and $\delta = 10$ (δ is the WED beyond which the voter is alienated). Let one candidate occupy $x_A = [13 \ 2]^T$ and the other occupy $x_B = [6 \ 5]^T$. Does citizen 1 vote? If he votes, which candidate does he prefer?

7.3* Suppose that the two candidates are in the same positions as in Exercise 7.2 ($x_A = [13 \ 2]^T$, $x_B = [6 \ 5]^T$), but consider a different voter 2, where $x_2 = [12 \ 4]^T$. Define "indifference" as follows:

The voter is indifferent if $|WED(x_A, x_2) - WED(x_B, x_2)| \leq 2$

Does voter 2 abstain out of indifference, or does he vote? Which candidate is closer to his ideal point in terms of measured WED?

Note: Exercises marked * are advanced material.

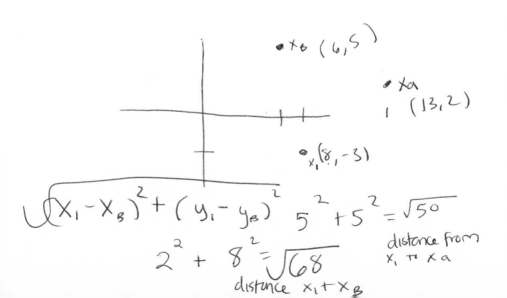

Recent advances

In the first section of this book we presented the classical model of analytical politics. The main result deriving from this model is the median voter theorem (MVT) in a single dimension. The MVT was then generalized to multiple dimensions. We next considered the basics of social choice and alternative voting systems. An important aspect of this inquiry was the attempt to identify the circumstances under which collective choices are coherent and normatively defensible as reflecting the will of the people. In the second section, we considered some extensions to the basic results, including accounting for voter uncertainty, candidate character, and the preferences that candidates themselves may have over policy outcomes. Finally, the basic model was extended to account for abstention, or withholding one's vote out of indifference or alienation. We concluded that while these are important marginal effects, the basic act of voting may have more to do with consumption than investment.

With the exception of the turnout decision, the model we have covered so far has mostly focused on *committee voting*, instead of *mass elections*. This model is useful as a starting point to analyze politics. Now we are going to consider some difficult problems that confront social scientists who wish to use the analytical model to understand real-world policy decisions. In Chapter 8, we focus on problems with the classical model of committee voting. In Chapter 9, we examine the model's applicability to mass elections.

The topics covered in this final section are these:

- Strategic, or sophisticated, voting
- Nonseparable preferences
- Probabilistic voting
- Directional theory
- Ideology

CHAPTER 8

Strategic voting, nonseparability, and probabilistic voting

Discretion is the better part of virtue,
Commitments the voters don't know about can't hurt you.
(Ogden Nash, *The Old Dog Barks Backward*,
1972, "Political Reflections")

In earlier chapters, we have presented a model of how people vote in a "committee" setting. As the reader will recall, the assumptions of committee voting are: (a) Each participant has full information about all possible alternatives and has well-defined *preferences* over those alternatives; (b) those preferences are *separable across issues,* so that even if the policy space is multidimensional, we can act as if issues are voted on one at a time; (c) each participant knows the preferences of all other participants; (d) all participants have *free, equal power to propose alternatives;* and (e) votes are assumed to be *sincere,* in the sense that if a member prefers alternative A to alternative B, he or she votes for A over B in a pairwise majority rule comparison.

We have also noted that this model is only a starting point. Real committee voting decisions are far more complicated. One complication is that the location of members' "ideal points" is the result of a variety of outside pressures and use of information, so that the ideal point is induced rather than being a primitive "preference."[1] Still, since we have taken member ideal points as exogenous, accounting for the origin or process of formation of the preference is not too difficult. All we need is that an ideal point exists.

A more difficult problem is the "agenda," or actual sequence of votes that leads to a decision. As John Kingdon points out:

It is important to keep in mind that in the process of setting the agenda and specifying the alternatives, a good many policy options are eliminated from consideration. There is a myriad of subjects that could conceivably be decided by Congress or by any other authoritative decision body. Governmental decision-makers, particularly congressmen, cannot attend to them all or even to a very large fraction of them. The subjects that do become part of the decisional agenda, therefore, represent only a part of the population of subjects that are potential agenda items. This selection of which subjects to address and which ones to overlook is a kind of structural "decision" of major consequence. . . . [When] a matter does reach the decisional agenda, *the process by which alternatives are evoked and seriously considered is also crucial.* (1981, pp. 282–3; emphasis added)

In this chapter we consider three advanced topics in the committee voting model that help us account for the complexity of both the voting decision and the process of agenda formation.[2]

Strategic voting

We have assumed that participants in political decision-making processes have reacted to each choice situation by casting a vote that reflects their "true," or sincere, preference. More specifically, given a vote between alternatives A and B, voter i votes for the alternative he most prefers. Of course, this makes sense if the present vote is the last one and no further choices will be presented.

Such a stopping rule is rarely in force, however. More often, a vote is really a choice between a set of future votes, the sequence of which depends on the "agenda" rule adopted by the organization. If political actors are sophisticated, they can recognize that a vote leads not to an outcome, but to another vote. Their preferences over outcomes can plausibly induce preferences over branches of an agenda "tree," as the following example makes clear.

Suppose the only three foods in the world were apples, broccoli, and carrots. Each type of food is sold only in large crates. Consider three people who, if they cooperate, will have just enough money to buy one, but only one, crate of food. The preference profiles of the three people, Mr. 1 (who loves apples), Ms. 2 (who loves carrots), and Mr. 3 (who loves broccoli), are listed in Table 8.1.

The premise of the example is that choice is collective: If they cannot agree on a food, all will go hungry, because no one has enough money to buy a crate alone. But the three disagree (as the reader can see from Table 8.1) about what to buy. After discussing the choices endlessly, they realize they will never reach a consensus, and no one is going to

Table 8.1. *Preference "lists" of three voters over apples, broccoli, and carrots*

Ranking	Person		
	Mr. 1	Ms. 2	Mr. 3
Best	Apples	Carrots	Broccoli
Middle	Broccoli	Apples	Carrots
Worst	Carrots	Broccoli	Apples

change his or her mind (if you don't like broccoli, you just don't like it; there is little room for persuasion). So, our three people decide to vote. They learned in ninth grade civics that voting is the only fair way to make collective decisions. Besides, they are all getting hungry.

The alert reader may feel sympathy at the naive hope that voting will solve the problem. The reason faith in voting is naive is that the preferences profiled in Table 8.1 do not admit of a Condorcet winner. By majority rule, apples are preferred to broccoli is preferred to carrots are preferred to apples, always by 2 to 1 margins. Say, for example, apples are voted against broccoli first. Mr. 1 and Ms. 2 both prefer apples to broccoli, Mr. 3 vainly dissents, and apples are selected. Apples are then compared with the remaining choice, carrots; Mr. 1 votes for apples, Ms. 2 votes for carrots, and Mr. 3 votes for carrots. It is quite possible that the three stop there, if they don't think things through, since nobody covered agenda manipulation in ninth grade civics. On the face of it, the "carrots preferred to apples preferred to broccoli" group preference seems fair enough.

If the first vote were between apples and carrots, then broccoli would be the collective choice (carrots beat apples, but lose to broccoli, in pairwise majority voting). If carrots and broccoli are the first comparison, then apples emerge as the favored food. The point is that there exists *some* agenda leading to *any* given outcome. Interestingly, this result is surprisingly general, as McKelvey (1976a, 1976b, 1986), Schofield (1978a, 1984), and McKelvey and Schofield (1986) showed. We can state the result in the form of a very much simplified theorem, which is more restrictive (and easier to understand) than the actual result.

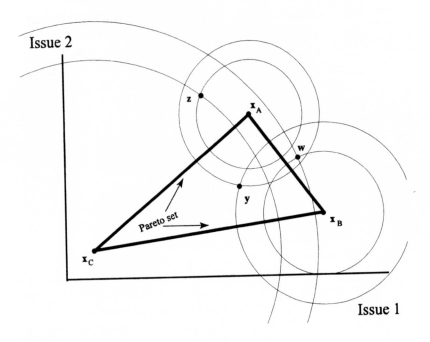

Figure 8.1. The existence of an agenda from **y** to **z**.

Chaos theorem. *Imagine a continuous policy space $\mathcal{P}$. Let the number of dimensions in $\mathcal{P}$ be at least three, assume decisions are by simple majority rule, and let there be at least three voters with proposal power. Let voting be sincere. If there is not at least one "median in all directions," it is possible to construct an agenda, or sequence of comparisons of pairs of alternatives, that leads to any alternative in the space.*

Intuitively, this theorem simply means that given a status quo **y** and any other alternative **z**, there exists an agenda (sequence of pairwise votes) that leads from **y** to **z**. Under some circumstances, in fact, this agenda has only one intermediate step **w**, so that a sophisticated agenda maker can go from **y** to **w** to **z**, no matter what values of **y** and **z** are chosen. We can illustrate such a "trajectory" in Figure 8.1: Beginning with **y**, a majority (B and A) prefers **w**. But then a majority (B and C) prefers **z** to **w**. What the chaos theorem says is that for any **y** and **z** there exists a **w** (where neither **z** nor **w** is necessarily contained in the Pareto set) that allows the agenda setter to go from **y** to **z**.

But wait just a minute. This result requires that the voters be completely ignorant of politics! Let us go back to our apples, broccoli, and carrots choosers. It is true that if no one knows social choice and an agenda is constructed at random by our hungry heroes, the choice could be *any one* of the three foods. In a way, this is "fair" because if the *agenda* is chosen at random, the implied outcome is (in effect) also randomly selected. If there is no median in all directions, a *naive choice over agendas* is tantamount to a *lottery over outcomes*.

If this kind of choice is routine, however, it seems unlikely that people could really fail to understand the underlying correspondence: Choosing an agenda implies a choice of an outcome. As Riker (1980) pointed out, if people disagree about outcomes and understand politics, their disagreement will take the form of a disagreement over the agenda, or institutions of choice more generally.

More fundamentally, what can we say from an ethical perspective about the "fairness" of the outcome if some people understand agendas, but others don't? The answer is disturbing: If only one person gets to pick the agenda and enforce a stopping rule, and if participants vote sincerely, there is no important difference between majority rule and dictatorship. Figure 8.2 contains the agendas selected by Mr. 1, Ms. 2, and Mr. 3. In each case the outcome is the same as if that person were dictator and had sole decision power. There is one sinister difference between dictatorship and a "monopoly agenda setter," however. Dictatorship is openly and definitionally undemocratic. By contrast, people naively voting on alternatives whose order is decided by an agenda setter may be unaware that the choice of outcome is, in effect, dictatorial.

Each alternative in the agenda is "considered," it is true, but the order of consideration dictates the outcome.[3] Getting to vote doesn't mean choice is democratic, though letting people go through the motions may imbue the choices of the agenda setter with an aura of legitimacy. To put it another way, there is nothing inherently "fair" about a sequenced majority rule decision. The trappings of democracy (people get to vote) may simply be the mechanism of manipulation.

There is some evidence that control of the agenda does confer just this sort of power on the "setter." Agenda control can be imbedded either in the rules of parliamentary procedure (see, e.g., Denzau and Mackay, 1983) or in proposals made by bureaucrats to elected officials

Panel (a): Mr. 1 wants apples to win

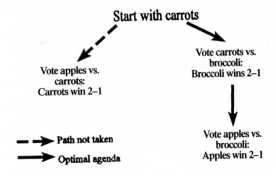

Start with carrots

Vote apples vs.
carrots:
Carrots win 2–1

Vote carrots vs.
broccoli:
Broccoli wins 2–1

Vote apples vs.
broccoli:
Apples win 2–1

Path not taken

Optimal agenda

Panel (b): Ms. 2 wants carrots to win

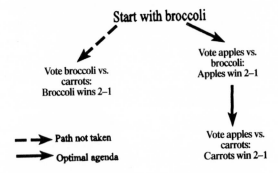

Start with broccoli

Vote broccoli vs.
carrots:
Broccoli wins 2–1

Vote apples vs.
broccoli:
Apples win 2–1

Vote apples vs.
carrots:
Carrots win 2–1

Path not taken

Optimal agenda

Panel (c): Mr. 3 wants broccoli to win

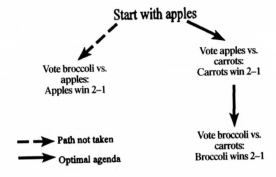

Start with apples

Vote broccoli vs.
apples:
Apples win 2–1

Vote apples vs.
carrots:
Carrots win 2–1

Vote broccoli vs.
carrots:
Broccoli wins 2–1

Path not taken

Optimal agenda

Figure 8.2. My agenda means my outcome.

(see, e.g., Niskanen, 1971; Romer and Rosenthal, 1978, 1979; Rosenthal, 1990). On the other hand, there have been claims that elected officials would not allow the sorts of rules that really give bureaucrats proposal power (Weingast and Moran, 1983; McCubbins and Schwartz, 1984; Shepsle and Weingast, 1987). More fundamentally, if "institutions" give real power to an agenda setter, there may be a contest over choice of institutions themselves (Riker, 1980); cycles over outcomes should be transformed into cycles over institutions. Still, if there is a monopoly agenda setter, that person can act as something close to a dictator if other participants vote their true preferences.

But wait just another minute; why assume people vote their sincere preferences in the face of agenda manipulation? What if the other participants know the power of the agenda setter? What if they recognize that voting over alternatives in the first stage is really voting over future agendas? Can't the *voters manipulate their votes,* in the same way the *setter can manipulate the alternatives?* The answer is obviously yes.

For that matter, why preclude strategic or sophisticated voting in any circumstance, not just when the agenda is set by someone else? Until we allow that voting might not be sincere, we *still* won't have captured the reality of political choice in committees. One of the first scholars to treat the difference between "sincere" voting (i.e., vote your true preferences) and "sophisticated" voting (vote strategically, in effect choosing over agendas rather than outcomes) was Farquharson (1969). There is considerable theoretical work (e.g., McKelvey and Niemi, 1978; Denzau and Mackay, 1981; Enelow, 1981) and empirical evidence (Enelow and Koehler, 1980; Denzau, Riker, and Shepsle, 1985) that claim sophisticated voting may be part of real-world political processes.

How would sophisticated voting work in our simple example of collective food purchase? We will suppose that Mr. 1 is the setter, for simplicity, since the exposition is the same for each participant. Mr. 1, of course, wants an outcome of apples, so he has the process begin with broccoli against carrots. Since he knows broccoli beats carrots, but loses to apples, this ensures the "right" outcome if the other participants cooperate by voting sincerely.

But suppose Mr. 3 has read Farquharson (1969) and recognizes that a first stage vote for broccoli over carrots is not the end of the process. Mr. 3 mentally looks ahead on the agenda tree in Figure 8.2 and notes that a first-stage vote for *broccoli* is really just a vote for *apples!* Mr. 3

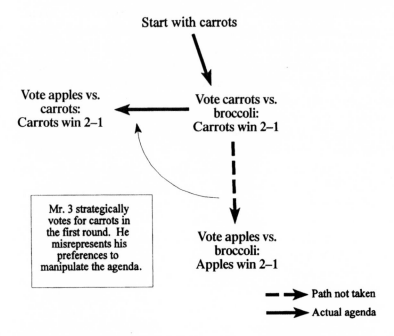

Figure 8.3. Mr. 3 votes strategically, and Mr. 1's agenda leads to carrots, Mr. 1's least-preferred alternative.

detests apples. He decides to vote strategically for carrots. Ms. 2 is happy to vote for carrots (her sincere preference is for carrots over broccoli, anyway). Consequently, carrots win the first round. Since Mr. 1's agenda specifies that the first-round winner is then voted against apples, the result is that carrots win again, this time on (sincere) votes by both Ms. 2 and Mr. 3. The agenda and new outcome are shown in Figure 8.3.

The point of this example is that the power of the agenda setter to dictate the sequence of votes may not be enough to ensure the setter his or her most-preferred outcome. If there are specific rules that force the elected body to accept the take-it-or-leave-it proposal, as the Romer and Rosenthal (1978, 1979) work assumes, then the setter has broad power. If the other participants aren't clever enough to recognize the need to choose sophisticated votes, then again the setter has his or her own way. But isn't it a little silly to base a theory on the presumption that people systematically make mistakes? Successful politicians understand politics. They recognize chances to vote for a particular sequence of future votes instead of the apparently simple issue at hand.[4]

The example in this section has dealt with simple majority rule. The logic of the example can be generalized to any voting procedure in an important theorem called the "Gibbard–Satterthwaite theorem." First, however, we will give a definition of a technical term, "strategy proofness," adapted from Mueller (1989, p. 395).

Strategy proofness. Suppose voter i is trying to decide how to vote. Let M_i be the "message" i gives the voting procedure when he states his true and sincere preference (so M_i could be a vote, a list of votes, or whatever is required by the voting procedure to register a preference). Let $\mathcal{M}_i$ be any distortion or strategic misrepresentation in M_i, so that $M_i \neq \mathcal{M}_i$. Now consider two outcomes of the actual application of the voting procedure, whatever it is:

> x is the outcome when voter i states M_i, and all other voters state their true preferences.
>
> y is the outcome when voter i states $\mathcal{M}_i$, and all other voters state their true preferences.

Then a voting procedure is strategy-proof, or immune to strategic voting, if and only if there is no achievable alternative y that voter i prefers to x, regardless of the distorted message $\mathcal{M}_i$ that i chooses. More simply, a voting procedure is strategy-proof if and only if the voter's best strategy is *always* to be sincere, regardless of what other voters do.

There is an important logical connection between voting procedures that are strategy-proof and social choice rules that obey the IIA axiom, which we discussed in Chapter 5.[5] Vickrey (1960), in his proof of Arrow's theorem, offered two conjectures. First, social choice rules satisfying IIA are also strategy-proof. Second, strategy proofness implies satisfaction of IIA.[6] This conjecture was correct, as was shown by Gibbard (1973) and Satterthwaite (1975).[7] A simple summary of the theorem is:

Gibbard–Satterthwaite theorem. *No voting rule that can predictably choose one outcome from many alternatives is strategy-proof, unless it is dictatorial.*

"Predictably" here means that the voting rule is not random, so that the voter can see some correspondence between the message or vote she reveals and the outcome. The Gibbard–Satterthwaite theorem is a classic social choice good news, bad news result. On the one hand, it means that all voting procedures (at least, all those that are not trivial or useless) are manipulable under many circumstances. Further, we cannot trust the particular votes or messages that voters deliver to represent their true preferences. This is bad news, because it means that voters often don't vote honestly, and the reasons have to do with the voting procedure itself, not the character of voters.

The good news is that "manipulation" (i.e., strategic voting) may be the mechanism that gives voters countervailing power over agenda setters. The apparent dictatorial power of those who manipulate the agenda is ameliorated by the ability of voters to manipulate their votes. Consequently, while the *means* of manipulation seems dishonest, strategic voting may actually ensure the "right" *end*. As we saw in our apples–broccoli–carrots example, simple agenda manipulation did not determine the outcome.

Multiple issues and nonseparable preferences: Order matters

The order in which alternatives are considered may determine the outcome, holding participants' preferences fixed. We have called the "order of consideration" the agenda and claimed that under some circumstances agenda control may give one participant disproportionate power. The agenda also matters in a multidimensional setting: The agenda determines the order in which policies or projects are considered. If preferences are not separable, the order of consideration may actually change issue-by-issue preferences, as we saw in Chapters 3 and 4.

What was shown earlier was that voting on each issue separately can solve the problem of multidimensional instability of majority rule. However, separating the issues in the *agenda* works only if *preferences* are also separable. The reason is that issue-by-issue voting reduces multidimensional choice to an unrelated series of unidimensional choices. Unfortunately (for the researcher, at least), separability of preferences among all issues is a very narrow and limiting assumption. What can we say if preferences are nonseparable and if (as in the preceding section) members recognize the implications of agendas?

Our answer needs to account for two obvious problems: First, nonseparability makes the outcome appear indeterminate, because preferences on each issue are conditional on what else has been decided. Second, voters have induced preferences over institutions (in this case, the agenda, or order of consideration of issues). The reason is that different agendas yield multidimensional outcomes given other participants' expected votes. These outcomes are closer to, or farther from, each voter's ideal point. More simply, if the order of consideration determines outcomes, then participants who care about outcomes will also care about the order of consideration.

Consequently, if there is a cycle in voting outcomes, there may be an induced cycle in attempts to choose the institutions that lead to choices. To put it another way, if the choice of agenda leads to a particular outcome, then disagreement over ultimate outcomes simply transfers to a disagreement over agendas, provided all participants are sophisticated.

As an illustration, let us consider again the legislative subcommittee from Chapter 3, faced with a choice of different appropriations for two projects. As the reader will recall, in the earlier discussion we argued that nonseparability forces consideration of conditional preferences, because the amount members expect to be spent on Project 1 affects their ideal preference for spending on Project 2. The reverse is also true: Project 1 preferences depend on Project 2 spending. In the preceding section we saw that the agenda may determine the outcome, but nonseparability makes the agenda even more important, though for a very different reason. The order of consideration can change conditional preferences, leading participants to favor different alternatives.

One theory that seeks to explain the stability of outcomes in legislatures (or, more accurately, in the U.S. Congress) is "structure-induced equilibrium" (SIE). Originally argued in two papers (Shepsle, 1979; Shepsle and Weingast, 1981), SIE theory notes the high potential costs of cycling and conflict in legislatures evokes an institutional response. Rules and practices will evolve to mitigate the problem of instability in a multidimensional policy space. The particular institution that SIE theorists have argued for is the committee system in the U.S. Congress, with a set of (arguably) disjoint jurisdictions over policy areas.[8]

The story SIE theorists use is that multidimensional instability is prevented, or at least ameliorated, by dramatically reducing the space any committee has jurisdiction over. Further, the status quo has a privileged position: It is usually voted last against the "perfected" amendment, or proposed change to policy, in parliamentary procedure. Consequently, the possibilities for cycling are diminished, and the power of committee members is enhanced.[9]

According to SIE theorists, committee proposals have a privileged status, within their recognized jurisdictions, because of "reciprocity," or the norm that floor members defer to committee members.[10] The basis of this agreement is that if I defer to you in your jurisdiction, you will defer to me in mine. Since each of us has a seat on a committee whose issue jurisdiction matters to our constituents, this reciprocity is self-enforcing and mutually advantageous. The proposals that come out of committees will either be that of the median member of the committee (if one believes Shepsle and Weingast, 1981; 1987) or the committee's expectation of the median of the floor (if one believes Krehbiel, 1991).

SIE theory holds a justifiably important place in theories purporting to explain legislative institutions and the importance of institutions in shaping outcomes. There is a largely unspoken premise to the argument, though, that is unrealistic. That premise is that preferences are separable. If we allow that preferences might be nonseparable, the prediction that policy will be the vector of medians of committee members in each respective jurisdiction breaks down.

That is not to say that the committee system has no role in creating or maintaining stability. It is just that the simple prediction that the outcome is the vector of medians has to be adjusted for the complexity of expectations in real legislatures. The role of expectations about the sequence of consideration is complexity was raised (though only implicitly) by Kramer (1972). The explicit criticism offered by Denzau and Mackay (1981) and Enelow and Hinich (1983b, 1983c) is both detailed and telling: One must be very careful not to interpret the SIE approach as a general answer, unless the question of forecasts by voters is also taken into account.

To see how the vector of medians prediction breaks down, recall the example of five members in an appropriations committee, members A, B, C, D, and E, from Chapter 3. Their ideal points (from Chapter 3)

Project 2 budget
(millions of $)

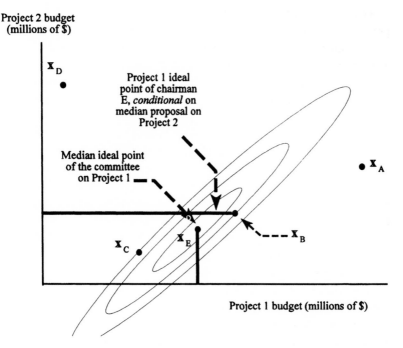

Figure 8.4. Medians of the committees are not the observed proposals, if preferences are nonseparable.

are depicted in Figure 8.4. Let us suppose that there are two subcommittees of this committee, each charged with making a recommendation for one project budget. The subcommittee for Project 2 is chaired by Ms. B (who happens to have the unidimensional median ideal point for Project 2), and the subcommittee for Project 1 is chaired by Mr. E (who likewise has the unidimensional median ideal for Project 1). Finally, let us suppose that all members, *except Mr. E*, have circular indifference curves (not depicted in Figure 8.4), but that Mr. E has sharply nonseparable preferences, as shown.

It is hard to predict the Project 2 subcommittee budget, because it may depend on expectations, logrolls, or other strategic considerations of real legislatures. For simplicity, however, let us stipulate that the Project 2 subcommittee recommends the unidimensional median favored by the subcommittee chair, Ms. B. The prediction of the naive SIE model is that the same approach (i.e., pick the unidimensional median) will then predict the budget for Project 1, *given* the Project 2 budget.

Yet this prediction is clearly wrong if preferences are nonseparable. The Project 1 budget will be larger than the simple unidimensional Project 1 median. Since the Project 2 budget ($80 million) exceeds Mr. E's ideal budget for Project 2 ($60 million), the conditional ideal of Mr. E for Project 1 also increases, because of complementarities in his preferences for the two projects.

The simplest version of SIE focuses on issue-by-issue voting. This focus is apparently made possible by the fact that committee jurisdictions in the U.S. Congress are disjoint, or nearly so. Still, this crucial simplification does not work unless preferences of committee members are also nonseparable.[11] More simply, what Kadane (1972) called "division of the question" (i.e., separating issues in the *agenda*) is one assumption about the process. Separability of *preferences* is another thing entirely. We could find that agendas separate issues and/or that preferences are separable across issues.

If preferences are nonseparable, then the median committee ideal point on any issue is conditional on either (1) other issues that have already been decided or (2) the *expected* decisions on other issues (Denzau and Mackay, 1981; Enelow and Hinich, 1983b, 1983c). As an example, imagine there is a change in the membership of one committee (call it Committee One) after an election, resulting perhaps from some new conservative members replacing liberal senior members. The new median position on the committee is implemented by the floor, if the norm of reciprocity (Weingast, 1979) operates. But this new policy in one dimension changes the conditional ideal points of all the other committees where members' preferences are nonseparable with respect to the newly changed policy. Consequently, if preferences are nonseparable, there is the potential that *all* the nation's policies change because of the electoral defeat of a *few members* on one committee.[12]

What happens if the preferences of members on Committee One are nonseparable? When all the other policies are adjusted, the location of the conditional median ideal point within One's policy jurisdiction is changed, too. The sequence of events can be summarized thus: (1) There is a change in the membership of Committee One, changing the median preference on the issue within its jurisdiction. (2) Other committees adjust policies in response. (3) Committee One readjusts, in response to the changes in other policies, or even changes in policies that members of One anticipate. There may be an equilibrium to this process of mutual readjustment, but there need not be: *The adjustment process can go on indefinitely.* (See Exercise 8.3.) Of course, the adjustments might be very large or so small as to be indiscernible. In any case, the smoothly functioning, "issue-by-issue" logic of the SIE model is greatly complicated when preferences are not separable.

Probabilistic voting

In Chapter 7, we claimed that the most promising form of statements about turnout may be "probabilistic," taking the form of an increased or decreased probability of voting. In this section, we will introduce what has been called "probabilistic voting" (Hinich, Ledyard, Ordeshook, 1972; Hinich, 1977; Coughlin, 1992), a theory that can generate the predictions of the preceding section.

Probabilistic voting has been widely misunderstood, partly because of the computational complexity of moving from deterministic decision rules to decisions described by a probability distribution. However, we have already seen (in Chapter 6) at least one example of a "rational" decision rule very much like probabilistic voting in the mixed-strategy equilibrium suggested by Ledyard (1984). Ledyard's voters randomized over the two strategies (vote or abstain) with only a small probability of voting in any given election. Nonetheless, as Ledyard showed, this strategy generated an equilibrium where turnout is large enough that the probability that one more voter will affect the outcome is negligible.

Probabilistic voting is, in general, simply a way of building in uncertainty about the behavior of the population of citizens. That doesn't mean individual voters use probabilities to decide how to vote, of course. On the morning of the election, the citizen may know for certain if he or she intends to vote, and for whom that vote will be cast. But there may be an automobile accident, snowstorm, or sprained ankle that prevents travel to the polls. The voter may even have a last minute change of heart on whom to support. The problem is that the researcher cannot hope to know the idiosyncratic decision rule used by each voter. In statistical terms, the key features of the voter's decision are "unobservable."

It is worth elaborating the sources of uncertainty about voter information, and choice rules, from the perspective of the *researcher*. A complete statement of the logic of probabilistic voting is given by Coughlin (1992). Paraphrasing Downs (1957, p. 212), Hinich and Munger (1994, p. 167) give a simplified summary of explanations of differences in the information that voters use, and the consequent differences in the way voters choose. The researcher's ability to model information use by voters accurately is limited, because:

- No externally generalizable rule guides voters' information search. Instead, each voter uses his or her unique, idiosyncratic experiences and values to guide the voting decision.
- Even if rules were general, voters would inevitably also have different samples from the complete set of information available. Since rules do differ, voters' opinions about candidates may differ strikingly.
- If information and perceptions of credibility were identical, opinions would be identical. Since information and beliefs differ, ex ante opinions about candidate behavior once in office may differ widely.
- As researchers, we can divide the set of determinants for a given individual's vote into those that *researchers* can identify and measure in some consistent fashion, and those that are *specific to each voter* and are unobservable to the researcher.

Probabilistic voting focuses on general tendencies of information use in the electorate, but allows that there may be idiosyncratic characteristics. For example, if $|x_i - x_A| < |x_i - x_B|$, we can say that voter *i* is *more likely* to vote for candidate A than for candidate B. More accurately, of the members of a *population* of voters who share ideal point x_i most will vote for A. Some voters will have different information or beliefs, but overall closeness is determinative.

Probabilistic voting builds in the researcher's uncertainty about atomistic voter decisions from the outset. The approach is a means of aggregating propensities to make choices based on observable characteristics of voters, candidates, and the features of the election. Thus, it is possible to compare the likelihood of certain outcomes with the deterministic predictions of the classical model. An illustrative comparison is given in Table 8.2.

Research on vote choice, including much of the work specifically based on the spatial model (e.g., Enelow and Hinich, 1982a, 1982b, 1984a, 1984b, 1989, 1994; Grofman, 1985; Enelow, Endersby, and Munger, 1993; Hinich and Munger, 1994), suggests that more than just spatial position "matters." Other important factors include the charac-

Table 8.2. *Comparison of the predictions of the classical and probabilistic voting models*

Feature of election	Prediction of classical spatial model	Prediction of probabilistic voting model
$\|x_A - x_i\| < \|x_B - x_i\|$	i votes for A	Voter i is *more likely* to vote for A. Probability rises with difference in closeness. If difference is small, i may vote for B, though A is "closer."
$\|x_A - x_i\| > \delta$ $\|x_B - x_i\| > \delta$	i alienated, abstains	i *more likely* to abstain; probability of abstention increases with distance to closest candidate position.
$\|x_A - x_i\| \approx \|x_B - x_i\|$	i indifferent, abstains	i *more likely* to abstain; probability of abstention increases as a function of the difference between candidate positions.

Note: A is the first candidate, whose position is x_A; B is the second candidate, whose position is x_B; i is the voter, whose ideal point is x_i.

ter of the candidate, perception of competence and probity, and loyalty to party or influence by campaign advertising. Probabilistic voting takes account of the multivariate aspects of political choice, but allows the observable factors in the spatial model to have predictable impacts. Monocausal explanations of human behavior are usually incomplete. Probabilistic voting assumes that the observer knows only *some* of the reasons why voters vote as they do.

It is useful to compare the predictions of the classical model and the probabilistic model graphically, in terms of the probability of voting for a particular candidate. The classical model is a "step function": If (i) candidate A is closer to the voter's ideal, in WED, and (ii) the voter is not alienated, then the voter votes for A with a probability equal to one. If condition (i) is not met, the voter votes for B or is indifferent. If condition (ii) is not met, the voter abstains, again with probability one.

For the sake of example, let us assume that the voter is not alienated ($\|x_A - x_i\| < \delta$, and $\|x_B - x_i\| < \delta$). Thus, we can analyze vote choice as follows: The voter will either vote for A, abstain out of indifference, or vote for B, depending on the value of the net candidate differential. Let us allow that the area of indifference may be "thick," so that the voter may abstain out of indifference if the candidates' positions are *almost* identical in terms of WED from x_i. (This situation was depicted in Figure 7.2.) Then we can illustrate the decision calculus of voters in panel (a) of Figure 8.5. As the figure shows, the voter votes for A, votes for B, or abstains, based on distance alone. No other factors, such as judgments about character, competence, or party are allowed to matter.

In panel (b), the predictions of the model are profoundly different. Voters with ideal points far from one of the candidate positions choose the other candidate with certainty, as before. (In principle, of course, the threshold where $0 < \text{Prob(B)} < 1$ might extend far enough to include all voters.) However, inside this threshold difference, any voter may pick any one of the three alternatives (vote for A, vote for B, abstain) with some positive probability. We claim the probability of choosing a candidate gets larger as the difference in perceived difference is bigger, but the voter may still choose one of the other two actions. In particular, a voter closer to A may vote for B, because factors other than simple distance matter.

The probabilistic voting approach is also useful because it affords a more accurate way of adding up expected votes. In providing advice to politicians, campaign consultants don't focus much on individual voters; they focus on groups. Some groups are likely to suppport one candidate, other groups are likely to support someone else. That doesn't mean every member of a group behaves in the same way, but overall different proportions of the groups are likely to support or oppose a given candidate. Further, support from a group may be "hard" (that group's members can be counted on to turn out, and not to change their minds) or "soft" (a high proportion of the group's members *say* they will vote for the candidate, but they may abstain or vote for someone else on a whim). Under the probabilistic approach, votes are counted as expected values, so that "soft" support counts less, just as it does in real politics. The following example makes this clearer.

Suppose there are five voters (1, 2, . . . , 5) and two candidates (A and B). Imagine that 1 and 2 are closer to A, and 3, 4, and 5 are closer to B. The classical model would predict that B wins the election, 3 to 2, and that would be the end of it. The probabilistic voting model, however, allows that voters may differ in the intensity of their support for candidates, based on other factors. Suppose that the breakdown of possible actions, by voter, is like that in Table 8.3. Since all we can predict is *expected* votes, it is clear that this race may be "too close to call," in

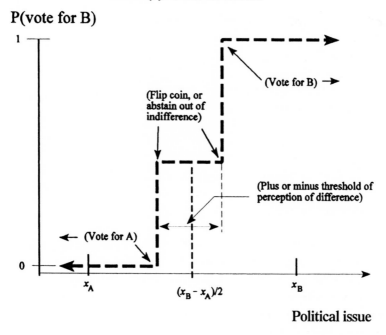

Panel (a): Classical model

P(vote for B)

(Flip coin, or abstain out of indifference)

(Vote for B) →

(Plus or minus threshold of perception of difference)

(Vote for A)

x_A $(x_B - x_A)/2$ x_B

Political issue

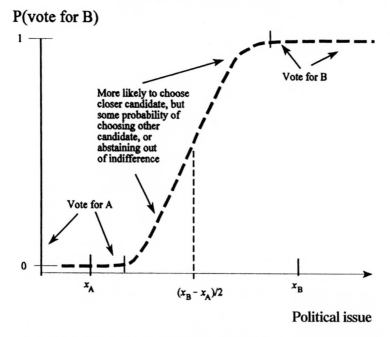

Panel (b): Probabilistic model

P(vote for B)

More likely to choose closer candidate, but some probability of choosing other candidate, or abstaining out of indifference

Vote for B

Vote for A

x_A $(x_B - x_A)/2$ x_B

Political issue

Figure 8.5. Comparing the classical and probabilistic models of vote choice.

Table 8.3. *Predicting outcomes as sums of expected values*

Voter	Probability of vote for A	Probability of vote for B	Probability of abstention (indifference)
1	1.00	0.00	0.00
2	0.80	0.05	0.15
3	0.10	0.45	0.45
4	0.05	0.60	0.35
5	0.00	0.95	0.05
Expected vote totals	1.95	2.05	1.00

the parlance of the electioneers. Notice that the "supporters" of B, whose vote was unquestioned in the classical model, are actually more equivocal than A's likely supporters. Candidate B's support is soft: There is a 1 in 20 chance that even voter 4 will cast his vote for A!

Real politicians must consider not just what people say they will do, but the likelihood they will go to the polls and do it. In our "early poll," based on the classical model, the prediction would have been 60% support for B, 40% for A (people rarely admit to pollsters they aren't going to vote). Assuming the probabilities in the table are independent, we can calculate some examples of the likelihood of other possible (though unlikely) outcomes:

A gets four votes, B gets none, one abstention: 0.0002
A gets one vote, B gets one, 4 abstentions: 0.0012
A gets three votes, B gets one, one abstention: 0.029
A and B each get one vote, three abstentions: 0.026

We don't have space to consider all the possible outcomes (there are fifty-four different outcomes with nonzero probabilities). The point is simple: Political contests can have surprising results, not wholly explained by the positions of the candidates and the ideal points of the voters.

The classical mode makes a useful simplification for the sake of pedagogy, but real politics is highly uncertain. Outcomes are the aggregation of many hard to predict choices by voters with myriad, possibly highly idiosyncratic decision rules. Fortunately, these idiosyncracies and many of the uncertainties that pervade real political choice can be incorporated into the model using probabilistic voting theory.

Conclusions

In this chapter we have examined some weaknesses of the classical model of analytical politics. The three topics we covered were (1) the implausibility of naive, or sincere, voting, (2) the implausibility of purely separable preferences in a multidimensional policy space, and (3) the implausibility of shared deterministic voting rules for all participants.

As we have shown, for each of these implausibilities there is an extension that makes the analytical model more realistic and general. These extensions are accomplished, however, only with a significant increase in the complexity of the model. We can summarize the differences in the results of the model as follows:

- Accounting for strategic voting allows committee members to have a sophisticated understanding of both political choice and the power of the agenda, but we are no longer able to make clear predictions about the outcome of majority rule processes with an agenda setter.
- Accounting for nonseparability makes the representation of preferences much more realistic, but makes the study of institutions whose apparent function is to "separate" issues much more complicated. We can no longer analyze one choice in isolation.
- Accounting for the diversity of voter decision rules and information in mass elections affords the researcher much greater flexibility in predicting vote choice. Probabilistic voting, however, is a self-consciously incomplete model of voter choice, because it allows that choices might be (a) idiosyncratic (with some shared elements), and (b) based on factors that have little to do with the classical model. These factors might include the perceived character of the candidate or other "nonspatial" attributes of the choice.

This is not meant to belittle the value of the extensions covered in this chapter. In each case, analytical political theorists have made good use of the perspectives we have covered here, and the value of the increased realism these extensions allow is obvious. It is important for the reader to recognize that the stylized model of earlier chapters is the one often criticized by opponents of rational choice. In fact, it is common to see current research question the assumptions made by analytical political theorists, and then quote some text from Downs (1957). Such criticisms may be correct, but they are anachronistic. The criticism of the original Downsian model of mass elections is blunted by understanding the extensions that this chapter has laid out.

EXERCISES

8.1 Assume that preferences for three foods (antipasto – A, brussels sprouts – B, and cauliflower – C) are given in the following table. Suppose all members vote sincerely and that Person 1 is the (politically knowledgeable) agenda setter. By prior agreement the agenda will consist of only two votes: One alternative against another, with the winner against the remaining alternative. The winner of the second contest becomes the group's choice. Which of the three alternatives is the group's choice? How can you be sure?

		Person	
Ranking	1	2	3
Best	A	B	C
Middle	C	A	B
Worst	B	C	A

8.2 Let all the facts of Exercise 8.1 remain the same, and use the same agenda as Person 1 used when all voting was sincere. However, allow all members to vote strategically (i.e., choosing over final outcomes rather than just the two alternatives being voted on). What is the outcome? Draw the sequence of votes in an "agenda tree," like those in Figure 8.2.

8.3* (Adapted from Enelow and Hinich, 1984b, Section 8.8). Suppose there are three voters, A, B, and C, with the following ideal points on two projects (i.e., there is a two-dimensional policy space).

$$\mathbf{x}_A = \begin{bmatrix} 25 \\ 55 \end{bmatrix} \quad \mathbf{x}_B = \begin{bmatrix} 100 \\ 100 \end{bmatrix} \quad \mathbf{x}_C = \begin{bmatrix} 120 \\ 40 \end{bmatrix}$$

Note: Exercises marked * are advanced material.

Let the corresponding matrix of salience and interaction weights
be:

$$(\text{Person A}) \begin{bmatrix} 1 & 0 \\ 0 & 1 \end{bmatrix} \quad (\text{Person B}) \begin{bmatrix} 1 & -9 \\ -9 & 1 \end{bmatrix} \quad (\text{Person C}) \begin{bmatrix} 7 & 0 \\ 0 & 1 \end{bmatrix}$$

(a) Suppose that (for some reason) all three voters expect that the Project 1 budget will be the median on that dimension: $x_{B1} =$ 100. Given this expectation, and assuming free proposal power, what will be the Project 2 budget if Project 2 is considered alone?

(b) Taking the new Project 2 budget you found in part (a), determine the Project 1 budget if the committee now votes, assuming free proposal power and a fixed Project 2 budget.

(c) Now start over: Taking the Project 1 budget from part (b) and assuming that all members believe that is the final budget, determine the Project 2 budget the committee will choose, assuming free proposal power. Why is it different from the budget you found in part (a)? Is there an equilibrium to this process, or will the committee cycle back and forth forever?

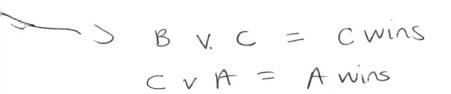

$$> \quad B \text{ v. } C = C \text{ wins}$$
$$C \text{ v } A = A \text{ wins}$$

CHAPTER 9

The nature of issues in mass elections

I remember standing at the polls one day, when the anger of the political contest gave a certain grimness to the faces of the independent electors, and a good man at my side looking on the people, remarked, "I am satisfied that the largest part of these men on either side mean to vote right." I suppose considerate observers, looking at the masses of men in their blameless, and in their equivocal actions, will assent that in spite of selfishness and frivolity the general purpose in the great number of persons is fidelity. The reason why any one refuses his assent to your opinion, or his aid to your benevolent design, is in you; he refuses to accept you as a bringer of truth, because, though you think you have it, he feels that you have it not. You have not given him the authentic sign.

(Ralph Waldo Emerson, "New England Reformers: A Lecture Read before the Society in Armory Hall," Sunday, March 3, 1844)

This book is about analytical politics. As we noted in Chapter 1, this phrase implies "breaking down" political phenomena into their components and considering theoretical propositions that unify or differentiate these phenomena. However, with only a few exceptions, such as the analysis of turnout in Chapter 7, what we have "analyzed" is voting in committees. In this final chapter, we discuss some recent advances in the ongoing attempt to apply analytical political theory to mass elections.

In discussing the classical spatial model, we have referred to Anthony Downs's 1957 book, *An Economic Theory of Democracy,* and Duncan Black's 1958 work, *The Theory of Committees and Elections.* It is tempting to categorize these two works as the origins of the "mass elections" model and the "committee voting" model, respectively. Crediting Black with the committee voting model is perfectly accurate. But the orthodox "Downsian" model of elections is different from what Downs intended.

180

Downs was trying to create a real theory of mass elections. The main goal of Downs's theory was accounting for the uncertainty and lack of information voters face in making political choices. Downs advances the rudiments of a spatial model in his chapters 1–4, and it is on this foundation that much of modern spatial theory, including the MVT, is built. The extensions of the spatial model were accomplished mechanically, taking issues as the dimension(s) of the relevant space.

What Downs was really arguing was that voters have too little information about parties or candidates to solve such a complex problem. Step outside the elaborate logical structure we have built around "issues" for a moment and think about what it all means. Just what is an issue? How many issues are there, really, in a mass election? To put it more formally, how many dimensions are there in the space where mass political competition takes place? How much information do voters have about those issues, and how do voters conceive of their choices in that space?[1]

An important early criticism of the spatial model of voting was offered by Stokes (1963). Among other things, Stokes objected to the Downsian model's assumption of "ordered alternatives" as a depiction of the space of political competition in mass elections. Stokes claimed that voters perceive issues diffusely, perhaps even as "either–or" choices or symbols, even if the underlying issues (tax rates, speed limits, spending on the military) may be continuous and measurable.

This criticism is fundamental, though it is better applied to the classical model than to Downs's own discussion.[2] The "what is an issue?" problem is very difficult for the classical model, because almost anything could be an issue.[3] Still, to be fair, the definition of an issue is very difficult for everyone. Scholars and pundits lament that campaigns aren't even "about" issues. In this context, an issue is some policy question that the scholar or pundit cares about. They think everyone else should care, too. It may be useful to restrict the definition of issues to policy questions that do manage to attract widespread attention in the political process.

Consider an example, prison overcrowding, used by Baumgartner and Jones (1993, chapter 7), Jones (1994, chapter 5), and Hinich and Munger (1994, chapter 6). All three of these works point out that there are many social problems, but that few become issues: No one pays attention. If the problem becomes an issue, the political system moves to a contest over whose language to use to describe the problem. Success in using the "right" language often guarantees the "right" solution, from the perspective of the disputants.

The problem with prison overcrowding is this: There are many more prisoners than beds in correctional facilities. This may be a real *problem,* but it is not necessarily an *issue* if neither politicians nor the media talk about it much. An event to focus attention, such as a court order dictating the release of felons for whom there is no room, can change the problem into an issue reported by the press or talked about by candidates.

Still, what is *the* issue? There are at least two possibilities: First, prisons are overcrowded, because (a) prisons are too small and (b) law enforcement is too lax, so that too many people commit crimes. The solution is to double spending on prisons and police enforcement. Second, prisons are overcrowded, because (a) too much money is being spent on punishment, rather than rehabilitation, and (b) there is too much spent on law enforcement, rather than poverty programs. The solution is to cut spending on prisons and enforcement, and then raise spending on job-training and welfare programs.

The problem this example creates in identifying the issue is obvious. Is the issue here prison overcrowding, the breakdown of law and order, or poverty? The answer may depend on how the issue is "framed" by the media and perceived by voters. In that case, there are no objective issues at all. How are we to portray issues in the political system *before* framing takes place? How can we model the way that mass publics perceive the choices presented to them? The classical spatial model does not address these problems very effectively, because it takes the issue space as given.

There is a further difficulty with the classical model. Mass democracy is rarely *direct,* because citizens only occasionally choose budgets and policies through referenda. Most mass democratic choice is *representative:* Voters choose representatives, who in turn decide policy questions. One might argue that we have reasonable models for how representatives choose. After all, the committee model, with its assumption of high interest, high information, and widespread proposal power, fits legislatures quite well.

But then we still need some model of how voters choose representatives. The answer given by the Downsian model, that voters choose the candidate closest to them in terms of distance (accounting for salience and nonseparability) in an n-dimensional issue space, seems much less realistic for mass elections than for committee voting. In this chapter, we consider two important alternatives to the classical model, *directional theory* and *ideology*. The reason these approaches are presented here as alternatives is that each questions the nature of issues, and choices presented to voters, in the classical model:

- *Directional theory* models voter responses to policy proposals as having two components: a direction (does the voter feel favorable or unfavorable to the policy?) and an intensity (how strongly does the person feel about the policy?). A voter evaluates a candidate using the sum of his or her responses to the stands of the candidate on each issue.
- Spatial theory based on *ideology* argues that the classical model imposes too many informational requirements on voters, and imposes too many requirements for commitment on parties. The space in which political competition takes place, therefore, is ideology, not policy. The "dimensions" of the ideological space are few, are latent, and are determined by the way that issues tend to cluster in voters' minds.

Directional theory

"Downsian" theory requires that voters perceive, and candidates occupy, positions in an n-dimensional policy space. Preferences are defined by the (weighted) proximity of a voter's ideal point to the alternative proposed. Many have claimed that the classical model of spatial preference representation makes inaccurate and misleading assumptions about voters and alternatives. Directional theory preserves some of the intuition of spatial theory, but requires far less information or cognitive exertion by voters.

There is no one directional theory, so it is useful to outline some key assumptions and illustrate their implications for political choice. Perhaps the first formal "directional" alternative to proximity models was suggested by Weisberg (1974), who noted that the idea of ordered, linear dimensions conflicted with voting behavior observed in legislatures.[4] Weisberg claimed the policy space is not a line, but a circle. If we visualize a circle with the status quo (or the voter) at the center,

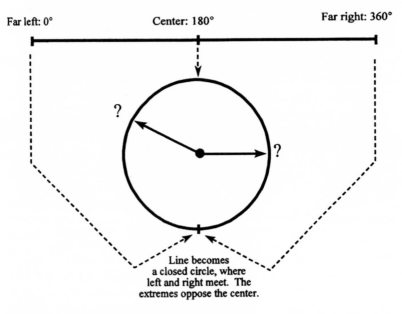

Figure 9.1. The left–right dimension transformed to a circle, where left meets right.

the choice of a direction (ranging from 0° to 360°) implies how policy will change.

Weisberg's "directional theory" assumed one dimension, a left–right scale that curves back on itself so that the extremes of left and right converge, as shown in Figure 9.1. The basic approach, however, can be extended to multiple dimensions simply by changing the conception from a circle to a *hypersphere,* or circle in *n*-dimensional space, as Matthews (1979) points out. Matthews analyzes the equilibrium properties of voting under this generalized representation of directional preferences.

A very different directional model is based on the theory and empirical findings developed in Rabinowitz (1978) and developed more fully in Rabinowitz and Macdonald (1989) and Macdonald, Listhaug, and Rabinowitz (1991, 1995). Rabinowitz (1978) used a nonmetric multidimensional scaling algorithm to place the implied voter ideal points and candidate issue positions in political issue spaces with two dimensions. What he found appeared to contradict the classical model's convergence prediction: Candidates took positions not in the middle but at the *periphery* of the distribution of voter ideal points.[5] What is the theoretical perspective of the Rabinowitz–Macdonald variant of directional theory?

Weisberg (1974) and Matthews (1979) assumed circular preferences, but modeled issues in the classical decision-theoretic fashion. For Rabinowitz and Macdonald, issues are in voters' minds no longer identical to the space of ordered alternatives. Instead, issues evoke a "symbol," and these symbols trigger a set of associations in the voter's mind. Rabinowitz and Macdonald (1989) claim that this "symbolic politics" model can be usefully applied even to everyday political issue voting:

Symbolic politics is by its nature associated with diffuse and emotionally laden reactions to issues. To the extent that issues are symbolic, the impact of issues should be modeled in terms of direction and intensity. But even if we assume a great deal of issue processing is not symbolic in nature, there are reasons to favor a directional (direction–intensity) paradigm for understanding mass cognition of issues. What is critical to the directional perspective is that the basic issue is conceptualized in diffuse fashion rather in terms of specific policy alternatives. . . . Based on [the empirical] findings accumulated over the last three decades, it is virtually inconceivable that the preferences for policy among the mass public go beyond a diffuse sense of direction. (pp. 94–5)

Discussion of an issue evokes two responses by voters in the directional model:

Direction: Is the reaction of the voters to the symbol positive, negative, or zero? For example, if the issue is a national health care system, voters might favor a system more like socialized medicine, or might oppose such a system.

Intensity: How strongly do voters feel about the issue? That is, if they favor a national health care system, what is the intensity of their preferences? Conversely, if they oppose such a move toward socialized medicine, what is the level of their emotional response?

This direction–intensity calculus can be applied to the candidate evaluation decision. Let us consider a representative voter *i*, who must decide which candidate to support. First, *i* judges whether each candidate stands on the same "side" (direction) of each issue as the voter herself. For some issues, the candidate and *i* may agree; on other issues, they take opposing positions. Second, *i* must make a judgment about (a) the intensity of her feelings about the issue and (b) the intensity of the candidate's professed commitment. Let us define SQ_j as the "neutral point" (in most cases, the status quo) for policy j. Then i's evaluation of a candidate A's stand on any given single issue j is:

$$(x_{Aj} - SQ_j) \times (x_{ij} - SQ_j) \tag{9.1}$$

If the voter and the candidate are both on the same "side" of the issue (both positive or both negative), the evaluation will be positive. The sign of the product in Equation 9.1 is the *direction* of the evaluation. Voters also evaluate the candidate based on the *magnitude* of the product (intensity). If the difference between either the candidate's location or the voter's location and the neutral point is small, the evaluation will be low in its intensity. To put it another way, directional theory requires intensity from both the candidate and the voter to generate a large effect.

There are two aspects of this model that differ fundamentally from the classical model, as an example will show. Suppose that there are three candidates (A, B, and C), each of whom takes a position for or against a national health care plan. (Since this is the only issue we will consider in the example, we will drop the j subscript.) Imagine that "positions" on the issue are identified by reactions to the extent of government involvement in delivery of, and financial support for, health care. The support scale has eleven points, centered on a neutral point of zero. Imagine that the four positions (x_A, x_B, x_C, and x_i) can be depicted as in Figure 9.2.

The proximity model would predict that the voter most prefers candidate B (a distance of two units from x_i), with candidate A (three units away) and candidate C (four units away) being ranked lower by the voter. Surprisingly, directional theory makes precisely the *opposite* set of predictions, with i most preferring candidate C, candidate A in the middle, and candidate B the worst. Using Equation 9.1, the evaluations of the candidates are as follows:

Candidate A: $(-4) \times (-1) = 4$
Candidate B: $(1) \times (-1) = -1$
Candidate C: $(-5) \times (-1) = 5$

The reason i would prefer A to B, though B is "closer," is intuitively plausible. Since the evaluation is directional, the apparent proximity is illusory: Voter i and candidate B are on opposite "sides" of the issue.

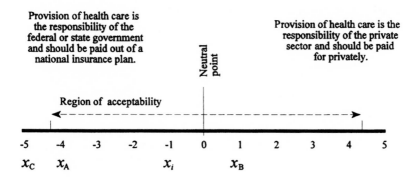

Directional model: Voter *i* likes C best and likes A better than B.
Ranking of candidates = *C, A, B*

Directional model with "region of acceptability": Voter *i* likes A best, doesn't like B, and thinks that C is "too extreme."
Ranking of candidates = *A, B, C*

Proximity model: Voter *i* likes B best and likes A better than C.
Ranking of candidates = *B, A, C*

Figure 9.2. The implications of the directional model contrasted with the classical proximity model on national health care.

The voter likes any candidate who is on her side of the issue more than any candidate on the other side.

Less easy to accept is the prediction of the directional model that C, the extremist, is preferred to A. After all, A and C are on the same "side" of the issue as *i*, but A is closer. Why would the voter prefer the more extreme candidate, when the voter herself appears quite moderate in her policy preferences?

The answer has two parts, and it is important to understand each. First, remember that the scale in Figure 9.2 is not an issue dimension! The eleven-point thermometer scale measures the *direction* and *intensity* of both the voter's self-described preferences and the voter's perceptions of the candidates' preferences or intentions. Consequently, candidate C is rewarded by the voter (according to directional theory) for taking a clear and deeply committed stand to an issue the voter slightly favors. The voter would like candidate C still more if the voter herself felt more strongly about the issue, of course. But for any voter who favors the left end of the health care policy scale, C is preferable to B.

Second, directional theorists have recognized that the prediction that extremism is always an advantage is unrealistic. What candidates should strive for is to take more intense stands than the other candidates, but avoid taking stands so extreme that voters reject them as irresponsible. As Rabinowitz and Macdonald point out:

> The driving force behind the directional model is the idea that people react to issues in a diffuse way rather than with a concern for the specifics of policy and the exact position the candidate advocates. A candidate, however, must convince voters of his or her reasonableness. Voters are wary of candidates who seem radical and project harshness or stridency. The label "extremist" can attach to such candidates and severely hamper the enthusiasm of potential supporters. This idea is incorporated in directional theory by introducing the concept of the *region of acceptability*. (1989, p. 108; emphasis in original)

The invocation of a *region of acceptability* to rescue the directional model from the patently false prediction "more extreme is better" seems ad hoc. Still, we have seen that a similar assumption has been used by classical spatial modelers to explain turnout: Voters were called "alienated" if all the candidates or alternatives were "too far" (more than an arbitrary constant δ) from the voters' ideal points.

In any case, for the purposes of our example, if C is perceived as "too extreme," or outside the region of acceptability, the prediction of the directional model would change: Candidate A would be preferred to C, because A receives the highest evaluation among those candidates whose perceived positions fall within the region of acceptability.

Electoral competition in the directional model

Throughout this book, we have emphasized that formal models give researchers a chance to analyze actual elections. Directional theory has some very interesting implications for the outcomes of elections. Perhaps the most important difference between the classical model and directional theory is the role of the center: The directional model implies that the center rarely commands much power in mass politics! Instead, a relatively noncentrist position, articulated by a strongly committed leader, will win elections and run the government.

If there are many issues, then the evaluation must account for trade-offs among the issues. Though it is possible to use a (diagonal) salience matrix $\mathbf{A}$, we will assume that $\mathbf{A} = \mathbf{I}$ for simplicity of the exposition.[6]

The reaction of a voter to a candidate is the sum of single issue evaluations across all of the m issues:

$$\sum_{j=1}^{J} (x_{Aj} - SQ_j) \times (x_{ij} - SQ_j) \tag{9.2}$$

What would spatial competition look like in a multidimensional space with a region of acceptability if voters behave in the way posited by directional theory?

Rabinowitz and Macdonald give two formal results that summarize the predictions of directional theory and highlight the differences between directional theory and classical proximity theory. Because the results are quite technical, but can be summarized intuitively, we will simply restate the results here:

Result 1. If the electorate is symmetrically distributed about the origin (neutral point) of the space, any candidate within the region of acceptability may win. That is, any "not too extreme" candidate is competitive with all other candidates similarly perceived as not too extreme. If more than one candidate is located within the region of acceptability, the election will turn on candidate- or election-specific factors. Stands on issues will not be the primary determinants of who wins.

This result is analogous to portions of the MVT proved earlier for the classical spatial model: If political competition drives candidates to the middle, it will appear that issues don't matter since all candidates look the same. Elections will be decided on other factors, according to the MVT. There is an important difference in the directional theory version, however: A symmetric distribution of voters renders the center not dominant, but irrelevant. Because voters are distributed symmetrically about the neutral point, their issue preferences as such all cancel out. The winning candidate is then the one who can persuade voters that she is more trustworthy, consistent, and committed.

Result 2. If the electorate is symmetrically distributed about a point (occupied by at least one voter) other than the origin of the space, a dominant political position exists. Define the direction toward the dominant point as established by the line segment between the current neutral point and the point around which voters are symmetrically distributed. Then the dominant position is the intersection of a line drawn in that direction and the region of acceptability. More simply, the most extreme position in the electorate's preferred direction of change will beat any other position in a pairwise majority rule contest.

The intuition behind this result is again reminiscent of the MVT, but again there are important differences. The MVT claimed that any status quo away from the center of the distribution of voters is unsupportable if there is free proposal power, because any such alternative will lose to a proposal closer to the median (if voter preferences are symmetric). To put it another way, the MVT says that if the polity finds itself pursuing policies different from what the "center" wants, policies are pushed toward the center.

Directional theory predicts that if the electorate has a clear directional preference (the center of the distribution of voters is different from the current neutral point), the best strategy for a candidate is to take as extreme a position as possible in the implied direction. Notice that the "direction" is complex because it is multidimensional. Further, the fact that the candidate takes this position and wins doesn't mean that that position becomes the new neutral point. It is quite possible that a candidate can win, but that a disparity remains in voters' minds between their perception of what government is doing and what they want.

This difference between movement to equilibrium, in the classical model, and movement toward equilibrium, in directional theory, is the defining distinction of the two models. Though differences in assumptions, as well as implications for measurement, make comparison of the two models difficult, a significant body of empirical work supports the view of political competition found in directional theory.

There have been some attempts to test "mixed" models, with elements of both directional and proximity motivations for voters (Merrill, 1993; Dow, 1995).[7] It is not yet clear whether a pure version of directional theory or one of the mixed variants is the best approach. One thing is clear, however: Directional theory is an important alternative conception of mass political behavior. It has implications for the nature of political choice and competition that differ broadly from the predictions of the classical model.

Ideology

One of the curious things about political opinions is how often the same people line up on opposite sides of different issues. The issues themselves may have no intrinsic connection with each other . . . yet the same familiar faces can be found glaring at each other from opposite sides of the political fence, again and again. It happens too often to be a coincidence, and it is too uncontrolled to be a plot. (Sowell, 1987, p. 6)

In real politics, choices cluster: "Liberals" favor welfare programs, support abortion rights, and advocate stricter environmental regulations; "conservatives" take opposite stands on *each* of these apparently separate issues. Consequently, one might argue that there are not really three issues (welfare, abortion, environment) at all. There is only one: liberal-conservative ideology.

The theory of mass politics based on ideology makes two claims that conflict with the classical model. First, the actual space in which choices are made is of much lower dimensionality than the complex space of "issues" in committee voting. Second, the dimensions of the space are not fixed, but are "latent," which means that the dimensions are determined by the way issues cluster in voters' beliefs or politicians' rhetoric. Ideologies serve as organizing principles, or guides to choice, in reducing the complex issue space to the much simpler space of mass-level political conflict.

Though there are many definitions of ideology, the one most useful for our purposes is that of Hinich and Munger (1994, p. 11): An ideology is "an internally consistent set of propositions that makes both proscriptive and prescriptive demands on human behavior. All ideologies have implications for (a) what is ethically good, and bad; (b) how society's resources should be distributed; and (c) where power appropriately resides."

Political choice based on ideology is not divorced from issues, because ideologies provide a set of "linkages" with the *n*-dimensional space of policies. These linkages are highly uncertain, however, and may differ across voters and over time. In a moment, we will see an example of how a spatial theory of ideology works. But first, it is important to establish the intellectual origins of the theory. Surprisingly, the originator of the critique of the classical, or "Downsian," model was Downs himself.

Downs was not a "Downsian"

I personally believe that the way information costs are treated [in *An Economic Theory of Democracy*] is perhaps the most important contribution. . . . It is more important than the spatial analysis of parties, although the latter has become much more famous. (Downs, 1993, p. 199)

Downs (1957, p. 96) defines ideology as "a verbal image of the good society and the chief means of constructing such a society." Note that this definition has two parts: *the ends* society should want, and the *means* for achieving these ends. For Downs, the reason that ideologies serve a vital purpose is that political decisions are made in an environment of pervasive uncertainty. The causal link between means and ends is clouded, and in any case the policies to be chosen by candidates after the election can only be guessed at by voters:

[A] voter finds party ideologies useful because they remove the necessity of his relating every issue to his own philosophy. Ideologies help him focus attention on the differences between parties; therefore, they can be used as samples of all the differentiating stands. With this shortcut a voter can save himself the cost of being informed upon a wider range of issues. (Downs, 1957, p. 98)

We can paraphrase the insight in this passage in the language of the spatial theory we have developed in earlier chapters. The cleavages between parties separate along simpler, more predictable lines than an n-dimensional policy space would imply, even if what voters care about is the n-dimensional space. If issues cluster by party ideology in just a few dimensions, then a reduced-dimensional policy space is no less accurate a representation of party conflict than the n-dimensional space. Conceiving of conflict in the simpler space is much easier for voters, however, and parties able to project their message in this fashion have a key competitive advantage. The bad news is that ideologies constrain the set of political choices available to voters, whether or not the voter herself is "ideological."

Another important function of an ideology is the ability to guide future action and predict positions on new issues. Cleavages among liberals and conservatives are predictable from the intellectual content (Downs's "verbal image of the good society") of the ideologies. More simply, an ideology doesn't just *list* the dimensions of conflict. It logically *implies* differences and cleavages.

Downs constructed a formal model of spatial competition among parties so he could make statements about the choices presented to voters. In other words, the model was designed to illuminate equilibrium. But the decision process Downs spells out for choices by voters rests squarely on the claim that mass behavior can be explained only using ideology. Yet Downs presented no real "model" of ideology, focusing instead on a model of spatial party competition. Most later scholars have understandably taken Downs's spatial model as the main contribution of his work.

A variety of scholars have recognized the potential importance of Downs's theory of ideology in its own right, however. Some, including North (1981, 1990), Kau and Rubin (1981, 1984), Higgs (1987), Hinich and Munger (1992, 1994), and Popkin (1994), have tried to capture the implications of ideology for policy making and the performance of societies over time. The goal in this chapter is much more modest: We will show how a spatial theory of ideology represents a fundamental departure from the classical model of mass political choice, particularly in the way it handles uncertainty and costly information.

Why are there linkages across issues?

There are at least three distinct theoretical justifications for ideologies, or links across issues: *communication, commitment,* and *budgets.* These theories are not mutually exclusive, so that more than one may apply to any given political context. Importantly, all three theoretical perspectives offer a justification for linkages across issues. Linkages across issues imply that there are relatively few independent dimensions in the space of political debate. The three justifications for linkage are:

- *Communication:* To provide voters with a message they can understand and use to make choices, parties must simplify their messages. Because only broad statements of principles can be used in advertising and position taking, the latitude for more subtle distinctions and differences is highly circumscribed. Ideologies are a means of solving problems of uncertainty and lack of information.
- *Commitment:* To be able to persuade voters that they can trust the party to do as promised after the election, parties must give reasons and explanations rather than just take positions. But explanations require some sort of overarching system of justification, as well as the advancement of values that can be applied to a variety of issues. Parties trade on reputations, but reputations are meaningful only if they provide a valuable signal. If parties act on their ideologies when such actions do not appear self-interested, reputations gain value.[8]
- *Budgets:* Increasing spending in one area of the budget forces either

decreases elsewhere or increased taxes or deficits. Thus, any change from the status quo forces a linkage to other issues, if only in terms of taxes or opportunity cost.

Ideology and the competition among parties

Parties mediate choices in representative democracy, but we haven't said much about them in this book.[9] Consider the following definition of a "party" from Hinich and Munger (1994, p. 85), itself adapted from several earlier definitions:

> **Party.** A group of citizens who (a) hold in common substantial elements of a political doctrine identified, both by party members and outsiders, with the name of the party; (b) choose candidates, either from within the group or by selecting outsiders, for political office with the object of carrying out this doctrine; and (c) organize the members of their delegation to the assembly of the political unit where the party is active.

Downs (1957) assumed either that there were precisely two parties or that the number was unimportant. A variety of scholars (see, just for the barest introduction, Lijphart, 1984; Grofman and Lijphart, 1986; Taagepera and Shugart, 1989; Sartori, 1994) have investigated the relation between the number of "effective" parties, the system by which representatives are elected, and the consequent performance of the electoral system. For our purposes, the number of parties can simply be taken as a result of the electoral institutions. From the perspective of voters, these voting rules (e.g., simple majority rule, Borda count) are fixed and exogenous. Parties are then collections of representatives who share all or parts of some political doctrine and seek to implement the policies implied by that doctrine (this simple definition is very close to that of Duverger, 1951). Parties are also citizens who identify with some or all of the political doctrine they associate with the party in the legislature.

Recall the earlier example of prison overcrowding. Suppose there are two parties, Right and Left. Some precipitating event has transformed prison overcrowding into an issue seized on by candidates from the party out of power. The party in power, which would have preferred that the problem not become an issue, must now try to characterize the problem in terms they prefer.

The Right's ideology might be simple: "Government should maintain law and order." The issues for the right then become lax law enforcement and the expansion of prison capacity. The Left's ideology, by contrast, might be "Government should help people who cannot help themselves." The issue for the left will be that there are too few economic opportunities and too little training in job skills for people already in prison.

The parties also have positions on many other issues. These positions are associated with the doctrines of the party, or its ideology. In a world where ideology presents the menu of choice, the issues are decided by the ideologies of the competing factions. The choices of voters are highly constrained, because representative democracy requires that they choose candidates from parties whose issue stands derive from ideology. What is the effective space in which mass-level political choice takes place, if ideologies determine the way issues cluster?

Consider Figure 9.3. If there are two parties, the effective space in which political choice takes place has only one dimension. The actual policies observed in the society along this dimension will reflect the proportion of seats of the two parties in the legislature. If there are three parties, the effective space is a two-dimensional plane, enough for complicated problems of social choice but far simpler than a space of issues.

Note that it doesn't matter how many issues there are: If there are just a few (cohesive) parties, there are just a few feasible dimensions of conflict. On the other hand, these dimensions of conflict are latent and depend on the way issues happen to cluster in that society. As Hinich and Munger (1994) point out, there are many different potential ways for issues to be linked, but only one of these linkages can be observed in a political system at a time.

Figure 9.3 is a gross simplification, of course, since real parties have internal factions that disagree, and governments may have different "branches," as in the United States federal government, where both the Congress and the president face popular elections of very different forms. Multiple institutions of government with overlapping or conflicting jurisdictions or powers offer a variety of choices for voters (see, e.g., Alesina and Rosenthal, 1995). Poole and Rosenthal (1996) docu-

Panel (a)

**If there are two parties,
the effective space for choice is a *line***

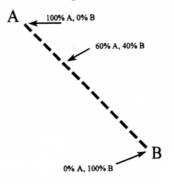

Panel (b)

**If there are three parties,
the effective space for choice is a *plane*.**

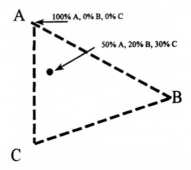

Figure 9.3. The effective space for "choice," given two or three parties.

ment the internal divisions, and empirical dimensions, that organize issue positions in the U.S. Congress and find that even with two parties there are occasionally two effective dimensions of choice. In terms of measurement of ideology, Poole and Rosenthal's work is fundamental. They show that if voters are presented with choices over parties, rather than direct choices over issues, the dimensionality of the effective choices presented voters in the United States is small, and almost never more than two.

Poole and Rosenthal (1991, 1996) analyze changes in the number of dimensions and the ability of one or two dimensions to explain variation in positions by members of the U.S. Congress since 1790. Changes in the prevailing ideological cleavage must take place both in individual beliefs and in the shared beliefs (ideologies) that link members into groups. Consider Table 9.1, excerpted from Poole and Rosenthal (1991), listing their measure of ideology (D-NOMINATE) from 1827 to 1860. The "% Correct" columns in the table describe the proportion of votes correctly predicted using a "cut point" based on the Poole–Rosenthal ideology measure.

To understand the table, it is important to consider context for a moment. Histories of this period reveal a fascinating preoccupation of members of Congress with the issue of slavery in the broader context of states' rights. Genovese (1961, 1972), for example, details the growing differences between the sets of ideas that northerners, westerners, and southerners had about the United States.

As Table 9.1 shows, the ability of any one or even two dimensions to classify votes declines dramatically in the early 1850s. The ideological divide that had organized U.S. politics since Andrew Jackson was breaking down. In fact, for the 32nd Congress (1851–2), even a large number of dimensions (ten, or more) does not classify members' votes very accurately.[10] Such complexity and idiosyncracy in voting patterns is most unusual. As Poole and Rosenthal (1996) show, with the exception of the 32nd Congress, two dimensions are always capable of explaining 80% or more of the variation in the votes of elected officials on most issues. In the next section, we will discuss a theoretical model consistent with this clustering phenomenon.

The relation between ideology and issues

There must be some correspondence in people's minds between ideological statements and predictions about the policies these statements imply.[11] This correspondence need in no way be *causal,* in the sense that everyone starts with issues and then infers ideology, or starts with ideology and then guesses at issues. The correspondence may be no more than a subconscious set of associations or stereotypes, based on the experience or socialization of the voter.[12] There is a key difference

Table 9.1. Performance of Poole–Rosenthal ideology model in classifying slavery votes, 1827–1860

Congress[a]	Years	1 Dimension: % Correct[b]	2 Dimensions: % Correct	Description of events
20th	1827–28	81	82	Andrew Jackson elected president; Tariff of Abominations; birth of Democrats; "nullification" doctrine raised
23rd	1833–34	76	79	Bank of U.S. dissolved; rise of the Whigs
24th	1835–36	81	86	Currency crisis causes regional tensions; different Whig factions nominate three separate candidates for president
25th	1837–38	84	91	Financial panic; "gag rule" prohibits abolitionist petitions in the House
26th	1839–40	80	88	Continuing currency problems; Whigs gain majority of seats in both chambers of Congress
27th	1841–42	84	90	Democrats regain control of the House in election of 1842
28th	1843–44	80	88	American Republican Party, forerunner of Know-Nothings; Texas annexed; Democrats regain control of Senate in 1844
29th	1845–46	73	89	Wilmot Proviso, outlawing slavery in territories obtained from Mexico; Mexican–American War (1846–8)
30th	1847–48	71	78	Free Soil Party presages new Republican coalition
31st	1849–50	75	82	Compromise of 1850: Texas and New Mexico admitted as slave states, Fugitive Slave Law extended under all parts of federal jurisdiction
32nd	1851–52	70	76	Whigs begin to disintegrate; Free Soil Party fails
33rd	1853–54	92	94	Kansas–Nebraska Act repeals Missouri Compromise (1820); Republican and "Know-Nothing" parties well-established; Republicans win control of House in elections of 1854
34th	1855–56	95	95	End of Whigs as party, in elections and in Congress; violent anarchy in "Bleeding Kansas"; Democrats retake House in 1856 elections
35th	1857–58	92	92	Dred Scott decision; financial "Panic"; Lecompton Constitution in Kansas; Lincoln–Douglas debates in Illinois; Republicans gain control of House in election of 1858
36th	1859–60	88	90	Brown's raid on Harper's Ferry; Democrats split into regional factions; Lincoln elected president; South Carolina votes to secede; Republicans win control of Senate in 1860 election

[a] Poole and Rosenthal (1991) include only those congresses that saw at least one recorded roll call vote on slavery.
[b] The "percent correct" refers to the proportion of votes by individual members correctly classified by the latent dimension(s) recovered by Poole and Rosenthal's MDS procedure (D–Nominate).

between belief systems of individuals and ideologies, however: Ideologies are *shared* belief systems.

If, as Downs claimed, an ideology were a weighted average of policy positions (where the weights differ across voters), there would be no coherence in ideological messages. Consequently, my "ideology" might be a shorthand rule or heuristic to help me choose among complicated alternatives, but it could not be a means of communicating in groups or organizing parties. If ideologies are shared belief systems, however, communication is possible and choice is more coherent.

Imagine that voters are aware of the abstract meanings of the words "liberal" and "conservative" and that it is possible to be more or less of either. That is, the statements "Party A is more liberal than party B" or "Candidate A is from the far left, while candidate B is much nearer the center" mean something to voters. What being liberal or conservative means depends, of course, on the historical and cultural context. In eighteenth-century England, the "liberals" favored a laissez-faire (hands off) economic policy. In the United States in the late twentieth century, many people associate liberals with increased government regulation of economic processes. In Russia in 1990, the "liberals" were those who favored market-oriented production and consumption patterns, while the "conservatives" advocated the old status quo Communist policies of state control over the means of production.

We are not assuming, then, that "liberal" and "conservative" mean the same things for all people at all times. All that is required is that *many voters,* in *one nation* at *one time,* have a *similar understanding* of what ideology means. However, what ideology "means" depends only partly on the aphorical statements used to justify the ideology and communicate it to voters. Ideologies also "mean" something in terms of policy, in a way first formalized by Hinich and Pollard (1981), and developed by Enelow and Hinich (1982b, 1984b).

To illustrate the link between abstract ideological positions and concrete policy positions, imagine that there are only two issues that concern a society: (1) how much to change spending on school lunches (to ensure poor children get at least one nutritious meal each day), and (2) how much to change spending on tanks (for protection against outside aggression). Imagine further that there are two parties, one of them "liberal" and the other "conservative." What are the implications of "liberalism" or "conservatism" for policy positions?

Interestingly, there is no clear answer, because the meaning of "ideology" is not fixed by theory or language. Instead, as a comparison of panels (a) and (b) in Figure 9.4 shows, the meaning of ideology is determined by the shared understanding of the correspondence between ideological statements and the associated policy positions. In panel (a), liberal means "libertarian," with a distrust of government generally. The conservative "nationalist" party pursues a corporatist conception of government, with a strong military and heavy investment in public schools and the vitality of the nation's youth.

In panel (b), the ideological dimension means something altogether different. This example could arise from a balanced budget requirement combined with a stricture against tax increases. The liberals want to increase school spending, in accordance with their philosophy of helping those least well off. But to finance this spending, the liberals will have to cut defense spending. Conservatives want to increase defense spending, but recognize they will have to cut school spending to find the money and meet the budget constraint.

Though these two examples are profoundly different in terms of their depiction of the understanding voters have of the correspondence between ideology and policy, they share one important characteristic: Ideologies impose *constraint,* to use the classic phrase of Converse (1963). Converse argued that ideologies do not constrain the beliefs of most people. And he was perfectly right, *given* his narrow definition of "ideologies" as internally consistent, highly structured belief systems. Converse seized on empirical inconsistencies among basic beliefs and expressed political preferences as evidence that "ideology" is a nonexistent concept. He argued that policy preferences are not structured by any shared beliefs.

There are three important problems with this perspective. First, there is a growing body of empirical evidence that voter beliefs are not *completely* unconstrained. In fact, as Feldman and Zaller (1992) have shown, when it comes to core political beliefs people struggle to reconcile apparently contradictory values so that their policy preferences are consistent. Beliefs and preferences are not perfectly inconsistent, as a cursory reading of the political behavior literature from the 1960s to the mid-1980s might lead one to believe. Recent research in voting behavior finds there is some shared structure in beliefs:[13]

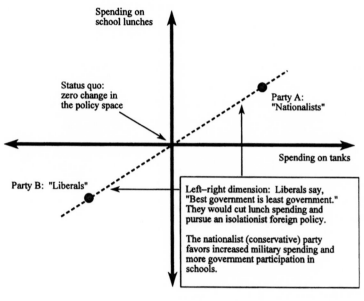

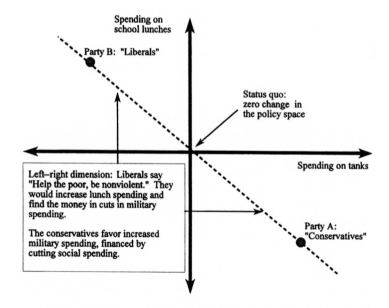

Figure 9.4. School lunches, tanks, and a left–right dimension: "Ideology" has no fixed meaning.

Contrary to the evidence of "ideological innocence," we argue that Americans do, for the most part, understand the philosophical underpinnings of the policies they endorse, and that, much more often than the belief systems literature would lead one to expect, Americans make use of cultural values and principles in explicating and justifying their political preferences. (Feldman and Zaller, 1992, p. 269)

The second problem with Converse's claim is that he defined the problem of political "choice" too narrowly, considering only how mass publics react to a given set of alternatives. But choices in representative democracies come from parties, so that the set of alternatives is highly constrained. If ideology determines the choices available, then voters must react to ideologies even if the voters themselves are not "ideological." As we saw in Figure 9.4, the choices on many issues may come down to which party (representing issue clusters) the voter likes best.

The third difficulty with Converse's argument is that it is too extreme. Arguments against the use of tightly integrated ideological constraint as an *axiom* of social science were well founded, of course, and Converse's contribution is justly recognized. There really is no reason to believe in general that beliefs are internally consistent across all citizens. But we are going too far if we refuse to entertain the possibility that ideological consistency is a *variable*. Different people, at a point in time, and some of the same people at different times, will exhibit variation in the level of constraint imposed by basic values.[14] In some ways, respect for basic values and the constraints these values impose on actions by citizens is the only thing that separates civilizations from the Hobbesian nightmare world of the war of all against all.

The spatial theory of ideology. Imagine that voters have preferences over n distinct issues. Each voter i, with ideal point $\mathbf{x}_i$ in the policy space, chooses between two candidates (A and B) based on their imputed platforms $\{\mathbf{x}_A, \mathbf{x}_B\}$ in $\mathcal{P}$. We will assume that the choice is based on a quadratic utility function and for notation use [] to mean the SED calculated between the two points:

$$U(\mathbf{x}_\alpha) = -[\mathbf{x}_i - \mathbf{x}_A]^2 \tag{9.3a}$$

$$U(\mathbf{x}_\beta) = -[\mathbf{x}_i - \mathbf{x}_B]^2 \tag{9.3b}$$

But the imputed platforms $\mathbf{x}_A$ and $\mathbf{x}_B$ have to come from somewhere. What is the source of voters' belief that these positions represent the likely policies of A and B if elected? Our claim is that though voters care about points in $\mathcal{P}$ (which has n dimensions), political competition takes place in the ideological space Π (with p dimensions, where $p \ll n$). Consequently, the choices voters can identify (and candidates can commit to) are constrained by ideology.[15] The mapping from the ideological space to the policy space can be expressed as a linear function of the various ideological dimensions. Though the model can handle multiple dimensions (see Enelow and Hinich, 1984; and Hinich and Munger, 1994), let us assume $p = 1$ for simplicity.[16] The imputed platform (for A, for example) can then be written as follows:

$$\mathbf{x}_A = \mathbf{b} + \mathbf{v}\pi_A \tag{9.4}$$

The $(n \times 1)$ $\mathbf{b}$ vector is the set of status quo policies. The $(n \times 1)$ $\mathbf{v}$ vector is the set of mappings from the ideological space to the policy space. The ideological position of each candidate is drawn from the set of feasible positions (i.e., $\pi_k \epsilon \Pi$, where in this case π_k is scalar).

The elements of $\mathbf{v}$ reflect the beliefs of voters that the prevailing ideology has implications for policies. For example, if $v_j \neq 0$, then voters believe abstract ideological statements are highly meaningful for policy j. Conversely, if $v_h = 0$, then issue h is not accounted for by the ideology of the prevailing party system. This does *not* mean voters don't care about the issue. Instead, if $v_h = 0$, then h is outside the issues voters associate with the orthodox political debate they hear from parties and candidates.

An example will clarify the status quo ($\mathbf{b}$) and mapping ($\mathbf{v}$) vectors. Consider again our earlier example of two policies: tanks and schools. T is spending on tanks for the military, a policy embraced by A, the party on the right, which advocates ideological position π_A. S represents spending on school lunches, advocated by party B, which runs on a leftist position π_B. We can depict the relation between ideological position and policy position graphically, as shown in Figure 9.5. Panel (a) presents a mapping from a left–right ideology on the horizontal axis to tanks on the vertical axis: Movements to the right represent increased military spending in voters' minds, so the slope of the linear relation is *positive*. Panel (b) depicts the analogous mapping from Π to S: Since rightists favor less school spending, the slope of the linear relation is *negative*.

The implied linkage between tanks and school lunches could have any of the origins discussed above. Budget laws may require offsetting

Panel (a)

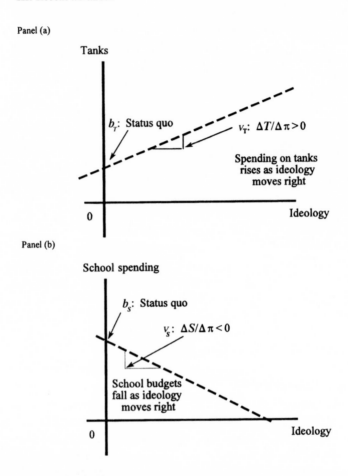

Figure 9.5. The relation between ideology and tanks (panel a) and between ideology and schools (panel b).

cuts to finance spending increases, parties may focus on their image as "tough" on foreign policy or "strongly supportive" of social programs, and so on. If issues are linked in this way, and this understanding of the linkage is shared by many people, ideology is a useful conception of political competition.[17]

The ideological model depicts the induced utility function, given a winning candidate (here, candidate A; the utility function if B wins is analogously defined), as follows:

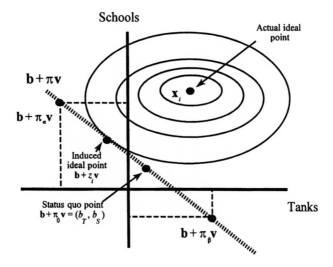

Figure 9.6. Voter i chooses A, the candidate closest to z_i in Π and closest to x_i in Ω.

$$U(\mathbf{x}_A) = U(\mathbf{b} + \mathbf{v}\pi_A) = -[\mathbf{x}_i - (\mathbf{b} - \mathbf{v}\pi_A)]^2 \qquad (9.5)$$

Thus, voters compare the utility of the candidates' positions, π_A and π_B, on the ideological dimension.

We can now consider voter utility in the policy space $\mathcal{P}$. This is exactly the same problem, in a slightly different informational setting. Suppose voter i has an ideal point $\mathbf{x}_i = (x_{i1}, x_{i2})$ and must choose between A and B. Let preferences around $\mathbf{x}_i$ be described by ellipsoidal indifference curves (preferences are not necessarily separable, nor are issues necessarily equally salient). The correspondence between the policy space $\mathcal{P}$ and the ideological dimension Π is given by Equation (9.4). We can depict this correspondence in Figure 9.6. The feasible positions in $\mathcal{P}$ are constrained to lie along Π, the ideological dimension. The status quo point in the policy space is represented by $\mathbf{b} = (b_T, b_S)$ and the status quo ideological position is π_0. Note that this correspondence is quite consistent with any of the three theoretical justifications given above, but is closest to the "budget" justification, particularly if the slope of the $\mathbf{b} + \mathbf{v}\pi$ line is $-\$1.00$.

The induced ideal point on the $\mathbf{b} + \mathbf{v}\pi$ line is $\mathbf{b} + \mathbf{v}z_i$, the point tangent to the highest attainable indifference curve. The corresponding ideal point in the ideological space Π is z_i (i.e., z_i is a scalar). The voter would prefer the policy position $\mathbf{x}_i$. But ideology constrains the positions that politicians can take and expect to be understood or believed, so $\mathbf{x}_i$ is not available to either politicians or voters.[18] The choice is between the partisans of the right, who favor tanks, and the partisans of the left, who favor school lunch programs. You can't get both, or neither, out of such a political system.

Consequently, in Figure 9.6 voter i chooses candidate A over B, because π_A is closer (in *weighted* Euclidean space) than π_B to $\mathbf{x}_i$. We will find it useful to define more formally the *induced ideal point* (denoted $\mathbf{b} + \mathbf{v}z_i$ in Figure 9.6) of voter i on the ideological dimension. Enelow and Hinich (1984b) show that if spatial preferences are based on SED, then the ideal point of a voter constrained to choose along a single ideological dimension is:

$$z_i = \frac{\sum_{k=1}^{m} v_k (x_{ik} - b_{ik})}{\sum_{k=1}^{m} v_k^2} \tag{9.6}$$

Thus, the voter's induced ideal point on the ideological dimension is a weighted sum of the differences between the voter's ideal point $\mathbf{x}_i$ and the status quo policy vector $\mathbf{b}$. The weights are a function of the ratio of the ideological mapping terms v_k to the sum of the squares of the weights on all issues. The expression in Equation (9.6) is a simple model of voter choice: Choose the candidate whose ideological position is closest to the induced ideal point z_i on Π.

We have claimed that ideology is an important mediating influence in voter choice among parties in representative democracies. A key difficulty with this formulation is the common usage of "ideology" to mean constraint or even sophistication in voters' belief systems. In fact, exactly the opposite is true; as Popkin (1994) points out:

Ideology is not the mark of sophistication and education, but of uncertainty and lack of ability to connect policies with benefits. . . . Parties use ideologies to highlight critical differences between themselves, and to remind voters of their past successes. They do this because voters do not perceive all the differences, cannot remember all the past performances, and cannot relate all future policies to their own benefits. But unavailability of data is not the only reason voters revert to default values. They do this when they are so satisfied with their past choices that they see no reason to collect any data. (pp. 51–2)

Ideology, constraint, and credibility

Ideology transmits information to voters and creates enthusiasm for political action. These two features alone are enough to make ideology a powerful competitive advantage in political discourse and in electoral politics. But there is an additional attribute of ideology, alluded to but not completely developed earlier, that makes it crucial for candidates and parties. This is its capacity to constrain the positions political actors can take. Campaigns, after all, must accomplish two things. First, they establish a candidate's or a party's position in the policy space. Second, and no less important, they persuade citizens that, once in office, the candidate or party will support or enact policies close to those they promised. Elections reflect the aggregation of individual voters' assessment of the candidate's or party's success in *both* of these endeavors.

Establishing credibility and commitment appears to be more important than simply taking a position. The reason is that debate centers on the ideological dimensions, not the policy space. Most voters know little of a candidate's actual policy stands, and establishing a position in the reduced-dimensional ideological space is more easily accomplished. The problem then quickly becomes convincing voters both that the candidate genuinely believes this position and will pursue it, and that it is the right thing to do.[19] Further, voters want to know about each candidate's character, integrity, ability to lead, and vision. The policy issues on which an elected official must decide are very difficult for voters to predict.

Consequently, voters must depend on the candidate's commitment to an ideological position as a guide for judgment. Future issues are unknowable, but the voter can try to ensure that the principles that the candidate will apply to deciding on new issues are the ones the voter also holds dear. The classical spatial model focused primarily on specific platforms, but campaigns appear to be about making general commitments to principles. Incumbents run on, and challengers run against, the record the incumbent has established. Even in open seat elections, there are party cues, endorsements by political elites, or prior experience by the candidates to give voters some means of guessing what the candidates claim they will do.

Classical spatial theory assumes that each politician chooses the position that maximizes his or her vote share given the expected platform of the opponent(s). This approach to modeling is extremely convenient and can be used to motivate experiments in which participants choose policy positions to maximize their payoffs. Such an approach is interesting from a scientific perspective, but may be of little use in describing real–world politics. For such an approach to work, voters must believe that a candidate who takes a position is likely to deliver that position. Analytical political theorists say that the candidate's promise must be "credible."

But why would anyone always believe the promises of politicians, whose public statements are often mocked as unreliable as guides to future behavior? One approach is to model voters' use of information. Recent work by Banks and Sobel (1987), Austen-Smith (1990), Banks (1990, 1991), Harrington (1992), and Chappell (1994) addresses how voters might rationally process candidate promises. This work is important, for it highlights the shortcomings in previous work in spatial models. But the signaling game approach simply substitutes an impossibly complex set of informational requirements for the impossibly unrealistic classical model of the campaign. Voters are assumed to know what they want on each of a large number of policy dimensions. Voters must also know just what candidates have promised to do. The only problem voters face is whether or not to believe the candidates.

By contrast, ideology offers two advantages that the games of asymmetric information lack. The first, noted by Downs, is that ideology serves as a means of reducing the costs of gathering information. What Downs did not recognize is the attenuated incentive to gather information, even on one's own most desired policies; voters simply do not know which policies are being considered, much less which position on these policies they most prefer. Ideology offers a means for parties and candidates to communicate, and for voters to decide, even when neither candidates nor voters know very much.

The logic of the classical model is a search for equilibria, or median positions. If the status quo is not an equilibrium, we imagine that at least one of the candidates changes his or her platform. But the primary goal of real campaigns is to persuade voters that the candidate or party will *not* move under any circumstances and is deeply committed to the promised platform. The fact is that voters evaluate candidates based on their reputations for probity, commitment, and consistency. Movement devalues these reputations. By constraining the possibilities for movement and by offering well-known justifications for particular clusters of policy positions, ideology solves the two key problems facing political systems: (1) How can politicians communicate their positions clearly? (2) How can politicians commit to those positions?

Conclusions

Both of the models in this chapter, directional theory and the ideology model, seem to have little to say about where alternatives come from. The great strength of the "Downsian" spatial model was its ability to say which proposals would win, and therefore to predict what positions candidates would take (if candidates wanted to win). The directional model takes "issues" as given and describes voters' reactions to them. The ideology model assumes even more preexisting structure for voter preferences, with linkages across issues and a lower-dimensional "ideological" space in which actual political debate takes place.

What these models do is make voter choice more realistic than the depiction of choice in the classical model. One possibility is that candidates' issue positions might be arrived at just as the classical model points out, but that the mass-level responses depicted by the models in this chapter provide a more realistic foundation for how voters choose once the alternatives are established. However, the logic of the two models actually implies an entirely different form of candidate strategy. Both directional theory and ideology theory are able to make predictions about what platform or set of proposals will win. The difference is that candidates may have only limited control over the set of characteristics or information that voters use in making their choices.

Final remarks

In this book, we have taken on a variety of normative and positive questions about human political action using analytical political theory. The theory itself is hard: It uses unfamiliar language and pitches its arguments in mathematical, or formal logical, terms. The hardest thing for many people is the use of simplifying assumptions, which make formal models seem far removed from real politics.

But that is what simplifying assumptions are for. Real politics is complicated, with lots of room for manipulation, bluffing, persuasion, and absurdity. Formal theories help social scientists explore "what if?" questions by deducing the implications of a set of premises. This approach has several advantages over other forms of theorizing. One of the most important advantages is the ability of analytical theory to help us evaluate claims about the quality of democratic choices and different ways of making those choices.

The key normative claim formal theorists have tried to evaluate is the existence of something like Rousseau's "general will." The general will must be a single choice, among mutually exclusive alternatives, achievable through democratic means and defensible based on ethical goals. The middle, or the center of the distribution of enfranchised citizens, is where political power is believed to reside. The contribution of analytical theory has been to make precise the consequences of different forms of choice and conflicting desires of citizens.

We first considered the concept of the median voter, under the assumption that government must choose just one policy. This use of the median as the definition of the center was then extended to account for the fact that government must in fact make many choices, all at once. Unfortunately, it turns out that the "middle" may not exist, if voters disagree. This is the worst possible news, since the only time we must really depend on voting is when there is disagreement. If we all agree, there is no real choice to be made: Government can simply implement the unanimous will of the people. The fact that there may be no defensible determinate choice in the face of disagreement means that democratic processes are most likely to fail when we need them most.

Further, this problem of indeterminacy of democracy is not confined to any one way of choosing. Arrow showed that *all* institutions of aggregation exhibit an inability to make a unique choice among three or more alternatives. The only exception is dictatorship, which "solves" the problem of disagreement in democracy by giving only one person a voice in choosing. What are the implications of this apparent incoherence of social choice rules?

One of the most famous scholars who contributed to the research reviewed in this book was William Riker. Much of his work questioned the validity of the "populist" interpretation of voting, which goes beyond advocacy of democracy simply as a way of choosing and attaches a moral force to the will of majorities. He argued:

Populism puts democracy at risk. Democracy requires control of rulers by electoral sanctions; the spirit of populism and populist institutions allows rulers to tamper with this sanction, thereby rendering it a weak defense against the tyranny of officials. The maintenance of democracy requires therefore the minimization of the risk in populism. . . . The main defense against populist excesses is the maintenance of the constitutional limitations. . . . It would probably help also to have a citizenry aware of the emptiness of the populist interpretation of voting. And surely a wide dissemination of the discoveries of social choice theory is a desirable additional defense. (Riker, 1982, p. 252)

We hope in this book to have helped disseminate some of the discoveries of social choice theory. In closing we would like to add one other thought: The faith that people have placed in political deliberation as a means of discovering truth is not wholly misplaced. Good democratic choices aren't impossible, but they are hard. We hope that knowing the limitations of institutions and rules will make making good choices a little easier.

Notes

CHAPTER 1

1. Schama (1989, p. 648).
2. The hierarchy described here was buttressed and legitimized by the ideological heritage of the Catholic Church, particularly its great thinkers, Augustine and Aquinas, themselves relying on Plato and, to a lesser extent, Aristotle.
3. As Monroe (1995) points out, the "collective wisdom" idea is better credited to Aristotle, though Rousseau most clearly develops it. Monroe cites Aristotle's *Politics,* book 3, chapter 11: "For it is possible that the many, no one of whom taken singly is a sound man, may yet, taken all together, be better than the few, not individually, but collectively."

CHAPTER 2

1. "Constitution" should not be taken here in the modern meaning of a document defining rights and constraining government. Instead, constitution means the way government is designed and justified. More generally, the words "class" in the quotations, or the word "preference" we use to describe Aristotle's citizens, should not be interpreted too literally. Modern ideas about government and citizens are very different from those of the Greeks in 400 B.C., and the use of Aristotle's "spatial theory" is intended more as an illustration than as a substantive interpretation of his theory.
2. By "unique," we mean that no person has more than one ideal point. Several (or all) members may share a single ideal point, however.
3. The mean may be important if voters try to "balance" in elections, as suggested by Alesina and Rosenthal (1995). The mode is important in a plurality rule system, if alternatives are discrete.
4. "CONVENTION. When n, the number of members, is odd, let us denote $O_{1/2 \cdot (n+1)}$ by O_{med}. When n is even and the chairman's optimum is at $O_{1/2n}$ or lower, let us denote $O_{1/2n}$ by O_{med}; or when n is even and the chairman's optimum is at $O_{1/2(n+1)}$ or higher, let us denote $O_{1/2(n+1)}$ by O_{med}" (Black, 1958, p. 18).

5. A closed interval is a line segment that contains its end points.

6. "THEOREM. If the members' curves are single-peaked, O_{med} will be able to get a simple majority over any of the other motions $a_1, \ldots, a_m$ put forward" (Black, 1958, p. 18). Though Black was the first to state the theorem clearly, he points out that the logic of the result has clear antecedents in earlier work. Black identifies Condorcet, Borda, and Dodgson as being perhaps the most important groundwork for the result. Interestingly, much of what we know about these antecedents comes from Black's own meticulous archival research, tracking down, translating, and reproducing the original documents in chapters 18–20 of *The Theories of Committees and Elections*. To put it more bluntly, Black might well receive more credit for his exposition of the MVT and its corollaries, save for two things: (1) He was a scholar of the first rank, and (2) he was an honest man.

7. Condorcet's "jury theorem," as argued in Grofman and Feld (1986) and Ladha (1992), states that the probability that a majority votes for the objectively "better" alternative (when the better state is unknown to anyone) goes to unity as the number of voters goes to infinity. This "voting system as consistent estimator of truth" approach is called the "epistemic interpretation" of democracy by Monroe (1995). Austen-Smith and Banks (1996) argue that even if there are only two alternatives and the other assumptions of the jury theorem are met, this conclusion makes unrealistic assumptions about the likely voting behavior of participants. In particular, the assumption that the probabilities of voting for the right alternative are parametric is shown to be inconsistent with rational behavior. These claims, however, are debatable, and counterarguments are offered by Ladha and Miller (1996).

8. Black (1958) examines this question exhaustively and finds that several people came very close to identifying the problem. The interested reader should examine "Part II" of Black (1958, pp. 156–238). However, we believe that in terms of the actual recognition of the definition of single-peakedness and its implications for stability in social choice, Duncan Black himself should receive great credit.

9. On the other hand, the assumption of single-peakedness need not be arbitrary or restrictive. Consider the standard utility maximization subject to a budget constraint in microeconomics, where one good is public and the other is private. Preference relations that are single-peaked are consistent with "normal" indifference curves, drawn assuming *quasi-concave* utility functions (see Glossary). In one dimension, non-single-peaked preferences require a violation of the standard *convexity* assumptions about indifference curves. However, in the more general case where there is more than one public good and more than one private good, it is quite possible to have non-single-peaked preferences even with quasi-concave utility functions. For a general discussion see Coughlin and Hinich (1984).

10. No, it doesn't! But for the sake of example we will ignore the fact that the

Security Council is actually a "collegium," with veto powers for all members, so that unanimity is required to pass any resolution.

11. In fact, the three discrete choices may not even satisfy the assumption of an ordered dimension. There is nothing inherently spatial about the Hun–Gats' choice problem. In that case (i.e., no ordered dimension), single-peakedness is a slightly different problem. One way to approach it would be this: Given alternatives, and preferences over those alternatives, is it possible to order the alternatives so that the associated preferences are single-peaked? If the answer is yes, single-peakedness is satisfied.

12. For background on Rousseau's ideas of the possibilities of representation, see Fralin (1978).

CHAPTER 3

1. This is a point of fundamental importance, both in rational choice theory and political psychology. One important recent development is the measurement of preferences that appear to drift or change depending on context (Zaller, 1992). However, this "framing" effect is precisely observationally equivalent to nonseparability under many circumstances, as Lacy (1996a, 1996b) has argued.

2. See also McKelvey (1976a, 1976b), Schwartz (1977), and Enelow and Hinich (1984b).

3. One other solution concept, the "uncovered set" (Miller, 1980; Feld et al., 1987), is commonly seen in technical articles. The definition of the "uncovered" set is the set of all feasible policy alternatives u such that, for all other feasible points y *either* (i) u beats y in a majority rule election, or (ii) there exists a feasible alternative $\tilde{y}$ such that u beats $\tilde{y}$ beats y in a majority rule election. The uncovered set can be, at most, the Pareto set, but it can be much smaller. If it is a singleton, the uncovered set is the Condorcet winner. For a review, see Mueller (1989).

   There are several other solution concepts, including the *yolk*, the *heart*, and the *Banks set*, that are beyond the scope of this book. For more information, see McKelvey (1986) and Schofield (1993). For an excellent overview of the technical literature, see Miller (1995).

4. There is an important sense in which this instability is an example of a more general indeterminacy of outcomes in games where there is disagreement over division of losses and gains. For very general but intuitive treatments of this problem, see Myerson (1991) and Brams and Taylor (1996).

5. A growing experimental literature on the "Pareto set," and the outcomes of voting processes in the laboratory, bears on this question. The original work was Fiorina and Plott (1978). For more recent experimental research, see Wilson (1986a, 1986b), Collier, McKelvey, Ordeshook, and Williams (1987), Eckel and Holt (1989), McKelvey and Ordeshook (1990), and the papers in Palfrey (1991), especially Plott (1991b). For a very different (but

potentially important) approach to mapping out patterns of positions taken by parties, see Kollman, Miller, and Page (1992).

6. There is some question whether the "distributive" efficiency form of legislative organization implied by the Shepsle–Weingast work actually explains the institutions we observe. For an aggressively opposing view, see Krehbiel (1991).

7. A median in all directions, if it exists, is the intersection of dimensional medians (or an element of the closed interval of same), but the reverse is not true.

8. One difficulty with the "structure-induced" equilibrium approach is the question of what members perceive to be their range of choices. Denzau and Mackay (1981) examine the role of expectations, considering whether there is a consistent agenda and whether members could predict that agenda. See also Enelow and Hinich (1983b, 1983c).

9. For an extended account of the role of redistribution and race in organizing much of American political conflict, see Poole and Rosenthal (1991, 1993, 1996). Fiorina and Shepsle (1982) give a critical review of the tensions over equilibrium models in analytical political theory.

10. McKelvey (1976a, 1976b) showed that if there is no median position, if voting is sincere, and the sequence of alternatives can be chosen by an outside agenda setter, then it is possible to choose an agenda (sequence of pairwise votes) that leads to virtually any outcome in the policy space. McKelvey and Schofield (1986) show that the stability of a political system may fundamentally depend on the number of different dimensions among alternatives.

CHAPTER 4

1. The Kelvin scale does have a nonarbitrary zero point, corresponding to $-273°$ Celsius. This zero point is theoretically rather than empirically anchored, because it represents the "temperature" where there is no heat, or where Brownian motion ceases completely. There is no way to produce this condition experimentally, since any insulator has heat conduction greater than zero, and only perfect insulation would produce $0°K$.

2. Technically $a_{12} = a_{21}$ means that the **A** matrix is symmetric. Intuitively, it means that the effect of the expected level of one policy on the marginal value of another is the same, regardless of which policy is fixed first. It is worth noting that there is nothing inherent in the model that requires **A** to be symmetric, however, and an interesting area for future research would be to consider the implications if order of consideration determines marginal valuation for this reason. Finally, in order for indifference curves to be ellipses, it must be true that $a_{11} \times a_{22} - a_{12} \times a_{21} > 0$. Since this condition has no obvious intuitive content for political preferences, we will simply mention it in passing.

3. Well, sort of. For the real proof, see Davis, DeGroot, and Hinich (1972) and McKelvey (1976a, 1976b).

CHAPTER 5

1. It is possible to question whether the "individually transitive, collectively intransitive" contradiction is a genuine paradox. Buchanan (1954, 1975), Tullock (1970), and Plott (1972) argue that "paradox" simply results from an indefensible insistence on an organic conception of societies. For a review, see Mueller (1989, pp. 388–92).

2. Coase (1960) points out that markets may allow enfranchisement of the downwind citizens, assuming transaction costs and wealth effects are negligible, and that distributional equity can be ignored. Coase's argument is that such arrangements can be noncollective, yet solve public problems. But this observation actually proves our point: Such a "market" requires a well-developed set of institutions for defining, enforcing, and transferring property rights, as well as a currency or accepted medium of exchange for effecting the transfer. Obviously, some collective decision, if only to define rights and afford some means for enforcing them, has taken place if a market solution can work.

3. It is commonly argued that both such activities do affect others, of course. "Immoral" sexual practices may offend others. If some people refuse to use helmets the result may be higher insurance rates for everyone. However, each of these may also be post hoc rationales. The point is that it is clearly possible, in principle, for the larger group to *determine* whether an action is private, quite separate from what the actors themselves believe.

4. The reader interested in pursuing public goods, externalities, and enfranchisement rules may find an extensive review in Mueller (1989).

5. There are many statements of Arrow's paradox. Ours is closest in spirit to that of Riker (1982, p. 18). An important general discussion, and some extensions, can be found in Sen (1970).

6. This statement is too strong. It is quite possible that societies are locked into conventions that nearly everyone knows are not Pareto optimal. See Schelling (1960), Lewis (1969), North (1981, 1990), Arthur (1989), and Denzau and North (1994).

7. It is important to note that rules requiring a fixed $K/N < 50\%$ vote apply only to access, and can allow but two alternatives: Reject the proposal, or pass the proposal along for further consideration. There is no inherent problem with access decisions if multiple alternatives "pass," since all this means is that the alternatives (bills, court cases, etc.) then continue through the process for disposition. The subject of concern in this book is for making a single choice among mutually exclusive alternatives. Consequently, we will restrict our attention to $K/N > 50\%$.

8. The KMVT we present is greatly simplified, compared with the more rigor-

ous treatments in Slutsky (1979). Slutsky's analysis has a different object, however, in that it compares mechanisms for achieving Pareto optimality in public goods provision with endogenous tax shares. The reader interested in the properties of different majorities required for decisiveness should also consult May (1952) and Sen (1970).

9. Quoted in Black (1958, p. 182), quoting from J. Mascart's *La Vie . . . de Borda* (1919).

10. Strategic voting is generally beyond the scope of this book. See Cox (1997) on the importance and breadth of strategic action in politics.

11. For an in-depth treatment of approval voting, see Brams and Fishburn (1984), and Brams and Nagel (1991). For some interesting background on approval voting, see Cox (1984b).

12. On the other hand, if each group selects only its first alternative as being acceptable, A will win, receiving eight votes compared with seven for B and six for C. Consequently, one might expect the middle and last groups to vote strategically, and include B and C in the acceptable category. This would ensure at worst a second-place rather than worst result for voters in those groups.

13. On "independence of path," see Plott (1973), Parks (1976), and Ferejohn and Grether (1977); on "multi-stage choice processes," see Schwartz (1986). For quite a different interpretation of the problem of social choice in general, see Nitzan and Paroush (1985).

14. For a variety of comparisons between PR and presidential systems, see Grofman and Lijphart (1992).

CHAPTER 6

1. If the object were to be *exactly* right, of course, the candidates would choose the modal median. However, the object is to be closest, so the mean median is the optimal platform. Nevertheless, there may not be any well-defined middle in a multi-dimensional space of legislator ideal points, as Goff and Grier (1993) point out.

2. Another possibility, beyond the scope of this book, is that the shape of the distribution is sharply bimodal, so that the identity of the median voter is highly discontinuous with respect to small changes in turnout. Further, the issue of how information is obtained is difficult. It is quite possible that campaigns all jealously guard their private knowledge of voter location. For an attempt to model this situation, see Ferejohn and Noll (1978).

3. As Calvert points out: "Candidates . . . may choose very different platforms in equilibrium if they have very different ideas about the probabilities of winning. However, this should properly be regarded not as a feature of the electoral institutions themselves, but as a direct result of the candidates' disagreement" (1985, p. 80).

4. For significant work on this point, see Ferejohn and Noll (1978), Ferejohn (1986), and Banks (1990, 1991).

5. It is quite possible that the distribution of expected positions is not symmetric, of course. A slightly different modification would allow the mean of the distribution of expected policy to differ from the candidate's announced positions. The latter possibility would require some prior distribution on candidate action, which might or might not be updated in response to new candidate messages. For one, relatively simple updating process using Bayes's rule, see Hinich and Munger (1994).

6. For some alternative ways of inducing voter beliefs over candidates, see Zaller (1992) or Jones (1994). Further, an important contribution to the experimental literature is the demonstration that voters may rely on endorsements or cues rather than direct experience (McKelvey and Ordeshook, 1985; Collier et al., 1987; Williams, 1994). The implication of this work is that elections may look as if all voters had accurate perceptions, even if only some have complete information.

7. A model that incorporates some of this reasoning (winning candidates must be extreme, but not "too" extreme) is the "directional theory" of Rabinowitz and Macdonald (1989). Hinich and Munger (1994) also make an argument for divergence, based on the need for a coherent heterodoxy, or opposition ideology, to defeat incumbents. Alesina and Rosenthal (1995) examine the implications of divergence of parties for the U.S. federal system of government.

8. For a discussion of the process of selection of candidates in U.S. presidential elections, see Aldrich (1980). For an example of a selection game at a more abstract level, see Hinich and Munger (1994, chapter 9). There is some persuasive, though indirect empirical evidence that elected officials pursue consistent policy goals, even if they are not subject to the reelection constraint. For a review of recent literature, see Bender and Lott (1996).

9. The reader interested in further learning may want to consult Binmore (1992) or Osborne and Rubinstein (1994). For an overview of the work game theorists have done, see Ordeshook (1989).

10. This assumption is called the "common knowledge" assumption. A more complete definition can be found in Binmore: "In game theory, something is common knowledge if everybody knows it; everybody knows that everybody knows it; everybody knows that everybody knows that everybody knows it; and so on. Game theorists usually assume that the rules of the game and the preferences of the players are common knowledge" (1992, p. 150).

11. The Nash solution concept (Nash, 1950) is a generalization of Cournot's equilibrium. But the dynamics of reaching an equilibrium, or moving from one equilibrium to another, are outside the logic of the Nash concept.

12. For a review of the political science literature on this question, see Bianco (1994). For a review of the "public choice" perspective, see Bender and Lott (1996).

13. Further, several authors have argued that no such variations in voting occur. See Lott (1987) and Lott and Davis (1992). For a different view, based

on the institutional implications of "discretion" as a goal of legislators, see Parker (1992). A more formal examination of the "rational" theory of leadership can be found in Frohlich and Oppenheimer (1971).

CHAPTER 7

1. We thank Gary Cox for calling our attention to this example of nonvoting.
2. According to the U.S. Constitution (Article I, Section 2, Part 1), "The electors in each State shall have the qualifications requisite for electors for the most numerous branch of the State legislature." Since state election laws differ, there can be wide variations in the definition of eligibility, even when voters are choosing among candidates for national office. Further, states have significant differences in registration requirements, purging of registration lists, and even poll hours. See Rosenstone and Wolfinger (1978), Wolfinger and Rosenstone (1980) and Cox and Munger (1989) for a discussion of some of these effects.
3. Some have argued that the registration decision is actually the key decision, and that analysis of turnout without accounting for differences in registration is misleading. See, for example, Kelley, Ayres, and Bowen (1967) and Erikson (1981).
4. Downs (1957) and Riker and Ordeshook (1968) model indifference. Ordeshook (1969), Hinich and Ordeshook (1969, 1970), and Hinich, Ledyard, and Ordeshook (1972) extend the Downsian model to account for alienation.
5. In principle, the radius of the circles depicting the regions of nonalienation might differ by candidate, since voters may care enough to vote for some candidates for reasons that have little to do with distance. This possibility can be accounted for using "probabilistic voting," as we discuss in Chapter 8.
6. We thank David Scocca for correcting and clarifying this diagram. In particular, Scocca made precise the curvature of the region of indifference, whereas the earlier Enelow and Hinich diagram made the borders of the region linear.
7. For a review of this literature, see Cox and Munger (1989).
8. Knack (1994) considers a variety of explanations for the effect of weather on turnout and outcomes.
9. We have also given short shrift to an important empirical perspective on the factors voters use in deciding among candidates: *retrospective* voting. According to this view (Key, 1966; Fiorina, 1989), voters evaluate the performance of the party or candidate now in office. If the incumbent has performed well (in the voters' judgment), he or she is returned to office. If the incumbent has botched things, voters vote for someone else, punishing poor performance after the fact. Retrospective voting is not completely contradictory to the classical spatial model, because there is an implicit comparison between the actual performance of incumbents and the expected performance of challengers. Still, the emphasis in the retrospective voting approach is clearly on the evaluation of the effectiveness of incumbents.

10. See also Barzel and Silberberg (1973).
11. Hinich (1981) goes further and conceives of voting as if it were an act of contribution. Contributions are usually thought of as monetary, but the time and effort required to vote can be thought of as a sacrifice by the voter for the sake of the candidate. Fiorina (1976) compares the "expressive" and investment-oriented, or "instrumental," motives for voting.
12. See Tullock (1967), Tollison, Crain, and Paulter (1975), and Silberman and Durden (1975). For a review, see Matsusaka and Palda (1993).
13. An interesting, and potentially important, new result is the "swing voter's curse" (Feddersen and Pesendorfer, 1996). They show that if other voters have private information (i.e., not all information about the alternatives is common knowledge), voters may be strictly better off abstaining than voting for either candidate, even if the costs of voting are not taken into account. This result hinges on the set of conditions that must be true about the world if the voter turns out to be the "swing" voter, or the vote that determines the outcome. For some policy implications on using polls, rather than votes, to determine public policy, see Brehm (1993). A more ambitious approach to "deliberative" decision making using polls is Fishkin (1991).
14. For a review of turnout over a longer period, see Aldrich (1976), Aldrich and Simon (1986), and Foster (1984).

CHAPTER 8

1. John Kingdon's classic book *Congressmen's Voting Decisions* (1981) lists what he believes to be the six most important factors in legislators' vote choices. These factors include: (1) desires of the constituency, (2) cues given by fellow members of Congress and by party leaders, (3) interest group pressures, (4) goals of the executive branch, (5) advice of staff, and (6) attention from the media.
2. "Agenda formation" incorporates changes in both public desires and interest group focus. For a review and some important new contributions, see Baumgartner and Jones (1993) and Jones (1994).
3. An important related result is the Romer and Rosenthal (1978, 1979) "setter" model, where the setter gets to choose a reversion level and then make a take it or leave it proposal.
4. One difficulty with this claim, of course, is that politicians may have to explain their vote on a specific issue, and it may prove difficult to explain that the vote was strategic. On the other hand, however, legislators who have won the trust of constituents may not need to make such explanations very often. For more on "trust," see Bianco (1994). Denzau and Munger (1986) describe the importance of different constituencies and levels of information in determining how voters' interests are represented.
5. For a more general discussion of the topics in this section, see Mueller (1989).

6. In fact, the result can be *derived* directly from Arrow's "impossibility" theorem and its proof, as was shown by Blin and Satterthwaite (1978) and Schmeidler and Sonnenschein (1978). For a useful and intuitive review of the technical basis of manipulability, see Kelly (1988, chapter 10, pp. 101–18). On the other hand, there are important differences between Arrow's result and the Gibbard–Satterthwaite impossibility conclusions (see, e.g., Border, 1984).

7. In his review of this literature, Schwartz (1986) points out that the Gibbard–Satterthwaite theorem applies to "resolute" voting rules, or rules that choose a single outcome from the choice set. Schwartz (1982) extends the theorem to (as he might say) "irresolute" collective choice processes.

8. This theory has spawned a contentious literature on the power of committees in the U.S. Congress. For a review, see Krehbiel (1991).

9. The argument is laid out in detail in Shepsle and Weingast (1987).

10. See Weingast (1979) and Niou and Ordeshook (1985).

11. It would be more accurate to say that the process of developing expectations about the package of all budgets becomes more important. See Denzau and Mackay (1981), Enelow and Hinich (1983b, 1983c), and Hinich (1986). For an experimental investigation of the applicability of structure-induced equilibrium to an abstract committee voting setting, see Wilson (1986a).

12. The question of whether anything like this actually happens is the subject of debate. For a recent review, see Shepsle and Weingast (1994) and Gilligan and Krehbiel (1994).

CHAPTER 9

1. The issue of issues is itself quite complicated. For a variety of perspectives on what constitutes an "issue" and for various typologies, see Riker (1959, 1963), MacRae (1965, 1970), Sundquist (1973), Zaller (1992), and Hinich and Munger (1994).

2. For a discussion of the differences between the "Downsian" (classical) model and Downs's model, see Hinich and Munger (1994).

3. Some wag has suggested that the definition of "issue" in political science is this: If someone at the University of Michigan asks someone else a question, and the answer is then coded and recorded by the Interuniversity Consortium for Political Science Research, that is an issue. Not surprisingly, there are many such issues. Whether these issues are actually distinct from each other in any global sense is another thing altogether.

4. In particular, Weisberg (1974) noted that in the Swedish Riksdag, members of "extreme" parties of the left and right would sometimes vote together in ad hoc coalitions against the center, or moderate members.

5. It might be objected that this "distribution on a circle" result is commonly found in multidimensional scaling procedures. This suggests that the fact that no voters appear in the middle of the issue space may be an artifact

of the *procedure* used to measure preferences, rather than a property of the preferences themselves. But the theoretical predictions of Rabinowitz's model have held up remarkably well in a wide variety of very different empirical tests (see, e.g., Poole and Rosenthal, 1984; Rabinowitz and Macdonald, 1989; Macdonald, Listhaug, and Rabinowitz, 1991, 1995; Macdonald and Rabinowitz, 1993; Merrill, 1993).

6. The question of whether a nondiagonal **A** matrix makes sense for directional theory is an open one and an interesting area for future research. The nature of interactions in directional theory are, at this point, unspecified. There is nothing in the logic of the model, however, that rules out such interactions. See Macdonald and Rabinowitz (1993) for some insights into linkages across issues in directional theory and Macdonald, Listhaug, and Rabinowitz (1995) for information on salience in directional models.

7. See also Iverson (1994) for a contrast of types of spatial models used in a comparative context.

8. The problem of commitment is long recognized in analytical politics. Three important treatments are Barro (1973), Ferejohn (1986), and Banks (1991). On the question of ideology as a filter and commitment device in particular, Kau and Rubin (1981) is the seminal work. Two other papers that follow this perspective are Lott (1987) and Dougan and Munger (1989).

9. Two important recent books on American parties and party control of legislative function are Cox and McCubbins (1993) and Aldrich (1995).

10. Our source for this information is Keith Poole, in private conversations.

11. Downs recognizes this, and offers the following explanation: "This dualism can be depicted on our graph of political space. . . . Each party takes stands on many issues, and each stand can be assigned a position on our left–right scale. Then the party's net position on this scale is a weighted average of all the particular policies it upholds. . . . Each citizen may apply different weights to the individual policies, since each policy affects some citizens more than others" (1957, pp. 132–3).

12. The "subconscious associations" may take any of a variety of forms, from a set of stereotypes the voter uses to interpret "liberal" and "conservative" to projections of the voter's own beliefs onto these concepts or labels. For an introduction to the political psychology literature on the formation of stereotypes by individuals, see Conover and Feldman (1982, 1984), Lau and Sears (1986), Krosnick (1991), Rahn (1993), and Zaller (1992).

13. There is significant support within the formal theory literature, also. See Enelow and Hinich (1984b, 1989, 1994), Enelow, Hinich, and Mendell (1986), and Hinich and Munger (1992, 1994).

14. For interesting evidence on this claim, see Budge (1994).

15. There is a crucial distinction between the "constraint" considered by Converse (1964) and that intended here. In Converse's "mass belief systems," constraint is imposed by coherent and consistent individual belief systems. Since this kind of constraint is rarely observed except among sophisticated citizens, beliefs do not appear to be coherent in this way. In our conception,

constraint is imposed by people's experience and their understanding of the regularities of political discourse. The notion of consistency is not logical, but is rather temporal: Similar messages have similar meanings.

16. The Poole and Rosenthal results show that, as an *empirical* matter, the dimensionality of the space of political debate is usually one. There is no theoretical reason to expect one dimension, rather than two or even three, is to be expected. The theory only implies we should expect many fewer ideological dimensions than there are issues.

17. To know whether an ideology is shared, researchers must grapple with difficult questions of both definition and measurement. A potentially path-
· breaking line of inquiry is suggested by Lupia (1994), who notes that decision rules and an understanding of cues need not be universal to achieve the benefits of the evolution of such rules. Whether ideologies are in fact one such kind of decision rule is part of the remaining research agenda.

18. In our example, this means that there is no party associated with the "more tanks–more school lunches" position.

19. For a review of recent work relating to information and democratic choice, see Ferejohn and Kuklinski (1990).

References

Aldrich, John. 1976. "Some Problems in Testing Two Rational Models of Participation." *American Political Science Review,* 20: 713–24.

Aldrich, John. 1980. *Before the Convention: Strategies and Choices in Presidential Nomination Campaigns.* Chicago: University of Chicago Press.

Aldrich, John. 1983a. "A Spatial Model with Party Activists: Implications for Electoral Dynamics." *Public Choice,* 41: 63–100.

Aldrich, John. 1983b. "A Downsian Spatial Model with Party Activism." *American Political Science Review,* 77: 974–90.

Aldrich, John. 1993. "Rational Choice and Turnout." *American Journal of Political Science,* 37: 246–78.

Aldrich, John. 1995. *Why Parties? The Origin and Transformation of Party Politics in America.* Chicago: University of Chicago Press.

Aldrich, John, and Dennis Simon. 1986. "Turnout in American National Elections." *Research in Micropolitics,* 1: 271–301. Greenwich, CT: JAI Press.

Alesina, Alberto, and Howard Rosenthal. 1995. *Partisan Politics, Divided Government, and the Economy.* New York: Cambridge University Press.

Aristotle, 1979. *Politics and Poetics* (translated by Jowett and Butcher). Norwalk, CN: Easton Press.

Arrow, Kenneth J. 1963. *Social Choice and Individual Values.* New Haven, CT: Yale University Press; 1st edition published by Wiley, 1952.

Arthur, W. Brian. 1989. "Competing Technologies, Increasing Returns, and Lock-in by Historical Events." *Economic Journal,* 99: 116–31.

Austen-Smith, David. 1990. "Information Transmission in Debate." *American Journal of Political Science,* 34: 124–52.

Austen-Smith, David, and Jeffrey Banks. 1996. "Information Aggregation, Rationality, and the Condorcet Jury Theorem." *American Political Science Review,* 90: 34–45.

Banks, Jeffrey. 1990. "A Model of Electoral Competition with Incomplete Information." *Journal of Economic Theory,* 50: 309–25.

Banks, Jeffrey. 1991. *Signaling Games in Political Science.* Chur, Switzerland: Harwood Academic.

Banks, Jeffrey, and J. Sobel. 1987. "Equilibrium Selection in Signaling Games." *Econometrica,* 55: 647–61.

Barro, Robert. 1973. "The Control of Politicians: An Economic Model." *Public Choice,* 14: 19–42.

Barry, Brian. 1970. *Sociologists, Economists, and Democracy.* London: Collier-Macmillan.

Barzel, Yoram, and Eugene Silberberg. 1973. "Is the Act of Voting Rational?" *Public Choice,* 16: 51–8.

Baumgartner, Frank, and Bryan Jones. 1993. *Agendas and Instability in American Politics.* Chicago: University of Chicago Press.

Beik, William. 1985. *Absolutism and Society in Seventeenth-Century France.* Cambridge: Cambridge University Press.

Bender, Bruce, and John Lott. 1996. "Legislator Voting and Shirking: A Critical Review of the Literature." *Public Choice,* 87: 67–100.

Bental, Benjamin, and Uri Ben-Zion. 1975. "Political Contribution and Policy: Some Extensions." *Public Choice,* 24: 1–12.

Bernhardt, M. Daniel, and Daniel E. Ingberman. 1985. "Candidate Reputations and the Incumbency Effect." *Journal of Public Economics,* 27: 47–67.

Bianco, William. 1994. *Trust: Representatives and Constituents.* Ann Arbor: University of Michigan Press.

Binmore, Kenneth. 1992. *Fun and Games: A Text on Game Theory.* Lexington, MA: Heath.

Black, Duncan. 1958. *The Theory of Committees and Elections.* New York: Cambridge University Press (reprinted 1987, Kluwer Academic, Netherlands).

Black, Duncan, and R. A. Newing. 1951. *Committee Decisions with Complementary Valuation.* London: Lowe and Brydon.

Blin, J.-M., and Mark Satterthwaite. 1978. "Individual Decisions and Group Decisions." *Journal of Public Economics,* 10: 247–67.

Bogdanor, Vernon, and David Butler, eds. 1983. *Democracy and Elections: Electoral Systems and Their Political Consequences.* New York: Cambridge University Press.

Border, Kim. 1984. "An Impossibility Theorem for Spatial Models." *Public Choice,* 43: 293–306.

Brams, Steven, and Peter Fishburn. 1984. *Approval Voting.* Boston: Birkhauser.

Brams, Steven, and J. H. Nagel. 1991. "Approval Voting in Practice." *Public Choice,* 71: 1–18.

Brams, Steven J., and Alan D. Taylor. 1996. *Fair Division: From Cake-Cutting to Dispute Resolution.* New York: Cambridge University Press.

Brehm, John. 1993. *The Phantom Respondents: Opinion Surveys and Political Representation.* Ann Arbor: University of Michigan Press.

Buchanan, James. 1954. "Social Choice, Democracy, and Free Markets." *Journal of Political Economy,* 62: 114–23.

Buchanan, James. 1975. *The Limits of Liberty: Between Anarchy and Leviathan.* Chicago: University of Chicago Press.

Buchanan, James, and Gordon Tullock. 1962. *The Calculus of Consent.* Ann Arbor: University of Michigan Press.

Budge, Ian. 1994. "A New Spatial Theory of Party Competition: Uncertainty, Ideology and Policy Equilibria Viewed Comparatively and Temporally." *British Journal of Political Science,* 24: 443–68.

Burnham, Walter D. 1965. "The Changing Shape of the American Political Universe." *American Political Science Review,* 59: 7–28.

Burnham, Walter D. 1970. *Critical Elections and the Mainsprings of American Politics.* New York: Norton.

Calvert, Randall. 1985. "Robustness of the Multidimensional Voting Model: Candidate Motivations, Uncertainty, and Convergence." *American Journal of Political Science,* 29: 69–95.

Chappell, Henry W. 1994. "Campaign Advertising and Political Ambiguity." *Public Choice,* 79: 281–304.

Coase, Ronald H. 1960. "The Problem of Social Cost." *Journal of Law and Economics,* 3: 1–44.

Coates, Dennis, and Michael Munger. 1995. "Legislative Voting and the Economic Theory of Politics." *Southern Economic Journal,* 61 (1995): 861–73.

Cohen, Linda, and Steven Matthews. 1980. "Constrained Plott Equilibria, Directional Equilibria, and Global Cycling Sets." *Review of Economic Studies,* 47: 975–86.

Coleman, James, and John Ferejohn. 1936. "Democracy and Social Choice." *Ethics,* 97: 26–38.

Collier, Kenneth, Richard McKelvey, Peter Ordeshook, and Kenneth Williams. 1987. "Retrospective Voting: An Experimental Study." *Public Choice,* 53: 101–30.

Conover, Pamela Johnston, and Stanley Feldman. 1982. "Projection and the Perception of Candidates." *Western Political Quarterly,* 35: 228–44.

Conover, Pamela Johnston, and Stanley Feldman. 1984. "How People Organize the Political World: A Schematic Model." *American Journal of Political Science,* 28: 95–126.

Converse, Phillip. 1963. "The Nature of Belief Systems in Mass Publics." In David Apter, ed., *Ideology and Discontent,* pp. 219–41. New York: Free Press.

Coughlin, Peter. 1992. *Probabilistic Voting Theory.* New York: Cambridge University Press.

Coughlin, Peter, and Melvin Hinich. 1984. "Necessary and Sufficient Conditions for Single Peakedness in Public Economic Models." *Journal of Public Economics,* 25: 323–41.

Cournot, A. A. 1897. *Researches into the Mathematical Principles of the Theory of Wealth.* New York: Macmillan; published in French in 1838.

Cox, Gary. 1984a. "An Expected Utility Model of Electoral Competition." *Quality and Quantity,* 18: 337–49.

Cox, Gary. 1984b. "Strategic Electoral Choice in Multi-Member Districts: Approval Voting in Practice?" *American Journal of Political Science,* 28: 722–38.

Cox, Gary. 1987. "Electoral Equilibrium under Alternative Voting Institutions." *American Journal of Political Science,* 31: 82–108.

Cox, Gary. 1990. "Centripetal and Centrifugal Incentives in Electoral Systems." *American Journal of Political Science,* 34: 903–35.

Cox, Gary. 1997. *Making Votes Count: Strategic Coordination in the World's Electoral Systems.* New York: Cambridge University Press.

Cox, Gary, and Mathew McCubbins. 1993. *Legislative Leviathan: Party Government in the House.* Berkeley: University of California Press.

Cox, Gary, and Michael Munger. 1989. "Contributions, Expenditure, Turnout: The 1982 U.S. House Elections." *American Political Science Review,* 83: 217–31.

Cox, Gary, and Michael Munger. 1991. "Putting Last Things Last: A Sequential Barriers Model of Turnout and Voter Roll-off." Typescript, University of North Carolina-Chapel Hill, Department of Political Science.

Davis, Otto, Morris DeGroot, and Melvin Hinich. 1972. "Social Preference Orderings and Majority Rule." *Econometrica,* 40: 147–57.

Davis, Otto, and Melvin Hinich. 1966. "A Mathematical Model of Policy Formation in a Democratic Society." In Joseph Bernd, ed., *Mathematical Applications in Political Science,* vol. 2, pp. 175–208. Dallas: Southern Methodist University Press.

Davis, Otto, and Melvin Hinich. 1968. "On the Power and Importance of the Mean Preference in a Mathematical Model of Democratic Choice." *Public Choice,* 5: 59–72.

Davis, Otto, Melvin Hinich, and Peter Ordeshook. 1970. "An Expository Development of a Mathematical Model of the Electoral Process." *American Political Science Review,* 64: 426–48.

Denzau, Arthur, and Robert Mackay. 1981. "Structure-Induced Equilibria and Perfect Foresight Expectations." *American Journal of Political Science,* 25: 762–79.

Denzau, Arthur, and Robert Mackay. 1983. "Gatekeeping and Monopoly Power of Committees: An Analysis of Sincere and Sophisticated Behavior." *American Journal of Political Science,* 27: 740–61.

Denzau, Arthur, and Michael Munger. 1986. "Legislators and Interest Groups: How Unorganized Interests Get Represented." *American Political Science Review,* 80: 89–106.

Denzau, Arthur, and Douglass North. 1994. "Shared Mental Models: Ideologies and Institutions." *Kyklos,* 47: 3–32.

Denzau, Arthur, William Riker, and Kenneth Shepsle. 1985. "Farquharson and Fenno: Sophisticated Voting and Home Style." *American Political Science Review,* 79: 1117–34.

Dougan, William, and Michael Munger. 1989. "The Rationality of Ideology." *Journal of Law and Economics.* 32: 119–42.

Downs, Anthony. 1957. *An Economic Theory of Democracy.* New York: Harper and Row.

Downs, Anthony. 1993. "The Origins of an Economic Theory of Democracy."
In B. Grofman, ed., *Information, Participation, and Choice,* pp. 198–201.
Ann Arbor: University of Michigan Press.

Duverger, Maurice. 1951. *Political Parties: Their Organization and Activity in
the Modern State.* London: Methuen.

Eckel, C., and C. Holt. 1989. "Strategic Voting in Agenda-Controlled Committee Experiments." *American Economic Review,* 79: 763–73.

Enelow, James. 1981. "Saving Amendments, Killer Amendments, and an
Expected Utility Theory of Sophisticated Voting." *Journal of Politics,* 43:
1062–89.

Enelow, James. 1992. "An Expanded Approach to Analyzing Policy-Minded
Candidates." *Public Choice,* 74: 425–45.

Enelow, James, James Endersby, and Michael Munger. 1993. "A Revised Probabilistic Spatial Model of Elections: Theory and Evidence." In B. Grofman,
ed., *An Economic Theory of Democracy in Historical Perspective,* pp. 125–
40. Ann Arbor: University of Michigan Press.

Enelow, James, and Melvin Hinich. 1982a. "Nonspatial Candidate Characteristics and Electoral Competition." *Journal of Politics,* 44: 115–30.

Enelow, James, and Melvin Hinich. 1982b. "Ideology, Issues, and the Spatial
Theory of Elections." *American Political Science Review,* 76: 493–501.

Enelow, James, and Melvin Hinich. 1983a. "On Plott's Pairwise Symmetry
Condition for Majority Rule Equilibrium." *Public Choice,* 40: 317–21.

Enelow, James, and Melvin Hinich. 1983b. "Voting One Issue at a Time: The
Question of Voter Forecasts." *American Political Science Review,* 77:
435–45.

Enelow, James, and Melvin Hinich. 1983c. "Voter Expectations in Multi-Stage
Voting Systems: An Equilibrium Result." *American Journal of Political Science,* 27: 820–27.

Enelow, James, and Melvin Hinich. 1984a. "Probabilistic Voting and the Importance of Centrist Ideologies in Democratic Elections." *Journal of Politics,* 46: 459–78.

Enelow, James, and Melvin Hinich. 1984b. *The Spatial Theory of Voting: An
Introduction.* New York: Cambridge University Press.

Enelow, James, and Melvin Hinich. 1989. "The Location of American Presidential Candidates: An Empirical Test of a New Spatial Model of Elections." *Mathematical and Computer Modeling,* 12: 461–70.

Enelow, James, and Melvin Hinich. 1994. "A Test of the Predictive Dimensions
Model in Spatial Voting Theory." *Public Choice,* 78: 155–69.

Enelow, James, Melvin Hinich, and Nancy Mendell. 1986. "An Empirical Evaluation of Alternative Spatial Models of Elections." *Journal of Politics,* 48:
675–93.

Enelow, James, and David Koehler. 1980. "The Amendment in Legislative
Strategy: Sophisticated Voting in the U.S. Congress." *Journal of Politics,*
42: 396–413.

Enelow, James, and Michael Munger. 1993. "The Elements of Candidate Reputation: The Effect of Record and Credibility on Optimal Spatial Location." *Public Choice,* 77: 757–72.

Erikson, Robert. 1981. "Why Do People Vote? Because They Are Registered." *American Politics Quarterly,* 9: 259–76.

Farquharson, Robin. 1969. *Theory of Voting.* New Haven, CT: Yale University Press.

Fedderson, Timothy, and Wolfgang Pesendorfer. 1996. "The Swing Voter's Curse." *American Economic Review,* 86: 408–24.

Feld, S. L., B. Grofman, R. Hartly, M. Kilgour, N. Miller, and N. Noviello. 1987. "The Uncovered Set in Spatial Voting." *Theory and Decision,* 23: 129–55.

Feldman, Stanley, and John Zaller. 1992. "Political Culture of Ambivalence: Ideological Responses to the Welfare State." *American Journal of Political Science,* 36: 268–307.

Ferejohn, John. 1986. "Incumbent Performance and Electoral Control." *Public Choice,* 50: 5–25.

Ferejohn, John. 1993. "The Spatial Model and Elections." In B. Grofman, ed., *Information, Participation, and Choice,* pp. 107–24. Ann Arbor: University of Michigan Press.

Ferejohn, John, and Morris Fiorina. 1974. "The Paradox of Not Voting: A Decision Theoretic Analysis." *American Political Science Review,* 68: 525–36.

Ferejohn, John, and David Grether. 1977. "Weak Path Independence." *Journal of Economic Theory,* 14: 19–31.

Ferejohn, John, and James Kuklinski, eds. 1990. *Information and Democratic Processes.* Urbana: University of Illinois Press.

Ferejohn, John, and Roger Noll. 1978. "Uncertainty and the Formal Theory of Campaigns." *American Political Science Review,* 72: 492–505.

Fiorina, Morris P. 1976. "The Voting Decision: Instrumental and Expressive Aspects." *Journal of Politics,* 38: 390–415.

Fiorina, Morris P. 1989. *Retrospective voting in American national elections* (3rd ed.). New Haven, CT: Yale University Press.

Fiorina, Morris P. 1994. "Divided Government in the American States: A By-product of Legislative Professionalism?" *American Political Science Review,* 88: 304–17.

Fiorina, Morris P., and Charles R. Plott. 1978. "Committee Decisions under Majority Rule: An Experimental Study." *American Political Science Review,* 72: 575–98.

Fiorina, Morris P., and Kenneth A. Shepsle. 1982. "Equilibrium, Disequilibrium, and the General Possibility of a Science of Politics." In P. C. Ordeshook and K. A. Shepsle, eds., *Political Equilibrium,* pp. 49–64. Boston: Kluwer Academic.

Fishkin, James. 1991. *Democracy and Deliberation.* New Haven, CT: Yale University Press.

Fort, Rodney. 1995. "A Recursive Treatment of the Hurdles to Voting." *Public Choice,* 85: 45–69.

Foster, Carroll B. 1984. "The Performance of Rational Voter Models in Recent Presidential Elections." *American Political Science Review,* 78: 678–90.

Fralin, Richard. 1978. *Rousseau and Representation: A Study of the Development of His Concept of Political Institutions.* New York: Columbia University Press.

Frohlich, Norman, and Joe Oppenheimer. 1971. *Political Leadership and Collective Goods.* Princeton, NJ: Princeton University Press.

Genovese, Eugene. 1961. *The Political Economy of Slavery.* New York: Random House.

Genovese, Eugene. 1972. *Roll, Jordan, Roll: The World the Slaves Made.* New York: Random House.

Gibbard, Allan. 1973. "Manipulation of Voting Schemes: A General Result." *Econometrica,* 41: 587–602.

Gilligan, Thomas, and Keith Krehbiel. 1994. "The Gains from Exchange Hypothesis of Legislative Organizations." *Legislative Studies Quarterly,* 19: 181–214.

Goff, Brian, and Kevin Grier. 1993. "On the (mis)Measurement of Legislator Ideology and Shirking." *Public Choice,* 76: 5–20.

Green, Donald, and Ian Shapiro. 1994. *Pathologies of Rational Choice Theory: A Critique of Applications in Political Science.* New Haven, CT: Yale University Press.

Grofman, Bernard. 1985. "The Neglected Role of the Status Quo in Models of Issue Voting." *Journal of Politics,* 47: 230–7.

Grofman, Bernard, and Scott Feld. 1988. "Rousseau's General Will: A Condorcetian Perspective." *American Political Science Review,* 82: 567–76.

Grofman, Bernard, and Arend Lijphart, eds. 1986. *Electoral Laws and Their Political Consequences.* New York: Agathon.

Grofman, Bernard, and Arend Lijphart, eds. 1992. *Parliamentary versus Presidential Government.* Oxford University Press.

Guizot, Francois. 1974. *Democracy in France.* New York: Howard Fertig.

Hamilton, James, and Helen Ladd. 1996. "Biased Ballots? The Impact of Ballot Structure on North Carolina Elections in 1992." *Public Choice,* 87: 259–80.

Harrington, Joseph. 1992. "The Revelation of Information through the Political Process." *Economics and Politics,* 4: 255–76.

Higgs, Robert. 1987. *Crisis and Leviathan: Critical Episodes in the Growth of American Government.* New York: Oxford University Press.

Hinich, Melvin. 1977. "The Median Voter Result Is an Artifact." *Journal of Economic Theory,* 16: 208–19.

Hinich, Melvin. 1981. "Voting as an Act of Contribution." *Public Choice,* 36: 135–40.

Hinich, Melvin. 1986. "Discussion of 'The Positive Theory of Legislative Institutions.'" *Public Choice,* 50: 179–83.

Hinich, Melvin, John Ledyard, and Peter Ordeshook. 1972. "Nonvoting and

Existence of Equilibrium under Majority Rule." *Journal of Economic Theory,* 4: 144–53.

Hinich, Melvin, and Michael Munger. 1992. "A Spatial Theory of Ideology." *Journal of Theoretical Politics,* 4: 5–30.

Hinich, Melvin, and Michael Munger. 1994. *Ideology and the Theory of Political Choice.* Ann Arbor: University of Michigan Press.

Hinich, Melvin, and Peter Ordeshook. 1969. "Abstentions and Equilibrium in the Electoral Process." *Public Choice,* 7: 81–106.

Hinich, Melvin, and Peter Ordeshook. 1970. "Plurality Maximization vs. Vote Maximization: A Spatial Analysis with Variable Participation." *American Political Science Review,* 64: 772–91.

Hinich, Melvin, and Walker Pollard. 1981. "A New Approach to the Spatial Theory of Electoral Competition." *American Journal of Political Science,* 25: 323–41.

Hotelling, Harold. 1929. "Stability in Competition." *Economic Journal,* 39: 41–57.

Iverson, Torben. 1994. "The Logics of Electoral Politics: Spatial, Directional, and Mobilizational Effects." *Comparative Political Studies,* 27: 155–90.

Jones, Bryan. 1994. *Reconceiving Decision-Making in Democratic Politics.* Chicago: University of Chicago Press.

Kadane, J. B. 1972. "On Division of the Question." *Public Choice,* 13: 47–54.

Kalt, Joseph, and Mark Zupan. 1984. "Capture and Ideology in the Economic Theory of Politics." *American Economic Review,* 74: 279–300.

Kalt, Joseph, and Mark Zupan. 1990. "The Apparent Ideological Behavior of Legislators: Testing for Principal–Agent Slack in Political Institutions." *Journal of Law and Economics,* 33: 103–31.

Kau, James, and Paul Rubin. 1981. *Congressmen, Constituents, and Contributors.* Boston: Martinus Nijhoff.

Kau, James, and Paul Rubin. 1984. "Economic and Ideological Factors in Congressional Voting." *Public Choice,* 44: 385–8.

Kelley, S., R. Ayres, and W. Bowen. 1967. "Registration and Voting: Putting First Things First." *American Political Science Review,* 61: 359–79.

Kelly, Jerry S. 1988. *Social Choice Theory: An Introduction.* Berlin: Springer Verlag.

Key, V. O. 1955. "A Theory of Critical Elections." *Journal of Politics,* 17: 3–18.

Key, V. O. 1966. *The Responsible Electorate.* Cambridge, MA: Harvard University Press.

Kingdon, John. 1981. *Congressmen's Voting Decisions* (2nd ed.). New York: Harper and Row.

Knack, Steve. 1994. "Does Rain Help the Republicans? Theory and Evidence on Turnout and the Vote." *Public Choice,* 79: 187–209.

Kollman, Ken, John Miller, and Scott Page. 1992. "Adaptive Parties in Spatial Elections." *American Political Science Review,* 86: 929–38.

Kramer, Gerald. 1972. "Sophisticated Voting over Multidimensional Choice Spaces." *Journal of Mathematical Sociology,* 2: 165–80.

Kramer, Gerald. 1973. "On a Class of Equilibrium Conditions for Majority Rule." *Econometrica,* 41: 285–97.

Kramer, Gerald. 1977. "A Dynamical Model of Political Equilibrium." *Journal of Economic Theory,* 16: 310–34.

Krehbiel, Keith. 1991. *Information and Legislative Organization.* Ann Arbor: University of Michigan Press.

Krosnick, Jon A. 1991. "The Stability of Political Preferences: Comparisons of Symbolic and Nonsymbolic Attitudes." *American Journal of Political Science,* 35: 547–76.

Lacy, Dean. 1996a. "A Theory of Nonseparable Preferences in Survey Responses." Typescript, Ohio State University, Department of Political Science.

Lacy, Dean. 1996b. "Nonseparable Preferences, Issue Voting, and Issue Packaging in Elections." Typescript, Ohio State University, Department of Political Science.

Ladha, Krishna. 1992. "The Condorcet Jury Theorem, Free Speech, and Correlated Votes." *American Journal of Political Science,* 36: 617–34.

Ladha, Krishna. 1996. "Hypothesis Testing and the Jury Theorem." In N. Schofield, ed., *Collective Decision Making: Social Choice and Political Economy,* pp. 385–92. Boston: Kluwer Academic.

Ladha, Krishna, and Gary Miller. 1996. "Political Discourse, Factions, and the General Will: Correlated Voting and Condorcet's Jury Theorem." In N. Schofield, ed., *Collective Decision Making: Social Choice and Political Economy,* pp. 393–410. Boston: Kluwer Academic.

Lau, Richard, and David Sears, eds. 1986. *Political Cognition: The 19th Annual Carnegie Symposium on Cognition.* Hillsdale, NJ: Erlbaum.

Laver, Michael, and Norman Schofield. 1990. *Multiparty Government: The Politics of Coalition in Europe.* New York: Oxford University Press.

Ledyard, John O. 1981. "The Paradox of Voting and Candidate Competition: A General Equilibrium Analysis." In G. Horwich and J. Quirk, eds., *Essays in Contemporary Fields of Economics,* pp. 54–80. West Lafayette, IN: Purdue University Press.

Ledyard, John O. 1984. "The Pure Theory of Large Two Candidate Elections." *Public Choice,* 44: 7–41.

Lewis, David. 1969. *Convention: A Philisophical Study.* Cambridge, MA: Harvard University Press.

Lijphart, Arend. 1984. *Democracies: Patterns of Majoritarian and Consensus Government in Twenty-One Countries.* New Haven, CT: Yale University Press.

Lott, John. 1987. "Political Cheating." *Public Choice,* 52: 169–87.

Lott, John, and Michael Davis. 1992. "A Critical Review and Extension of the Political Shirking Literature." *Public Choice,* 74: 461–84.

Lott, John, and Robert Reed. 1989. "Shirking and Sorting in a Model of Finite-Lived Politicians." *Public Choice,* 61: 75–96.

Lupia, Arthur. 1994. "Shortcuts versus Encyclopedias: Information and Voting

Behavior in California Insurance Reform Elections." *American Political Science Review,* 88: 63–76.

Macdonald, Stuart E., and George Rabinowitz. 1987. "The Dynamics of Structural Realignment." *American Political Science Review,* 81: 775–96.

Macdonald, Stuart E., and George Rabinowitz. 1993. "Ideology and Candidate Evaluation." *Public Choice,* 79: 59–78.

Macdonald, Stuart E., Ola Listhaug, and George Rabinowitz. 1991. "Issues and Party Support in Multiparty Systems." *American Political Science Review,* 85: 1107–31.

Macdonald, Stuart E., Ola Listhaug, and George Rabinowitz. 1995. "Political sophistication and models of issue voting." *British Journal of Political Science,* 25: 453–84.

MacRae, Duncan. 1965. "A Method of Identifying Issues and Factions From Legislative Votes." *American Political Science Review,* 59: 909–26.

MacRae, Duncan. 1970. *Issues and Parties in Legislative Voting: Methods of Statistical Analysis.* New York: Harper and Row.

Matsusaka, John, and Filip Palda. 1993. "The Downsian Voter Meets the Ecological Fallacy." *Public Choice,* 77: 855–78.

Matthews, Steven A. 1979. "A Simple Direction Model of Electoral Competition." *Public Choice,* 34: 141–56.

May, K. O. 1952. "A Set of Independent, Necessary, and Sufficient Conditions for Simple Majority Decision." *Econometrica,* 20: 680–4.

McCubbins, Mathew, and Thomas Schwartz. 1984. "Police Patrols and Fire Alarms." *American Journal of Political Science,* 28: 165–79.

McKelvey, Richard. 1976a. "General Conditions for Global Intransitivities in Formal Voting Models." *Econometrica,* 47: 1085–111.

McKelvey, Richard. 1976b. "Intransitivities in Multidimensional Voting Bodies and Some Implications for Agenda Control." *Journal of Economic Theory,* 30: 283–314.

McKelvey, Richard. 1986. "Covering, Dominance, and Institution-Free Properties of Social Choice." *American Political Science Review,* 30: 283–414.

McKelvey, Richard, and Richard Niemi. 1978. "A Multistage Game Representation of Sophisticated Voting for Binary Procedures." *Journal of Economic Theory,* 18: 1–22.

McKelvey, Richard, and Peter Ordeshook. 1985. "Sequential Elections with Limited Information." *American Journal of Political Science,* 29: 480–512.

McKelvey, Richard, and Norman Schofield. 1986. "Structural Instability of the Core." *Journal of Mathematical Economics,* 15: 179–98.

Merrill, Samuel, III. 1993. "Voting Behavior under the Directional Spatial Model of Electoral Competition." *Public Choice,* 77: 739–56.

Miller, Nicholas. 1980. "A New Solution Set for Tournaments and Majority Voting: Further Graph Theoretical Approaches to the Theory of Voting." *American Journal of Political Science,* 24: 68–96.

Miller, Nicholas. 1995. *Committees, Agendas, and Voting.* Chur, Switzerland: Harwood Academic Publishers.

Monroe, Burt L. 1995. "Fully Proportional Representation." *American Political Science Review,* 89: 925–40.

Morton, Rebecca. 1991. "Groups in Rational Turnout Models." *American Journal of Political Science,* 35: 758–76.

Mueller, Dennis. 1989. *Public Choice II.* New York: Cambridge University Press, 1989.

Myerson, Roger. 1991. *Game Theory: Analysis of Conflict.* Cambridge, MA: Harvard University Press.

Nagler, Jonathan. 1991. "The Effect of Registration Laws and Education on U.S. Voter Turnout." *American Political Science Review,* 85: 1393–1406.

Nash, John. 1950. "Equilibrium Points in *N*-Person Games." *Proceedings of the National Academy of Sciences,* 36: 48–9.

Nelson, Douglas, and Eugene Silberberg. 1987. "Ideology and Legislator Shirking." *Economic Inquiry,* 25: 15–25.

Niou, Emerson, and Peter Ordeshook. 1985. "Universalism in Congress." *American Journal of Political Science,* 29: 246–58.

Niskanen, William. 1971. *Bureaucracy and Representative Government.* Chicago: Aldine–Atherton.

Nitzan, Shmuel, and Jacob Paroush. 1985. *Collective Decision Making: An Economic Outlook.* New York: Cambridge University Press.

North, Douglass. 1981. *Structure and Change in Economic History.* New York: Norton.

North, Douglass. 1990. *Institutions, Institutional Change, and Economic Performance.* New York: Cambridge University Press.

Olson, Mancur. 1965. *The Logic of Collective Action.* Cambridge, MA: Harvard University Press.

Ordeshook, Peter. 1969. *Theory of the Electoral Process.* Ph.D. dissertation, Department of Political Science, University of Rochester, Rochester, NY.

Ordeshook, Peter. 1989. *Game Theory and Political Theory.* New York: Cambridge University Press.

Osborne, Martin J., and Ariel Rubinstein. 1994. *A Course in Game Theory.* Cambridge, MA: MIT Press.

Palfrey, Thomas, ed. 1991. *Laboratory Research in Political Economy.* Ann Arbor: University of Michigan Press.

Palfrey, Thomas, and Keith Poole. 1987. "The Relationship between Information, Ideology, and Voting Behavior." *American Journal of Political Science,* 35: 511–30.

Palfrey, Thomas, and Howard Rosenthal. 1983. "A Strategic Calculus of Voting." *Public Choice,* 41: 7–53.

Palfrey, Thomas, and Howard Rosenthal. 1985. "Voter Participation and Strategic Uncertainty." *American Political Science Review,* 79: 62–78.

Parker, Glenn. 1992. *Institutional Change, Discretion, and the Making of Modern Congress.* Ann Arbor: University of Michigan Press.

Parks, Robert. 1976. "Further Results on Path Independence: Quasi-Transitivity and Social Choice." *Public Choice,* 26: 75–87.

Plato. 1956. *The Republic,* In *Great Dialogues of Plato,* translated by W. H. D. Rouse, edited by E. H. Warmington and P. G. Rouse. New York: New English Library (Mentor).

Plott, Charles. 1967. "A Notion of Equilibrium and Its Possibility under Majority Rule." *American Economic Review,* 57: 787–806.

Plott, Charles. 1972. "Ethics, Social Choice Theory, and the Theory of Economic Policy." *Journal of Mathematical Sociology,* 2: 181–208.

Plott, Charles. 1973. "Path Independence, Rationality, and Social Choice." *Econometrica,* 41: 1075–91.

Plott, Charles. 1976. "Axiomatic Social Choice Theory: An Overview and Interpretation." *American Journal of Political Science,* 20: 511–96.

Plott, Charles. 1991a. "Will Economics become an Experimental Science?" *Southern Economic Journal,* 57: 901–20.

Plott, Charles. 1991b. "A Comparative Analysis of Direct Democracy, Two-Candidate Elections, and Three-Candidate Elections in an Experimental Environment. In T. Palfrey, ed., *Laboratory Research in Political Economy,* pp. 134–56. Ann Arbor: University of Michigan Press.

Plott, Charles, and M. Levine. 1978. "A Model of Agenda Influence on Committee Decisions." *American Economic Review,* 68: 146–60.

Poole, Keith, and Howard Rosenthal. 1984. "The Polarization of American Politics." *Journal of Politics,* 46: 1061–79.

Poole, Keith, and Howard Rosenthal. 1991. "Patterns of Congressional Voting." *American Journal of Political Science,* 35: 228–78.

Poole, Keith, and Howard Rosenthal. 1993. "Spatial Realignment and the Mapping of Issues in U.S. History: The Evidence from Roll Call Voting." In William Riker, ed., *Agenda Formation,* pp. 13–40. Ann Arbor: University of Michigan Press.

Poole, Keith, and Howard Rosenthal. 1996. *Congress: A Political-Economic History of Roll Call Voting.* New York: Oxford University Press.

Popkin, Samuel. 1994. *The Reasoning Voter: Communication and Persuasion in Presidential Campaigns* (2nd ed.). Chicago: University of Chicago Press.

Rabinowitz, George. 1978. "On the Nature of Political Issues: Insights from a Spatial Analysis." *American Journal of Political Science,* 22: 793–817.

Rabinowitz, George, and Stuart Macdonald. 1989. "A Directional Theory of Issue Voting." *American Political Science Review,* 83: 93–121.

Rahn, Wendy. 1993. "The Role of Partisan Stereotypes in Information Processing about Political Candidates." *American Journal of Political Science,* 37: 472–96.

Rawls, John. 1971. *A Theory of Justice.* Cambridge, MA: Harvard University Press.

Riker, William. 1959. "A Method for Determining the Significance of Roll Calls in Voting Bodies." In J. C. Wahlke and H. Eulau, eds., *Legislative Behavior,* pp. 123–49. New York: Free Press.

Riker, William. 1963. *The Theory of Political Coalitions.* New Haven, CT: Yale University Press.

Riker, William. 1980. "Implications from the Disequilibrium of Majority Rule for the Study of Institutions." *American Political Science Review,* 74: 432–46.

Riker, William. 1982. *Liberalism against Populism: A Confrontation between the Theory of Democracy and the Theory of Social Choice.* San Francisco: Freeman.

Riker, William. 1986. *The Art of Political Manipulation.* New Haven, CT: Yale University Press.

Riker, William. 1990. "Heresthetic and Rhetoric in the Spatial Model." In James M. Enelow and Melvin Hinich, eds., *Advances in the Spatial Theory of Voting,* pp. 46–65. New York: Cambridge University Press.

Riker, William, and Peter Ordeshook. 1968. "A Theory of the Calculus of Voting." *American Political Science Review,* 62: 25–42.

Romer, Thomas, and Howard Rosenthal. 1978. "Bureaucrats vs. Voters: On the Political Economy of Resource Allocation by Direct Democracy." *Public Choice,* 33: 27–44.

Romer, Thomas, and Howard Rosenthal. 1979. "Political Resource Allocation, Controlled Agendas, and the Status Quo." *Public Choice,* 33: 27–44.

Rosenstone, Steven, and Raymond Wolfinger. 1978. "The Effect of Registration Laws on Voter Turnout." *American Political Science Review,* 72: 22–45.

Rosenthal, Howard. 1990. "The Setter Model." In James M. Enelow and Melvin Hinich, eds., *Advances in the Spatial Theory of Voting,* pp. 199–234. New York: Cambridge University Press.

Rousseau, Jean Jacques. 1973. *The Social Contract,* translated by G. D. H. Cole. London: Dent; first published 1762.

Rudé, George. 1964. *Revolutionary Europe: 1783–1815.* New York: Harper and Row.

Russett, Bruce, and Samuel Shye. 1993. "Aggressiveness, Involvement, and Commitment in Foreign Policy Attitudes." In D. Caldwell and T. McKeown, eds., *Diplomacy, Force, and Leadership,* pp. 41–60. Boulder, CO: Westview.

Sartori, Giovanni. 1976. *Parties and Party Systems.* Cambridge: Cambridge University Press.

Sartori, Giovanni. 1994. *Comparative Constitutional Engineering: An Inquiry into Structures, Incentives, and Outcomes.* New York: New York University Press.

Satterthwaite, Mark. 1975. "Strategy-Proofness and Arrow's Conditions: Existence and Correspondence Theorems for Voting Procedures and Social Welfare Functions." *Journal of Economic Theory,* 10: 187–218.

Schama, Simon. 1989. *Citizens: A Chronicle of the French Revolution.* New York: Knopf.

Schelling, Thomas. 1960. *The Strategy of Conflict.* Cambridge, MA: Harvard University Press.

Schmeidler, David, and Hugo Sonnenschein. 1978. "Two Proofs of the Gibbard–Satterthwaite Theorem on the Possibility of a Strategy-Proof Social Choice Function." In H. W. Gottinger and W. Leinfeller, eds., *Decision Theory and Social Ethics,* pp. 227–34. New York: Reidel.

Schofield, Norman. 1978a. "Instability of Simple Dynamic Games." *Review of Economic Studies*, 45: 575–94.

Schofield, Norman. 1978b. "The Theory of Dynamic Games." In P. Ordeshook, ed., *Game Theory and Political Science*, pp. 119–64. New York: New York University Press.

Schofield, Norman. 1984. "Social Equilibrium and Cycles on Compact Sets." *Journal of Economic Theory*, 33: 59–71.

Schofield, Norman. 1985. *Social Choice and Democracy.* Heidelberg: Springer Verlag.

Schofield, Norman. 1993. "Party Competition in a Spatial Model of Coalition Formation." In W. Barnett, M. Hinich, and N. Schofield, eds., *Political Economy: Institutions, Competition, and Representation*, pp. 135–74. New York: Cambridge University Press.

Schwartz, Thomas. 1977. "Collective Choice, Separation of Issues and Vote Trading." *American Political Science Review*, 71: 999–1010.

Schwartz, Thomas. 1982. "No Minimally Reasonable Collective Choice Process Can Be Strategy-Proof." *Mathematical Social Sciences*, 3: 57–72.

Schwartz, Thomas. 1986. *The Logic of Collective Choice.* New York: Columbia University Press.

Sen, Amartya K. 1970. *Collective Choice and Social Welfare.* London: Holden-Day.

Shepsle, Kenneth. 1979. "Institutional Arrangements and Equilibrium in Multidimensional Voting Models." *American Journal of Political Science*, 23: 27–60.

Shepsle, Kenneth. 1991. *Models of Multiparty Electoral Competition.* Chur, Switzerland: Harwood Academic.

Shepsle, Kenneth. 1994. *Cabinet Ministers and Parliamentary Government.* New York: Cambridge University Press.

Shepsle, Kenneth, and Barry Weingast. 1981. "Structure Induced Equilibrium and Legislative Choice." *Public Choice*, 37: 503–19.

Shepsle, Kenneth, and Barry Weingast. 1987. "The Institutional Foundations of Committee Power." *American Political Science Review*, 81: 85–104.

Shepsle, Kenneth, and Barry Weingast. 1994. "Positive Theories of Congressional Institutions." *Legislative Studies Quarterly*, 19: 149–80.

Silberman, Jonathan, and Garey Durden. 1975. "The Rational Behavior Theory of Voter Participation: The Evidence from Congressional Elections." *Public Choice*, 23: 101–8.

Slutsky, Steven. 1979. "Equilibrium Under α-Majority Voting." *Econometrica*, 47: 113–25.

Smithies, A. 1941. "Optimum Location in Spatial Competition." *Journal of Political Economy*, 49: 423–39.

Sowell, Thomas. 1987. *A Conflict of Visions.* New York: Morrow.

Stokes, Donald. 1963. "Spatial Models of Party Competition." *American Political Science Review*, 57: 368–77.

Sundquist, James. 1973. *Dynamics of the Party System: Alignment and Realignment of Political Parties in the United States* (rev. ed.: 1983). Washington, DC: Brookings Institution.

Taagepera, Rein, and Matthew Shugart. 1989. *Seats and Votes: The Effects and Determinants of Electoral Systems.* New Haven, CT: Yale University Press.

Tocqueville, Alexis de. 1969. *Democracy in America.* Edited by J. P. Mayer, translated by G. Lawrence. Garden City, NY: Anchor.

Tollison, Robert, W. Mark Crain, and Paul Paulter. 1975. "Information and Voting: An Empirical Note." *Public Choice,* 24: 39–43.

Tollison, Robert, and Thomas D. Willett. 1973. "Some Simple Economics of Voting and Not Voting." *Public Choice,* 16: 59–71.

Tullock, Gordon. 1967. *Toward a Mathematics of Politics.* Ann Arbor: University of Michigan Press.

Tullock, Gordon. 1970. *Private Wants, Public Means: An Economic Analysis of the Desirable Scope of Government.* New York: Basic.

Tullock, Gordon. 1981. "Why So Much Stability?" *Public Choice,* 37: 189–202.

Uhlaner, Carole. 1989a. "Rational Turnout: The Neglected Role of Groups." *American Journal of Political Science,* 33: 390–422.

Uhlaner, Carole. 1989b. "'Relational Goods' and Participation: Incorporating Sociability into a Theory of Rational Action." *Public Choice,* 62: 253–85.

Vickrey, W. 1960. "Utility, Strategy, and Social Decision Rules." *Quarterly Journal of Economics,* 74: 507–35.

Weingast, Barry. 1979. "A Rational Choice Perspective on Congressional Norms." *American Journal of Political Science.* 23: 245–62.

Weingast, Barry, and Mark Moran. 1983. "Bureaucratic Discretion or Congressional Control? Regulatory Policy-Making by the Federal Trade Commission." *Journal of Political Economy,* 91: 775–800.

Weisberg, Herbert. 1974. "Dimensionland: An Excursion into Spaces." *American Journal of Political Science,* 18: 743–76.

Williams, Kenneth. 1994. "Spatial Elections with Endorsements and Uninformed Voters: Some Laboratory Experiments." *Public Choice,* 80: 1–8.

Wilson, Rick. 1986a. "Forward and Backward Agenda Procedures: Committee Experiments on Structurally Induced Equilibrium." *Journal of Politics,* 48: 390–409.

Wilson, Rick. 1986b. "Results on the Condorcet Winner: A Committee Experiment on Time Constraints." *Simulation and Games,* 17: 217–43.

Wittman, Donald. 1977. "Candidates with Policy Preferences: A Dynamic Model." *Journal of Economic Theory,* 14: 180–9.

Wittman, Donald. 1983. "Candidate Motivations: A Synthesis of Alternatives." *American Political Science Review,* 77: 142–57.

Wittman, Donald. 1990. "Spatial Strategies when Candidates Have Policy Preferences." In James M. Enelow and Melvin Hinich, eds., *Advances in the Spatial Theory of Voting,* pp. 66–98. New York: Cambridge University Press.

Wolfinger, Raymond, and Steven Rosenstone. 1980. *Who Votes?* New Haven, CT: Yale University Press.

Zaller, John. 1992. *The Nature and Origins of Public Opinion.* New York: Cambridge University Press.

Glossary

Arbitrary: An arbitrary selection from a set is used as an example. Something like, "Pick a card, any card" to start a card trick. A selection is arbitrary only if it doesn't matter which is chosen.

Assumptions: Premises, taken as true within the context of a logical argument, where some conclusion is deduced. The truth value of such premises is deduced from the truth or falsity of the conclusions.

Classical left–right dimension: Used by Anthony Downs to describe a dimension of differences in views of ideal forms of economic organization, ranging from the "left" (government ownership of the means of production) to the "right" (pure laissez-faire economics).

Classical spatial model: The decision-theoretic model of voter behavior, using the assumption that preferences can be represented with a weighted quadratic loss function based on distance.

Closed interval: On a line segment, all the points between the end points of the segment, including the end points.

Committee voting: A decision process with the following properties: informed voters, voting directly for alternatives rather than candidates, significant stakes by voters on outcomes, and a presumption of participation by all voters. Additional properties that may be assumed include simple majority rule and free proposal power, but there can be other forms of committee voting with neither of these properties.

Complementarity: An interaction between preferences for two or more alternatives. Positive complementarities mean that more (less) of one alternative makes the voter want more (less) of another alternative. Negative complementarities mean that more (less) of one alternative makes the voter want less (more) of another alternative.

Condorcet winner: An alternative that beats any other alternative in a pairwise majority rule election.

Continuous: A continuous curve is smooth and has no gaps or breaks. Another way of thinking about continuity is that for any two points that are elements of a set on a line segment, there is another point that lies between the two points that is also an element of the set.

Corollary: A result that follows almost immediately from a theorem, with little or no additional assumptions and few logical steps.

Decisive set: A group G is decisive for an alternative A versus another alternative B if A is collectively preferred (chosen by the group) to B under every preference pattern in which all the members of G prefer A to B, whatever the preferences of nonmembers of G. In particular, if all members of G like A over B, all nonmembers like B over A, and the society chooses A, G is decisive for that pair of alternatives.

Deduction: The logical process of arriving at a conclusion from a set of premises.

Democracy: Democracy means many different things. The important thing to remember is that there is no single, dominant process of democracy. At the most fundamental level, democracy is simply rule by the people.

Dictator: A decisive set with a single member, decisive for all pairs of alternatives.

Discrete: A discrete set of elements is "countable," so that it is possible to assign integers uniquely to elements. Discrete sets are not continuous.

Enfranchised: Given the effective power to vote. Alternatively, an enfranchised person is one whose opinion has a positive weight in some collective decision.

Equilibrium: Generally, a situation with no tendency to change without the agency of some outside force. Equilibrium requires that actions are either independent or mutually consistent.

Ideal point: The outcome that a voter judges to be best, of all the feasible alternatives.

Institutions: Rules of the game, or restrictions on the process of choice.

Majority rule equilibrium: One alternative, or a set of alternatives, that cannot be defeated by another alternative in a pairwise majority rule election. It is possible that other alternatives tie the majority rule equilibrium, but none can command a strict majority against it. If the win set of an alternative is empty, that alternative is a majority rule equilibrium, and vice versa. Likewise, any "median in all directions" is a majority rule equilibrium, and vice versa. If the majority rule equilibrium is unique, it is a Condorcet winner.

Mass elections: A decision process with the following properties: many uninformed voters, insignificant stakes by voters on outcomes, and no presumption of participation by all voters. Generally, mass elections are conceived as choices over bundles of policies called "candidates," though referenda are also mass elections.

Models: A representation of a complex structure that aids in understanding. In this book, models are mental mock-ups of a political process, much like an architect or shipbuilder might create a mock-up to understand a design.

Nash equilibrium: A set of actions by all the participants of a game such that the action of each person is the optimal response to all the other players' actions. The "actions" may be a choice (a vote, a proposal) or a contingent sequence of moves (called a "strategy"). A Nash equilibrium is a situation where no player, acting alone, can improve his or her lot by acting differently.

Necessary condition: A requirement if a conclusion is true. Suppose that A is true only if B is true. Then B is a necessary condition. However, B could be true and A could still be false, unless B is also a sufficient condition for A.

Normative theory: A theory about what ought to be.

Oligarchy: Rule by a few.

Open interval: On a line segment, all the points between the end points of the segment, not including the end points.

Paradox: A surprising result, arising from a contradiction or inconsistency of seeming innocuous premises.

Plott conditions: Pairwise symmetry of ideal points around a median position. The Plott conditions are sufficient, but not necessary for the existence of a majority rule equilibrium.

Politics: This word is often used to mean maneuvering among individuals for power or resources. This is not the meaning intended here. Instead, politics means the process of deciding policies or actions in a democratic society.

Positive theory: A theory about what is, or about how and why phenomena occur.

Preferences: Set of reactions of a citizen to alternatives. Presented with two alternatives A and B, a citizen may prefer A to B, prefer B to A, or be indifferent between them. A citizen's set of preferences is the list of all these reactions to all pairs of alternatives, ranked from best to worst (though ties, or indifference, may occur). The basis of preference may be taste, psychological factors, or reason.

Result: A conclusion, which may be supported either deductively or inductively. A deductive result is one in which the conclusion follows from the premises, with clearly identified necessary and sufficient conditions.

Separability: A feature of preferences. Separable preferences mean that the citizen's reaction to changing levels of one alternative is independent of the expected level of any other alternative.

Sincere voting: Voting one's own preferences, regardless of the expected actions of others.

Single-peaked preferences: Single-peaked preferences decline monotonically as alternatives are more different from the ideal. If changing alternatives in any constant direction lowers utility for some distance, and then increases utility, preferences are not single peaked.

Status quo: The present government policy, whether it is the result of a conscious decision process in the past or simply historical accident.

Strategic voting: Voting to produce the most desired outcome from a decision process, rather than to express sincere preferences over the alternatives immediately presented.

Sufficient condition: A conclusion must be true whenever a sufficient condition is true. Suppose that A always follows from B. Then B is a sufficient condition for A. However, A could also be true if B is not true, if B is not also a necessary condition.

Symmetry: A feature of preferences, implying that differences from the ideal point are disliked equally, whether the differences are positive or negative.

Theorem: A deductive result that is not self-evident, but can be proved to follow logically from a defined set of assumptions.

Transitivity: The logical linkage in a chain of preference longer than two alternatives, when only pairwise comparisons are available. For example, if A is preferred to B, and B is preferred to C, A is preferred to C only if preferences are transitive.

Unique: The property of being the one and only element of a set. For example, an ideal point is unique if only one person has maximum satisfaction at that point. A median point, however, can be unique if there are no other median points, even if several voters share the median point as their ideal point. In the latter case, the median point is unique but the ideal point is not.

Win set: The intersection of the alternatives that a decisive set of voters all prefer to the status quo. Any element of the win set of z (written $W(z)$) would defeat z if the two were voted on. Win sets can be defined for any majority, from 0% to 100%, but the usual presumption is that the decision rule is 50% + 1, so that the decisive set is any simple majority of the enfranchised voters.

Solutions to selected exercises

CHAPTER 2

2.1 Arrange the positions in order $\{-2, 2, 6, 9, 9\}$ to see that the median is 6 (there are two points smaller than 6 and two points greater). The mean, or average, is the sum of the above positions divided by the number of positions (five): 24/5.

2.2 By the definition of symmetry, changes in either direction will yield similar changes in a voter's utility. The two voters with positions less than 3 will clearly vote for it, and the two with positions greater than 8 will choose it. The middle voter at position 6 has symmetric preferences, so equal changes in either direction yield equal changes in utility; since 3 is further away than 8, the median voter will choose 8 (closer is better) and 8 will win 3 to 2.

2.3 If 7 is added to the committee, then no unique median exists; 6 and 7 are both medians. If this new committee is asked to choose between 8 and 3, then 8 will again be chosen.

2.4 Order the positions to find the median $\{-4, -3, 6, 7, 21\}$. By definition, 6 must be the median. If one replaces 7 with 25 the new ordering is $\{-4, -3, 6, 21, 25\}$ and the median stays the same. The mean, however, changes (increases).

2.5 Probably not. One can imagine a society in which a few outliers change the mean from the true middle of society. Instead, one might want to argue that the mode is most important, insofar as Aristotle is arguing for a large, vigorous middle class.

2.6 The three measures of central tendency are in general not the same

245

for a given distribution. One can easily imagine distributions where they happen to be the same: for example, the set $\{5, 5, 5, 5, 5, 5\}$ or $\{1, 2, 3, 4, 5\}$.

2.7 The median income is likely a better indicator of where the middle class is due to the effect that outliers have upon the mean. A small group of very rich people can move the mean higher than it would be naturally; alternatively, a small group of very poor people can move it lower. In general, if the mean is higher than the median it means the distribution is weighted to the right (i.e., the rich in this example); if the mean is lower than the median, the distribution is weighted to the left (i.e., the poor).

2.8 *Proof by Contradiction:* Assume n is odd, and that two medians exist (or there is an interval bounded by $\{x, y\}$). Suppose $x < y$. By definition, the number of points to the left of x must be the same as the number to the right of y (if the number to the left of x if less than the number to the right of y, then x is not a median; the opposite case also holds for y). Thus, n_l for $x + n_r$ for y is some even number (since $n_l = n_r$ we are in effect doubling one of them, which proves the result is even). The only other numbers that have been excluded from the set are x and y; adding them makes n even (since all we have done is add 2 to an already even number). This results in a contradiction (n is odd), proving the result.

CHAPTER 3

3.1 **z** is not a Condorcet winner, as its win set is not empty.

3.2 If the issues are separable, then the median for issue 1 is 5 and the median for issue 2 is 10. The ordered pair is thus (5,10), but this is no surprise given the result that voting on separable issues one at a time results in the same outcome regardless of order.

3.3 There is a Condorcet winner at (5,10), which is also a median in all directions.

CHAPTER 4

4.1 For such a problem, SED is a linear transformation of WED. If the SED is $((x_1 - y_1)^2 + (x_2 - y_2)^2))^{1/2}$, then the WED is $[\lambda(x_1 - y_1)^2 + \lambda(x_2 - y_2)^2)]^{1/2}$.

4.2 Since a_{12} is < 0, we are left with a negative interaction term. If x_1 (equal to 20) is $> x_{i1}$, then the conditional ideal on x_{i2}^* is larger than x_{i1}; if $x_1 < x_{i1}$, the opposite will hold.

4.3 Assume one of the two points is the origin. Then, the key to the proof is to realize that if there are three dimensions (x, y, z), one can apply the Pythagorean theorem not only to the plane described by (x, y), but also to the right triangle created by the vector reaching from the origin to the point (x, y) and the side $(0, z)$. Applying the Pythagorean theorem twice yields:

$$\sqrt{[(x^2 + y^2)^{1/2}]^2 + z^2} = \text{the equation for SED}$$

One can easily broaden this result to any two points, rather than the origin and another point, by transformation of the origin.

CHAPTER 5

5.1 What we want to find is a K such that no other position could receive a K-majority. Take for example, $K = 9$ (which is $n/2 + 1$). The position 9 would thus be a KMVT, supplanting 7 in an election. The smallest K, which would maintain 7 as the status quo, is thus $K = 10$.

5.2 First round $x_A = 2$, $x_B = 2$, $x_C = 1$; second round $x_A = 3$, $x_B = 2$. Then x_A gets a score of 10, $x_B = 11$, and $x_C = 9$. Member C would win the election.

CHAPTER 6

6.1 The general formula for voter preference is WED from Chapter 4. Given this, candidate B wins 3 to 0 based upon the position $[2\ 3]^T$.

6.2 From Equation 6.5, the candidate with the least distance and variance will win the election. If the variance for candidate R is 2, then R will win the election. In fact, R's variance could be as high as 14 to be insured of winning (at 14, there would be a coin toss to determine the victor).

6.3 Given the discussion of Nash equilibrium in the chapter, the candidates will converge upon the median in all cases. Thus, all the elections will result in a tie, giving them an expected utility of at least $1/2$ (representing the chance that they win); if a candidate doesn't move (e.g., because the position is far from the ideal), the candidate's expected utility is less, because he or she will certainly lose the election (W in the utility function) and receive little utility from the ending policy position (x in the utility function).

CHAPTER 7

7.1 Given Equation 7.1, any of the governor's initiatives would increase a factor in the equation, thus increasing the number of probable voters. And as these initiatives focus on the first two factors, they will have a larger impact than factors 3 and 4 (once you get a person to the voting booth, it is likely he or she will actually vote).

7.2 Using the formula for WED, the citizen prefers candidate A to B ($50^{1/2}$ to $68^{1/2}$) and will vote since the distance to the candidate is less than 10.

7.3 Again, using the formula for WED, the voter is a distance of $5^{1/2}$ from candidate A and $37^{1/2}$ from B. Subtracting these terms yields a difference greater than 2, indicating the voter is not alienated.

CHAPTER 8

8.1 If person 1 is strategic and can set the agenda, the first pairwise contest will be B against C. C loses to B 2 to 1. The second contest would be B against A. B loses to A 2 to 1. The cycle could continue, but the malevolent person A has the ability to stop after these two votes.

8.2 Consult Figure 8.1 – one can make a 1 to 1 substitution of vegetables and find the answer (i.e., the two problems are isomorphic).

Index

Adams, John, xi
affine transformations, 79
agendas, 157–71, 221
  preferences over, 161–5, 167–8
agenda setter with
  proposal power, 161–4, 177, 216, 221
Aldrich, John, 69, 146, 149, 152, 219, 221, 223
Alesina, Alberto, 68, 195, 213, 219
approval voting, 100, 106–9
Aquinas, Thomas, 213
Aristotle, 21–3, 37, 63, 69, 99, 213
Arrow, Kenneth, 92, 95–8, 165, 210, 217, 222
  see also paradox, Arrow's
Arthur, Brian, 217
assumptions, 4, 8, 22, 27, 30, 210
Augustine, Saint, 213
Austen-Smith, David, 122, 208, 214
Ayres, R., 149, 220

Banks, Jeffrey, 122, 208, 214, 218, 223
Barro, Robert, 223
Barry, Brian, 146
Barzel, Yoram, 221
Baumgartner, Frank, 181–2, 221
Bayes's rule, 219
Beik, William, 10
Bender, Bruce, 219
Bental, Benjamin, 127
Ben-Zion, Uri, 127
Bernhardt, M. Daniel, 122
Bianco, William, 132, 219, 221
Binmore, Kenneth, 219
Black, Duncan, ix, xi, 21, 33, 34, 36, 37, 62, 106–7, 180, 213, 214, 218
Blin, J.-M., 222

Borda count, 100, 106–9, 113
Borda, Jean-Charles, 106, 108, 214, 218
Border, Kim, 222
Bosnia, U.N. involvement in, 37–41
Bowen, W., 149, 220
Brams, Steven, 215, 218
Brehm, John, 221
Buchanan, James, 68, 100–2, 217
Budge, Ian, 223
Burke, Edmund, 50, 63, 136
Burnham, Walter, 69, 140

Calvert, Randall, 121, 127–8, 131, 218
campaign messages, 122–33, 142, 174
candidates with policy preferences, 115, 118, 127–34, 219
Cartesian product, 52, 73
chaos, 71, 111, 160
Chappell, Henry, 208
coalition governments, 111
Coase, R. H., 217
Coates, Dennis, 133
Cohen, Linda, 87
Coleman, James, 44–5
collective decisions, 94, 217
Collier, Kenneth, 215, 219
commitment by candidates, 122–33, 193, 202, 207, 208–9, 223
  technology of, 126–7
committee voting, 12, 127–8, 155, 157, 180
complementarities, 51, 57–61, 83–6, 170
Condorcet, Marquis de, 90–1, 95, 106, 214
Condorcet winner, 62, 65, 66, 71–2, 86, 90–2, 215

249

Printed in the United States
55548LVS00004B/268-312